Dynamic fiscal policy

Dynamic fiscal policy

Alan J. Auerbach
UNIVERSITY OF PENNSYLVANIA
NATIONAL BUREAU OF ECONOMIC RESEARCH

and

Laurence J. Kotlikoff
BOSTON UNIVERSITY
NATIONAL BUREAU OF ECONOMIC RESEARCH

Cambridge University Press
Cambridge
London   New York   New Rochelle
Melbourne   Sydney

Published by the Press Syndicate of the University of Cambridge
The Pitt Building, Trumpington Street, Cambridge CB2 1RP
32 East 57th Street, New York, NY 10022, USA
10 Stamford Road, Oakleigh, Melbourne 3166, Australia

© Cambridge University Press 1987

First published 1987

Printed in the United States of America

Library of Congress Cataloging-in-Publication Data
Auerbach, Alan J.
Dynamic fiscal policy.
Bibliography: p.
Includes index.
1. Fiscal policy – Mathematical models. 2. Finance, Public – Mathematical models. 3. Equilibrium (Economics) – Mathematical models. 4. Macroeconomics – Mathematical models. I. Kotlikoff, Laurence J. II. Title.
HJ131.A94 1987   339.5′2   8624447
ISBN 0 521 30041 X

British Cataloguing-in-Publication applied for.

To Gay and Dayle

Contents

List of illustrations	*page* x
List of tables	xi
Preface	xiii
Acknowledgments	xv

1. Introduction   1
   - A. Key issues   2
   - B. Key findings   4
   - C. Background   5
   - D. The need for a dynamic general equilibrium simulation model   6
   - E. A dynamic, perfect foresight general equilibrium model   10
   - F. Organization of the book   13

2. The two-period life cycle model: an introduction to the general model   16
   - A. The two-period model: a Cobb–Douglas example   17
   - B. Illustration of a dynamic fiscal policy transition – a temporary tax cut   22
   - C. Deficiencies of the two-period model   24

3. Modeling the economy   26
   - A. Household behavior   26
   - B. The impact of taxation on household behavior   32
   - C. Firm behavior   35
   - D. Government behavior   38
   - E. Equilibrium under perfect foresight   41
   - Appendix: Effect of taxation on household behavior   42

4. Simulation methodology   46
   - A. Solution method   46
   - B. Parameterization of the model   50
   - C. Conclusions   54

Contents

5.	Tax reform – choice of the tax base	55
	A. Key points	55
	B. Conceptual issues	57
	C. Simulation results	64
	D. Welfare effects of structural tax reform	74
	E. The relative efficiency of alternative tax structures	77
	F. Announcement effects	82
	Appendix: LSRA transfers	87
6.	Deficits, government spending, and crowding out	88
	A. Short-term tax-cut policies	89
	B. Balanced budget increases in government consumption	97
	C. Deficit-financed increases in government consumption	101
7.	Economic versus accounting definitions of deficit finance and the potential for fiscal illusion	103
	A. Summary	109
8.	Progressive taxation	111
	A. Modeling progressive taxes	112
	B. The impact of progressive taxation on economic decisions	113
	C. Sensitivity analysis	118
	D. Welfare and efficiency effects of progressivity	122
	E. The choice of tax base, once again	124
	F. Progressive taxes and intragenerational redistribution	125
9.	Investment incentives	127
	A. Distinguishing savings and investment incentives	128
	B. Adjustment costs, investment, and stock market values	134
	C. Simulation results	136
	D. Announcement effects	140
	E. The impact of disguised wealth taxation	141
10.	Social security	145
	A. Social security and savings	146
	B. Including social security in the simulation model	150
	C. Simulating the transition to unfunded social security	151
	D. The efficiency gains from benefit-tax linkage	154
	E. Conclusions	160

11.	Effect of a demographic transition and social security's policy response	162
	A. The U.S. social security system's policy responses to the demographic transition	164
	B. Modeling demographics	166
	C. Specifying a time path of fertility change	167
	D. Baseline simulations: the economic effects of a demographic transition	168
	E. Including social security in the demographic transition	171
	F. Social security policy responses to the demographic transition	174
	G. Summary and conclusion	178
12.	Summary and conclusion	180
	References	183
	Index	191

Illustrations

Figure

2.1	Capital accumulation in a two-period life cycle model	page 19
2.2	The impact of a tax-cut policy on steady state capital	21
4.1	The model and its solution	48
5.1	The savings effect of a compensated switch from wage to capital income taxation	61
5.2	Age-earnings and age-consumption profiles in the base case steady state	65
5.3	The impact on capital formation of tax reform	67
5.4	The welfare effects of tax reform	75
5.5	The effects on capital formation of preannounced switches to consumption taxation	83
5.6	The effects on capital formation of preannounced switches to wage taxation	84
5.7	The welfare effects of preannounced switches to consumption taxation	85
5.8	The welfare effects of preannounced switches to wage taxation	86
8.1	Lifetime profiles of marginal and average tax rates under different tax bases	116
8.2	Comparison of labor supply and consumption profiles under proportional and progressive income taxation	118
9.1	The impact on Q of savings and investment incentives with and without adjustment costs	138
9.2	The impact on interest rates of savings and investment incentives	139
9.3	The impact on Q of immediate and 5-year preannounced savings and investment incentives with adjustment costs	142

Tables

Table

2.1	The transition arising from a one-period tax cut	*page* 24
5.1	The base case steady state	64
5.2	Structural tax change	66
5.3	Structural tax reform – steady state sensitivity analysis	68
5.4	Steady state changes in the capital stock and factor returns (parameters)	69
5.5	Sensitivity analysis of structural tax reform: consideration of nonlinearities	71
5.6	Sensitivity analysis of structural tax reform: level of initial steady state income tax rate (percent)	73
5.7	Efficiency gains or losses from switching from income to wage taxation	77
5.8	Efficiency gains or losses from switching from income to consumption taxation	78
6.1	Crowding out under alternative short-term income tax–cut policies	92
6.2	The intergenerational welfare effects of short-term tax cuts: welfare changes	94
6.3	Five-year income tax cut with and without adjustment costs	96
6.4	Crowding out from balanced budget increases in government consumption	99
6.5	The choice of tax bases in financing balanced budget permanent increases in government consumption	100
6.6	Crowding out from debt-financed permanent increases in government consumption	102
8.1	Effects of progressive taxation – 15 percent proportional income tax revenue benchmark	115

8.2	Effects of progressive taxation – 25 percent proportional income tax revenue benchmark	119
8.3	Sensitivity analysis of effects of switching to progressive income taxation	121
8.4	Efficiency gains of a switch from income taxation (percentage of lifetime wealth)	124
9.1	The impact of adjustment costs: switch from 15 percent proportional income tax to specified tax regime	137
9.2	Announcement effects: switch in year 6 from 15 percent proportional income tax to specified tax regime	141
10.1	Simulating unfunded social security under different tax bases	152
10.2	Welfare effects of unfunded social security (wealth equivalents, in percent)	154
10.3	Efficiency gains from linking social security benefits to payroll taxes	158
10.4	LSRA steady state and transitional values of capital and labor	160
10.5	Efficiency gains from social security benefit–payroll tax linkage, LSRA versus no LSRA	161
11.1	Population age structure in transition	169
11.2	Characteristics of demographic transitions without social security	169
11.3	Welfare effects of demographic transitions: equivalent variations as percentage of resources spent on adult consumption and leisure	172
11.4	Characteristics of demographic transitions with social security	173
11.5	Effects of reducing social security's replacement rate	175
11.6	Effects of increasing social security's retirement age	176
11.7	Immediate taxation of social security benefits	177
11.8	Accumulation of social security trust fund	178

Preface

Our objective in writing this book is to share a new perspective on the macroeconomic effects of fiscal policies. This new perspective is grounded in the microeconomics of intertemporal choice and the macroeconomics of savings and growth. It emphasizes that fiscal policy is not a one-time event with one-time outcomes, but a time path of choices leading to a time path of macroeconomic reactions. The timing of macro policy responses can be quite surprising to those accustomed to textbook Keynesian and other static models. Short-run policy responses can be exactly opposite to long-run responses, policies that have very significant long-run outcomes can have barely discernible short-run impacts, and delays in implementing policies can enhance or greatly impair their effectiveness.

Linking present and future fiscal policies and present and future macro outcomes is the simple fact that people live for many years. Current saving and labor decisions are influenced by perceptions of future as well as current policies, and these current decisions not only have immediate macro consequences, but they also influence the economy's future macro equilibrium.

The new perspective arises from our own recent research as well as that of a number of other economists. This research focuses on the timing and effects of policy changes, the relationship of current saving and labor supply decisions to future economic well-being, the role of expectations, the structural similarities of alternative fiscal policies, the effects of fiscal decisions on the stock market and on other asset values, and the integration of microeconomic decisions and macroeconomic outcomes.

The late 1960s witnessed an extensive analysis of fiscal policy within neoclassical growth models. But the new research, in addition to addressing different issues, employs a new technology – namely, computer simulation models – to illustrate in concrete terms the implications of theoretical propositions. By demonstrating dynamic macroeconomic responses to fiscal policy with numerical examples rather than with equations or phase diagrams, the new technology opens this subject to a much larger audience. It is our hope that this book will be read, in part or in full, by readers ranging from policy analysts to our own colleagues working in macroeconomics and public finance.

To address a wider audience, we have presented topics covered in the book in a "tell-and-show" format. The "tell" part provides the theoretical basis for the "show" part's simulation results. We repeatedly use the simple two-period life cycle model to illustrate theoretical issues. The "show" part presents results from a 55-period life cycle simulation model.

Those using this book for undergraduate teaching should find the two-period model an excellent classroom aid. We have found that undergraduates can readily follow the two-period model without calculus and can use hand calculators to simulate policy changes. The two-period model is presented in detail in Chapter 2 and is used at the beginning of Chapters 5, 9, and 10. With an understanding of the basic mechanisms of the life cycle model, undergraduates can follow the intuition behind the 55-period model simulation results even if they have only skimmed Chapters 3 and 4. These somewhat more technical chapters present the 55-period model and discuss its solution algorithm.

The macro general equilibrium simulation model developed in this book is derived strictly from micro behavior and assumptions about government policy. Hence, the model is useful for sharpening one's economic intuition concerning the relationship between micro choices and macro outcomes. Indeed, it seems fair to say that, for newcomers to economics, mastering this book's contents will provide a firm grounding in a good deal of neoclassical micro- and macroeconomics.

For those well versed in economics, the book offers some unexpected findings concerning the likely economic effects of fiscal policies. We, at least, were surprised to learn that deficits are likely to cause short-run "crowding in" and lower short-term interest rates; that investment incentives are likely to hurt capitalists while increasing investment; that business tax cuts may be self-financing; that the degree of tax progressivity is as important as the choice of tax base for issues of savings and efficiency; that official government deficits are highly unreliable measures of the government's true economic debt policy; and that although baby "busts" such as those under way in the United States are bad for the social security system, they are, on net, likely to be beneficial to the economy.

The book also demonstrates a variety of important propositions, which, although fairly well known to public finance economists, may be of special interest to the general reader. One such proposition is that enhancing investment incentives in the presence of an income tax is structurally equivalent to introducing a consumption tax. Another is that a consumption tax represents a combination of a wage tax and a tax on wealth. A third is that instituting an unfunded social security system is structurally similar to running official deficits through tax cuts.

In the course of examining the many surprising results contained in this book, we hope the reader will come to share our appreciation of the dynamics and potential effectiveness of fiscal policies.

Acknowledgments

The research underlying this book was conducted between 1980 and 1986. During this period of developing and enhancing the book's computer simulation model we were greatly assisted by David Reitman, Andrew Myers, and Jonathan Skinner. Their technical expertise, economic intuition, and sense of humor were invaluable to the project, and we enjoyed working with them.

We are also grateful to the National Bureau of Economic Research, the National Science Foundation, the U.S. Department of Health and Human Services, the Brookings Institution, and Data Resources, Inc. for supporting various phases of the project. We particularly appreciate Martin Feldstein's decision to finance the initial development of the model.

Merri Ansara and Jane Konkel provided excellent assistance in typing the manuscript, and Anne Monahan was, as always, extremely helpful in supervising the preparation of the manuscript.

James Poterba and Bill Samuelson carefully read the first draft of the book, and the current version reflects their detailed and helpful comments. We also thank David Bradford, Michael Boskin, Fischer Black, Ken Judd, John Laitner, and Robert E. Lucas for helpful comments, suggestions, and discussions.

CHAPTER 1

Introduction

This book examines the effects of fiscal policy on the economy. Fiscal policy refers to the actions of government in collecting and spending private resources. As its title suggests, the book is concerned with the dynamic aspects of fiscal policy. These include the effects of fiscal policies on capital formation, economic growth, and intergenerational equity; the influence of long-run expectations on short-run outcomes; and the restrictions imposed by current policies on the set of feasible future policies.

Dynamic analysis has recently gained favor over static analysis in various fields of economics. It is particularly appropriate for the study of fiscal policy, which, at least in the United States, is frequently adjusted and altered. Such changes are often explicitly legislated in advance, but when not pre-announced they may often be surmised from current fiscal conditions. That fiscal variables are continually modified is not surprising. Current policy changes alter the course of the economy and invariably require additional policy changes in the future. But the anticipation of such future changes also alters current outcomes; indeed, the current impact of fiscal decisions cannot be determined without considering the entire future time path of fiscal policy.

A dynamic perspective is also crucial in weighing the short-run benefits of particular policies (e.g., tax cuts) against long-run losses (e.g., crowding out) and in evaluating the economic efficiency of alternative policies. Economic efficiency refers to the potential for improving the welfare of some segment of society without reducing that of another. Static analysis is ill-equipped to examine economic efficiency because it ignores a vast segment of society, namely, all future generations. Dynamic analysis considers both current and future generations and permits one to distinguish policies that truly improve economic efficiency from those that simply redistribute resources across generations.

In addition to including the time dimension of fiscal policy, any persuasive analysis of this subject should include the general equilibrium effects of policy choices on endogenous economic variables such as interest rates, wages, and saving. Studying fiscal policy in a dynamic general equilibrium model involves a number of issues that are not present in static models. These include treatment of expectations, aggregation of the behavior of overlapping generations, and solving for the equilibrium transition path of the economy. The difficulties in obtaining either qualitative or quantitative analytical results in any but extremely simple and highly unrealistic dynamic models influenced our decision to use a computer simulation model to study the dynamics of fiscal policy. Although this methodological approach to analyzing fiscal policy issues is commonplace, the model developed here appears to be unique in that it can be used to study the effects of a wide range of important fiscal policies on intertemporal general equilibria under the assumption of rational expectations.

The numerical simulation technique is required because of the complexity of the problems studied here. Nevertheless, the model has few components, and these are easily described. As a consequence, the simulation results are highly intuitive and easily understood by tracing the effects of policy changes through the different parts of the model.

A. Key issues

The book examines many types of fiscal policies, including deficit finance, changes in the level and timing of government spending, choice of the tax base, tax progressivity, investment incentives, and social security. In addition, the book considers the interaction of demographic change and fiscal choices, the effect of fiscal policies on the stock market, particularly investment incentives, and the question of whether conventional measures of government debt are intrinsically well defined.

To provide a better sense of the scope of this book, we list below some of the questions to be addressed.

1. *Savings, welfare, and the choice of tax base*

    Would a switch in the tax base from income to consumption increase savings and welfare in the long run?
    How would the outcome be different if the alternative tax base were labor income, rather than consumption?
    Do policies that lead to increased savings in the long run also improve individual welfare in the long run?

2. *Efficiency gains from dynamic tax reform*

    To what extent do policies that improve long-run welfare succeed in doing so through transfers in resources from earlier

1 Introduction

generations rather than through increases in economic efficiency?

Do fiscal policies exist that offer Pareto efficiency gains, that is, that improve the welfare of at least one generation without lowering that of others?

How large are the efficiency gains or losses from switching tax bases?

3. *"Crowding out" and deficits*

How much private investment is displaced by deficits associated with tax cuts of different sizes and durations?

How fast does crowding out occur?

What is the impact of deficit finance on short- and long-term interest rates?

Is it possible for investment to increase when a deficit occurs?

How does the type of tax cut that induces a deficit influence the degree of crowding out?

How useful are reported government deficits as measures of intergenerational redistribution and fiscal stimulus?

4. *Business tax incentives*

What types of business tax incentives have the greatest "bang for the buck" in terms of increased investment per dollar of revenue loss?

What is the impact of investment incentives on the stock market and interest rates?

How do adjustment costs to investment influence the efficacy of fiscal policy?

How do changes in investment incentives influence the effective base of taxation?

5. *Tax progressivity*

How serious are the efficiency costs of progressive taxation in comparison with the costs of proportional taxation?

How much is labor supply and savings reduced by the progressivity of the tax system?

How does increasing the progressivity of different taxes shift the burden of taxation across generations?

4   Dynamic fiscal policy

6.   *Announcement effects*

Can early announcement of policy changes mitigate or reverse their intended effects?

How does the anticipation of different fiscal policy changes affect short-run economic behavior?

In what cases is early announcement of a policy shift beneficial?

7.   *Demographic shifts*

What economic changes, particularly in capital formation and factor prices, should occur when fertility rates undergo major changes?

How does such a demographic shift affect the financial viability of social security and the distribution across generations of the burden of financing social security?

What changes in the social security system are required to offset the effects of a major increase in the ratio of retirees to workers?

B.   Key findings

These and numerous other questions are addressed in the following chapters using both theoretical analysis and the results of the simulation model. The key findings are as follows:

Deficits arising from income tax cuts of short duration "crowd in" saving and investment in the short run even though saving and capital formation are crowded out in the long run by such policies.

Consumption taxation stimulates considerably greater savings than income or wage taxation.

Most of the long-run welfare gains that would result from a move to consumption taxation are due to intergenerational transfers of the tax burden rather than gains in economic efficiency.

Officially reported government deficits can be highly misleading indicators of the "tightness" or "looseness" of fiscal policy.

Investment incentives can lead to substantial declines in stock market values.

Investment incentives can be self-financing in the sense that short-term revenue losses are offset by long-term increases in revenues with no required increase in personal or business tax rates.

1 Introduction

The degree of tax progressivity is as important as the choice of the tax base in influencing saving and capital accumulation.

Despite adverse consequences for social security, projected demographic changes such as those under way in the United States are likely to improve significantly the welfare of future generations because of capital deepening and a decline in the number of young children supported per adult.

C. Background

Recent research into the effects of fiscal policy has been particularly active in a number of areas, albeit without having achieved a broad consensus. The ensuing debates and controversies have motivated the choice of many of the topics covered in this book.

1. *Savings, labor supply, growth, and government policy*

One of the central questions explored here is to what extent can government policies affect the rate of capital accumulation and the supply of labor in the economy. Capital accumulation and labor supply are two of the main sources of economic growth. Both growth and measured saving have been quite low in the United States in recent decades.[1] Various studies (e.g., Feldstein, 1974) have suggested that government fiscal policy is in large part responsible for discouraging saving. Their particular concern is the crowding out caused by government debt policies and the disincentives to saving and labor supply generated by high marginal tax rates.

2. *The choice of tax base*

As has become increasingly apparent, the choice of the tax base – whether it be income, consumption, wages, or capital income – has important implications for the distribution of welfare among individuals in society and for the efficient operation of the economy. The United States, like most other industrialized countries, derives a large part of its revenue from the individual income tax. During the past two decades proposals to replace the tax on income with a tax on personal consumption have received serious attention from economists and government officials. This discussion was influenced by the arguments of Fisher (1939), Kaldor (1957), and

---

[1] For a presentation and discussion of different U.S. saving measures see Kotlikoff (1984a), Auerbach (1985), or Boskin and Kotlikoff (1985). Auerbach (1984) considers the relationship between reduced saving and growth in the United States in the 1970s.

others before them dating back to Hobbes (1651). Proponents of the consumption tax argue that not only would it be more equitable, simpler to administer, and less distortionary, but it would also promote saving. Opponents believe that it would reduce the progressivity of the tax system, while discouraging labor supply through increased marginal tax rates on wage and salary income.

3. *Social security and the demographic transition*

The impact of social security on the U.S. economy and the effects of economic and demographic change on social security are receiving considerable attention. From a rather minor fiscal institution in the 1940s, social security has grown enormously in the ensuing years. Social security taxes are now the second largest source of U.S. government revenues, and social security benefit payments represent almost three-quarters of all U.S. government transfer payments. Although social security is credited with greatly improving the welfare of the postwar generation of the elderly, some say that its implicit form of deficit finance accounts in large part for the recent declines in the U.S. saving rate. Others have voiced concerns about the potential impact of social security's payroll tax, which they see as highly distortionary.

Greater attention has focused on the substantial increases in the ratio of the elderly to the younger population that will occur in the United States in the first half of the next century and considerably sooner in Japan and some European countries. The financial squeeze on social security associated with the projected rise in the ratio of beneficiaries to contributors has prompted a variety of reform proposals. These include increases in payroll taxes as needed over time, large-scale benefit cuts, and the early accumulation of a massive social security trust fund.

D. **The need for a dynamic general equilibrium simulation model**

Harberger (1962) was among the first researchers to analyze the effects of fiscal policy using a general equilibrium approach. He was concerned with the effects of a corporate tax in an economy with two production sectors (corporate and noncorporate), two factors of production (capital and labor), and a representative household that supplies the productive factors and purchases the output of the two sectors. Despite the simplicity of his model, it is only possible to obtain general analytical expressions for the effects of taxation in the case of infinitesimal tax changes.

1 Introduction

These expressions are quite complicated when there are nonzero tax rates in the initial economy (Atkinson and Stiglitz, 1980).

Simulation analysis is the only alternative available when it is necessary to analyze large policy changes in models that are too complicated for simple analytical solutions. To solve such models one must specify explicitly the key parameters, such as the elasticity of substitution in production of capital for labor. Obviously, if the model is to be as realistic as possible, the numerical estimates of these parameters should be culled from the empirical literature. Given such a parameterization, one can usually obtain an exact numerical solution for the equilibrium of the economy for any given fiscal policy and compare the results for different fiscal policies. This is the essence of the numerical simulation approach.

Simulating the model for alternative policies takes the place of the comparative static exercises that are performed with analytical models. In addition, one can conduct sensitivity analysis of the numerical simulation model by examining the impact of plausible variations in parameter values. Often the results of such sensitivity analysis are very robust to reasonable parameter changes, even though this outcome could not be foreseen prior to performing the simulation experiments. In other cases results are quite sensitive to small changes in particular parameters. This, too, is useful information, for it indicates which parameters need to be empirically estimated most precisely.

1. *Early simulation models*

The model used in this book is a large-scale dynamic simulation model. In contrast, most of the initial simulation studies of fiscal policy utilized static models. Although such models are not suitable for analyzing the types of questions considered below, the earlier work provides important insights into the problems of obtaining solutions to numerical simulation models and the potential uses of such models.

The best known of the early simulation models are those developed by Shoven, Whalley, and various collaborators (Shoven and Whalley, 1972; Shoven, 1976; Fullerton, Shoven, and Whalley, 1983; and Ballard et al., 1985). These models have been used to study the incidence and efficiency effects of a variety of fiscal regimes in both closed and open economies.[2] In the earliest application of these models an important element of the research involved ensuring that a solution could be found with a computational algorithm. Scarf's (1967, 1973) algorithm was important in this context because it guaranteed convergence to an equilibrium, as long as

---

[2] This research is surveyed in some detail in Ballard et al. (1985).

at least one existed. Subsequently, alternative algorithms that were computationally more efficient proved successful in the solution of large models. One such method is utilized in the present analysis.[3]

2. Steady state simulation models

Generally missing from this earlier generation of large-scale general equilibrium simulation models is the element of time, which is needed to understand the effects of government policy on savings and growth. Although the production sectors of the economy are disaggregated in great and careful detail in the early models, future production and consumption are either left out or treated in a less than satisfactory manner. As will become clear from the description of the model used here, tracing out the dynamic path of an economy presents the researcher with special methodological problems.

An alternative approach was developed to avoid such problems while still making it possible to analyze a subset of questions concerning saving and growth. This approach characterized individual saving behavior more fully, but was limited only to finding a solution for the position of the economy in its long-run stationary (or, in the presence of trend growth, steady) state, when each year is the same as the previous one. In the stationary state, since nothing changes, the role of expectations and the process of economic adjustment cannot be considered, nor can issues relating to short-run outcomes, the timing of policy, or the behavior of different cohorts. The stationary state approach can be used, however, to consider the long-run effects on the economy of changes in economic conditions, including most fiscal policies.

In general, such models have been much less concerned with a disaggregation of markets than have the static large-scale models and have relied on the life cycle model of saving developed by Modigliani and Brumberg (1954) and by Ando and Modigliani (1963). For example, papers by Tobin and Dolde (1971, 1981), Sheshinski (1978), and Kotlikoff (1979) examine the impact of social security on steady state labor supply and savings, while Summers (1981a) presents a steady state simulation analysis of the effects of changing the tax base from income to consumption.

3. Limitations of steady state analyses

As emphasized below, the steady state characteristics of an economy, although they reflect its long-run position, can be misleading if used to

---

[3] In fact, computing technology has advanced to the point where the simulation model described below is available for use on personal computers.

1 Introduction

compare alternative fiscal policies. For example, in the base case simulations of Chapter 5, the wage tax is associated with higher long-run capital per capita than the income tax, although the income tax is economically more efficient. Because of the intergenerational redistribution generated by different tax systems, future generations in the long run may be better off simply because members of earlier generations suffered. There is no way to consider this intergenerational redistribution without examining the economy's dynamic transition path from one tax regime to another.

4. *Myopic dynamic models*

A general equilibrium model of the dynamic transition must incorporate forward-looking behavior into the actual determination of the time path of prices and policy variables facing households and firms. Hence, the solution of the dynamic transition path presents problems that are much more imposing than finding the equilibrium of a single steady state. If, however, one makes the extreme simplifying assumption that individuals behave "as if" economic conditions were not changing, the economy's dynamic path can be solved forward recursively, one year at a time, without regard to the impact of future conditions on current behavior.

Although this assumption of "myopia" or "static expectations" is not satisfactory when the economy is changing every year, it does provide some insight into how the economy might look in the short run after a policy change and how long the economy might take to adjust to such a change. Miller and Upton (1974) provided perhaps the first dynamic simulations to be based on a life cycle model assuming such static expectations. Summers (1980) extended his own steady state calculations to the transition path of the economy after a change in tax structure, again under the assumption of myopia. Seidman (1983) has continued this line of research, examining some of the questions considered in this book.

In myopic dynamic simulation models, however, it is difficult to perform meaningful calculations of the welfare effects of changes in fiscal policy. Since individual households are assumed to ignore the economic impacts of such changes, one cannot separate the effects of the policy itself from the effects of such irrational household behavior. In addition, consistent application of the myopic expectations hypothesis requires that agents ignore, or fail to perceive, future policy changes. In the simulation of policies such as temporary tax cuts, the assumption of myopic expectations can lead to dramatically different short-run responses from those arising in the same model, but with rational households.

E. A dynamic, perfect foresight general equilibrium model

In a series of articles (Auerbach and Kotlikoff, 1983a, b, c, d, 1985a, b; Auerbach, Kotlikoff, and Skinner, 1983) we developed a life cycle dynamic simulation model that solves for the economy's path under the assumption that households and firms rationally take account of future changes in economic conditions. In fact, individuals in the model have perfect foresight; along the solution path of the economy described by the model individuals and firms make decisions based on correct expectations of future economic variables.

Although perfect foresight may, at first, strike the reader as an extrem. assumption, it appears to be a useful benchmark for analyzing behavior, just as the assumption that consumers optimally choose among commodities appears useful in elementary demand analysis. The assumption of fully rational perfect foresight provides a useful benchmark because deviations from full rationality are not likely to be systematic. Thus some households may overestimate future wages and others underestimate them. In contrast to the rational expectations assumptions, the assumption of myopic expectations implies that all households are irrational in a particular manner.

1. *Households*

The life cycle model developed by Modigliani and Brumberg (1954) and Ando and Modigliani (1963) provides the basic theoretical framework for modeling household behavior. According to this theory, households rationally choose levels of current and future consumption and leisure. The life cycle model examined here is a "pure" life cycle model in that households are assumed neither to leave bequests nor to receive inheritances. Each household is represented by an adult who lives for 55 years. (In versions of the model designed to address demographic change, children are also present in the household.) The adult chooses a path of consumption and labor supply over his lifetime that is optimal, given his preferences and lifetime budget constraint. The labor supply decision encompasses not only the decision of how much to work in any given year, but also whether to work at all or to retire.

The extent to which the pure life cycle model without bequests characterizes actual behavior is a matter of considerable controversy. There is uncertainty about whether the wealth accumulation of households follows the "hump saving" pattern of net saving during middle age followed by dissaving during retirement (Mirer, 1979; King and Dicks-Mireaux, 1982; Bernheim, 1981) and whether most of the economy's capital stock can be traced to prior life cycle asset accumulation (Tobin, 1967; White,

1 Introduction

1978; Darby, 1979; Kotlikoff and Summers, 1981, 1987; Modigliani, 1983, 1984). A number of authors have suggested that an accurate description of aggregate saving behavior must treat the bequest motive, liquidity constraints, and the absence of competitive annuities markets.[4] Although each of these considerations may be significant, the basic life cycle model remains an important benchmark for studying fiscal policy.

2. Firms

The production sector of the simulation model is characterized by a single representative firm that uses capital and labor in production. Although there is a single homogeneous labor input, workers of different ages are assumed to differ in their skill levels; that is, some workers provide more of the homogeneous labor input per unit of time than do others. The representative firm hires factors and sells output competitively and is rationally valued by the stock market. The firm's investment decisions are governed by current and future after-tax profitability, subject to the restrictions imposed by short-run adjustment costs. The first model of a present value maximizing firm with adjustment costs is due to Eisner and Strotz (1963). Grunfeld (1960) first explicitly linked the investment decision to the observed market value of the firm. Jorgenson (1963) first showed how to incorporate the U.S. business tax structure into the theoretical model in a realistic way. The inclusion of adjustment costs gives rise to a "q" model of investment, as first described by Tobin (1969) and Lucus and Prescott (1971) and examined by Hayashi (1982), Abel (1979), Poterba (1984), Summers (1981b, c, d), and others.

3. Government

Government in the model consists of two institutions. One, the fiscal authority, provides general public services and has the power to levy taxes of all sorts and to issue short-term debt. In addition to levying a progressive income tax, the fiscal authority can levy progressive taxes on capital income, labor income, or consumption; and it can provide investment incentives. The second institution is the social security system, which, as in the United States, levies its own payroll taxes to finance its provision of retirement benefits.

A key requirement of the model is intertemporal government budget balance; that is, the model does not permit consideration of economically infeasible policies such as perpetual increases in the budget deficit. Built into the model is the requirement that debt issued today must, eventually, be paid off, or, more fundamentally, that government consumption

---

[4] For further discussion and references to this literature see Kotlikoff (1984a).

through time must be financed by a reduction through time in the consumption or leisure of at least one generation. This aspect of fiscal policy has come to be recognized in the economics literature (Blinder and Solow, 1973; Auerbach and Kotlikoff, 1983a; Sargent and Wallace, 1981), but its policy implications are still not fully appreciated.

4. *What's not included*

Despite the complexity of the model just described, it would be a hopeless task to attempt to include all the interesting aspects of economic behavior in a simulation model (even with the rapidly declining costs of computation). The model was originally designed to study a particular set of fiscal policy questions and has been extended to other issues such as labor supply distortions and demographics. Still, there are certain interesting macroeconomic questions for which the model in its current form would not be a suitable tool of analysis. It will be useful to mention some of these at the outset so that the model's limitations as well as its strengths are understood by the reader.

There is only one type of government debt in this model and no money. Hence, the question of inflation and the distortions caused by the interaction of real and nominal magnitudes cannot be addressed. That money is not required in a model of this type has led monetary economists over the years to a variety of explanations for money demand. Recent research has emphasized the role of transactions costs and constraints requiring money as a means of payment,[5] but this is still an unresolved area, as is the entire issue of why labor and financial contracts are often not indexed in the presence of inflation. Introducing money into the model in a satisfactory way would constitute an enormous task. Introducing it in an ad hoc fashion (for example, by entering money holdings directly as an object of consumer preferences) would be relatively simple, but probably misleading.

Although money is excluded, financial variables are determined in the model. The value of the stock market plays a significant role in the model, particularly in the presence of investment incentives. In general the model provides considerable insight into the interconnections of financial and real variables.

The model does not directly incorporate government optimization decisions; hence, the problem of dynamic inconsistency of government policies (Calvo, 1978b; Kydland and Prescott, 1977) is ignored. In comparing the welfare effects of different simulated policies, we are implicitly

---

[5] See, e.g., Grossman and Weiss (1983).

1 Introduction

assuming that any policy that is feasible (in terms of satisfying the government's revenue requirements) can also be made credible.

Because the model's labor market is competitive and there are no constraints on the behavior of firms or workers, there is no scope for "involuntary" unemployment as defined by Keynes (1936) and by subsequent writers who have focused on the role of labor contracts in the determination of short-run employment fluctuations.[6] As with the rational for money, the nature of labor market equilibria or disequilibria remains a complicated and controversial area of research in macroeconomics. For the types of questions addressed in this book, however, the omission of involuntary unemployment is less serious than would be the case if one were attempting to treat issues of short-run stabilization policy.

One of the reasons why both money and unemployment are difficult to include in this model is that the existence of each in the real economy is related to uncertainty about the future. Although very simple stochastic simulation models have been used to analyze fiscal policy,[7] introducing uncertainty into this model seems computationally infeasible.

Since there is only one country present in the model, it is not possible to consider the impact of policy on exports, imports, exchange rates, or foreign investment. Finally, since the model has a single production sector it cannot take into account the effects of policy on particular markets, for example, housing.[8]

F. Organization of the book

This introduction is followed by eleven chapters. Chapter 2 presents a simple two-period life cycle model that will familiarize the reader with the terminology used in the book and identify various issues involved in solving a dynamic general equilibrium simulation model. Chapter 3 presents a detailed description of the model used throughout the book. This is a life cycle model with 55 overlapping generations of adults, competitive production, and the government institutions characterized above. Chapter 4 provides a technical discussion of the algorithm used to find the equilibrium of the simulation model.

Chapters 5 through 11 are concerned with theoretical discussions and simulation results. Chapters 6 and 7 deal with the effects of deficit finance. Chapter 6 presents simulations measuring the impact of deficits on private investment, interest rates, and welfare under a variety of assumptions about the source of the deficit and the parameters of the private

---

[6] See Azariadis and Stiglitz (1983) for a survey of such work.
[7] For example, see Auerbach (1986), Kotlikoff, Shoven, and Spivak (1986).
[8] See Gavhari (1985) for a steady state analysis of fiscal policy effects on housing.

production technology. Chapter 7 deals with the ambiguities inherent in the way fiscal deficits are customarily measured.

Chapters 5, 8, and 9 present simulations pertaining to different issues of tax structure. Chapter 5 considers the choice of alternative tax bases, including total income, consumption, labor income, and capital income. The simulations in Chapter 8 demonstrate the effects of progressive taxation. Chapter 9 focuses on business tax incentives and the important distinction between policies that are good for the stock market and policies that are good for investment.

Chapters 10 and 11 deal primarily with the impact of social security on the economy. Chapter 10 analyzes the effects of social security on saving, labor supply, and the welfare of individuals of different ages. Chapter 11 considers the repercussions of changes in the birth rate on the economy in general and on the social security system in particular.

Chapter 12 provides a summary of the book's findings, conclusions about their implications for the conduct of future fiscal policy, and an evaluation of recent fiscal policy from the perspective developed in the book.

Readers familiar with the life cycle model and its implications may choose to skip Chapter 2 or skim it for material that is unfamiliar. Those who are familiar with our previous simulation work may treat Chapter 3 in a similar fashion. The discussion in Chapter 4 will be of greatest interest to those concerned with developing and solving simulation models. Familiarity with the material in this chapter is not assumed in the subsequent chapters. Chapters 5 through 11 may be read independently, although Chapter 7 is best read after Chapter 6, Chapters 8 and 9 after Chapter 5, and Chapter 11 after Chapter 10.

Throughout the book we have tried to keep the analysis as simple as possible and the technical jargon to a minimum. In most cases what appear at first to be fairly complex results have straightforward intuitive explanations, which we attempt to provide. Enhancing the reader's understanding of the dynamics of fiscal policy is, indeed, the main purpose of this book and explains our reliance on simulation methodology. The simulation model is ideal for showing what can happen, although not necessarily what will happen. The simulation results should not be mistaken for empirical estimates, which they are not. Simulation analysis is certainly no substitute for empirical research. Rather, it provides a method of exploring the full implications of economic relations and empirical findings.

Although one should not take literally the absolute magnitudes of simulated variables, the simulation results are likely to permit more reliable inferences concerning the relative effects of alternative policies. For some policy choices a qualitative ranking of alternatives may be all that is needed. An example of this is our finding that consumption taxation is virtually always more conducive to savings than income taxation.

For other policy decisions, an understanding of fiscal mechanisms and the timing of fiscal outcomes may be most important. Thus legislators and others concerned with fiscal policy should be aware that enhancing investment incentives is equivalent to introducing a consumption tax, that unfunded social security is covert deficit finance, that significant crowding out from tax cuts occurs gradually, that increasing the progressivity of income taxation redistributes resources toward the elderly, and that baby "busts" have beneficial as well as adverse economic consequences. These and related lessons from the simulation model are the source of our interest and excitement in this book, as we hope they are for the reader.

CHAPTER 2

The two-period life cycle model: an introduction to the general model

Many of the key features of the 55-period life cycle model used to study dynamic fiscal policy can be illustrated with a simple two-period model. In this model, one young and one old generation exist at any point in time. For simplicity assume that individuals in this two-period economy work full time when young and are retired when old. Also assume that neither the population nor productivity grows and, for the moment, that there is no government. Since the old do not work, they finance their old age consumption out of savings they accumulated when young. The young choose their current consumption and anticipated old age consumption on the basis of their preferences and their lifetime resources. Since parents in this life cycle model are assumed to spend their old age resources (their savings plus income earned on their savings) entirely on their old age consumption, there are no bequests, gifts, or other forms of net intergenerational transfers to the young. As a consequence, the young have no nonhuman wealth, and the lifetime resources of the young correspond to the labor earnings they receive when young.

If one adopts the convention that output is produced, income is received, and consumption occurs at the end of each period, the tangible wealth of the economy at the beginning of any period consists of private assets held by the elderly. Since the elderly consume all available resources in their possession at the end of their last period of life, the capital stock available to the economy in the next period consists of savings by the current young that they bring into the next period (their old age).

The supplies of productive factors to the economy thus consist of the labor supply of the current young plus the capital supplied by the elderly (the savings of last period's young generation). These factors are supplied to the production sector of the economy. The output of the production sector in turn is paid out to the productive factors as returns to capital and labor. In this model, equity and debt are perfect substitutes. Hence, the elderly are completely indifferent between exchanging their capital for stocks or bonds at the beginning of their second period and receiving a return of principal plus capital income in the form of dividends and proceeds from the sale of their shares in the case of stocks and in the form of interest plus principal payments in the case of bonds.

2 The two-period life cycle model

Since the production sector is competitive, factors (labor and capital) are hired to the point where marginal revenue products equal factor payments. For the economy to be in equilibrium, the time path of factor demands must equal the time path of factor supplies.

A.   The two-period model: a Cobb–Douglas example

1.   *The supply of savings*

The workings of the two-period model and the conditions for dynamic general equilibrium will become clearer if we consider a two-period model in which both the utility and production functions are Cobb–Douglas:

$$U_t = C_{yt}^{\beta} C_{ot+1}^{1-\beta} \tag{2.1}$$

$$Y_t = K_t^{\alpha} L_t^{1-\alpha}. \tag{2.2}$$

Equation (2.1) expresses the lifetime utility of a member of generation t as a function of consumption when young, C_{yt}, and consumption when old, C_{ot+1}. The economy's production function relates output per young worker, Y_t, to capital per young worker, K_t, and labor per young worker, L_t. L_t is exogenously supplied by each young worker and is measured in units such that $L_t = 1$. Equation (2.3) gives the lifetime budget constraint of an individual who is young at time t.

$$C_{yt} + C_{ot+1}/(1 + r_{t+1}) = W_t, \tag{2.3}$$

where W_t is the wage earned in period t, and r_{t+1} is the period $t+1$ return on savings. Equation (2.3) states that the present value of consumption equals the present value of labor earnings. It can also be expressed as

$$C_{ot+1} = A_{t+1}(1 + r_{t+1}), \tag{2.3'}$$

where A_{t+1}, the assets (net wealth) of the old at time $t+1$, equals the saving carried out by these elderly when they were young, $W_t - C_{yt}$. Maximization of (2.1) subject to (2.3) yields consumption demands. In particular, $C_{yt} = \beta W_t$ and the supply of capital by the household sector, A_{t+1}, can be written as

$$A_{t+1} = (1 - \beta) W_t. \tag{2.4}$$

Profit maximization by representative firms in the economy implies the following expressions relating factor demands to factor returns:

$$W_t = (1 - \alpha) K_t^{\alpha} \tag{2.5}$$

$$r_t = \alpha K_t^{\alpha - 1}. \tag{2.6}$$

The condition for equilibrium in the market for capital is given by

$$K_t = A_t. \tag{2.7}$$

This condition must hold for each period t if the economy is to be in dynamic equilibrium. Since the assets supplied at time t depend on the consumption-saving decision made by the young at time $t-1$, which in turn is based on perceptions of r_t (which enters the budget constraint of generation $t-1$), the dynamic equilibrium, if it occurs, will depend on the expectations of successive young generations about economic conditions when they are old. Since this is a certainty model, the assumption of rational expectations reduces to that of perfect foresight. The condition of dynamic perfect foresight equilibrium can now be described as a time path of wage rates (W_t) and returns to capital (r_t) that (1) is correctly foreseen by the household sector and (2) induces a time path of supply of capital that equals the time path of demand for capital forthcoming at these factor prices.

2. Dynamics

Combining expressions (2.4), (2.5), and (2.6) provides a relationship between capital at time $t+1$ and capital at time t:

$$K_{t+1} = K_t^\alpha (1-\alpha)(1-\beta). \tag{2.8}$$

This expression can also be derived from the national income account identity that the change in the capital stock (national investment) equals national saving:

$$K_{t+1} - K_t = Y_t - C_{y,t} - C_{o,t} = K_t^\alpha - \beta W_t - K_t(1 + r_t). \tag{2.8'}$$

Equation (2.8') together with (2.5) and (2.6) implies (2.8). In the economy's steady state, capital per worker is constant, as are all other economic variables. The steady state level of capital $\hat{K}$ can be determined from (2.8) by setting $\hat{K} = K_{t+1} = K_t$. The derivative of K_{t+T} with respect to K_t evaluated at $\hat{K}$ is given by

$$dK_{t+T}/dK_t = \alpha^T. \tag{2.9}$$

The condition for local stability is that α is less than 1. In this case there is no long-run (for very large values of T) impact on the amount of capital arising from a temporary increase or decrease in the capital stock. Equation (2.8) can also be expressed as

$$K_{t+1}/K_t = (\hat{K}/K_t)^{(1-\alpha)}, \tag{2.10}$$

where $\hat{K} = [(1-\alpha)(1-\beta)]^{1/(1-\alpha)}$ is the steady state value of K. Since $1-\alpha$ is positive, K_{t+1} exceeds K_t when K_t is less than the steady state value $\hat{K}$;

2 The two-period life cycle model

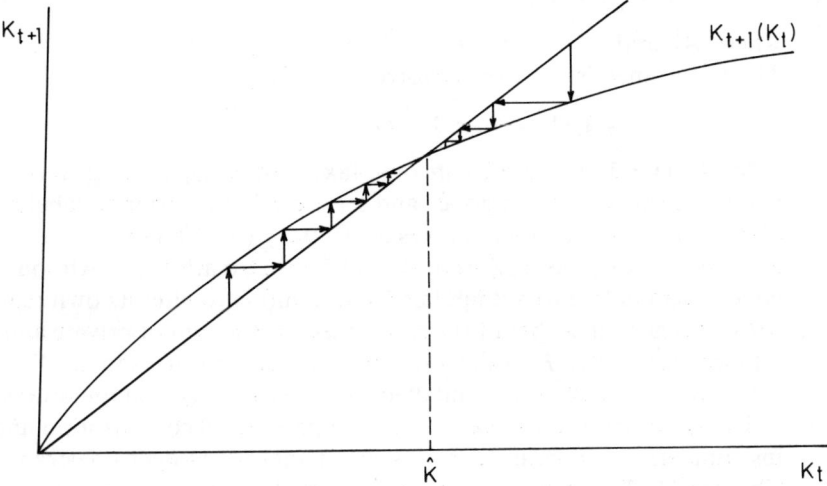

Figure 2.1. Capital accumulation in a two-period life cycle model.

that is, capital accumulation is positive when the economy's capital stock is beneath its steady state value. (This ignores the possibility of zero capital examined by Costrell, 1981.) There is capital decumulation, however, when the economy's capital stock exceeds its steady state value. Figure 2.1 provides a graph of the relationship between K_{t+1} and K_t. Around the steady state value $\hat{K}$ the evolution of the capital stock can be traced using the 45-degree line (following the arrows) and noting that the diagram is valid for analyzing capital formation between any successive periods.

3. Inclusion of the government

The inclusion of fiscal policy alters the model in two ways. First it changes lifetime budget constraints, with after-tax prices and after-tax lifetime resources substituted for their pre-tax values. Second, the capital stock now corresponds to total national net wealth, that is, the net wealth of the government plus the private sector.

Consider, as an example, how the model's equations are altered if the government is levying a proportional income tax at rate τ_t and also has a negative net worth; that is, there is outstanding government debt. The lifetime budget constraint is now written as

$$C_{y,t} + C_{o,t+1}/[1 + r_{t+1}(1 - \tau_{t+1})] = W_t(1 - \tau_t) \tag{2.3''}$$

and the equilibrium condition in the market for capital is now:

$$K_t = A_t^p + A_t^g, \tag{2.7'}$$

where A_t^p and A_t^g are private and government net worth, respectively. The government's net worth evolves according to

$$A_{t+1}^g = A_t^g(1+r_t) + \tau_t Y_t - G_t. \tag{2.11}$$

In (2.11) $\tau_t Y_t$ is period t income taxes, while G_t is the government's period t consumption of goods and services. The decision to label particular government receipts as taxes is arbitrary (see Chapter 7); hence, the division of K_t between A_t^p and A_t^g in (2.7') is also arbitrary. Although the government is free to manipulate its accounting to alter its own reported net worth as well as that of the private sector, the sum of private and government net worth, K_t, is invariant to pure accounting changes. The budget constraint (2.3') is also unaffected by accounting manipulations.

The government's choice of the time path of its consumption and tax instruments is constrained by its intertemporal budget constraint (see Chapter 3). This constraint requires that the present value of the government's outlays equals the present value of its receipts plus its initial net worth. While restricting the set of feasible policies, the government's long-term budget is consistent with a wide range of short- and medium-term policies. In particular, the government can permit debt to grow for a long time at a faster rate than the economy, although indefinite use of this policy is not feasible in this model, since under such a policy debt would eventually exceed national wealth and the capital stock would be negative.

For any particular government policy, the perfect foresight assumption requires that households correctly foresee the time path of government policy variables entering their budget constraints; for example, as suggested by equation (2.3"), the generation that is young at time t must correctly foresee both r_{t+1} and τ_{t+1}. Perfect foresight, although not required by the model, may be needed by the government if it is to implement effectively its desired fiscal program. For example, if the government myopically believes that the future level of capital, income, and other real variables will always be those that are currently observed, it may be unpleasantly surprised to learn that quite different tax rates are required in the future from those anticipated.

The government's policy affects both the time path of the economy and its steady state stability. In some cases, it is possible to characterize the evolution of the economy's capital stock in response to fiscal policy with a nonlinear first-order difference equation. For example, consider a policy of keeping government assets (debt, if A_t^g is negative) and government consumption constant at $\hat{A}^g$ and $\hat{G}$, respectively, and adjusting the tax rate τ_t each period to produce cash flow budget balance each period, namely,

2 The two-period life cycle model

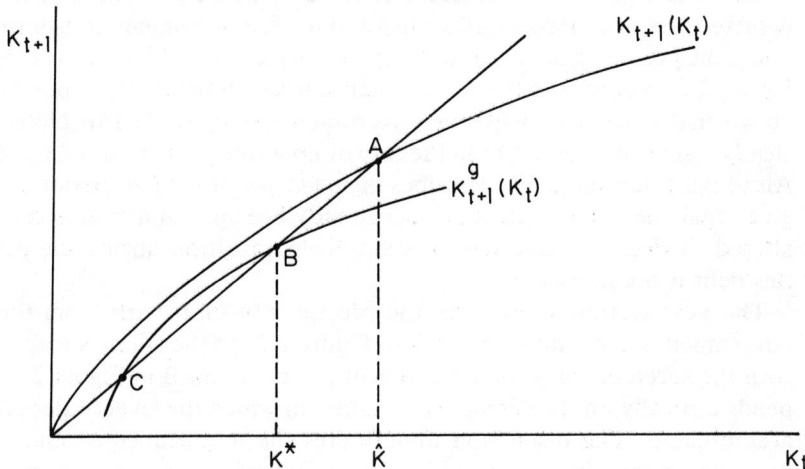

Figure 2.2. The impact of a tax-cut policy on steady state capital.

$$\tau_t = (\hat{G} - r_t \hat{A}^g)/Y_t. \tag{2.12}$$

Equations (2.7′) and (2.12) plus the formula for the savings of the young when they maximize utility subject to (2.3′) imply

$$K_{t+1} = K_t^\alpha [1 - (\hat{G} - \alpha K_t^{\alpha-1} \hat{A}^g)/K_t^\alpha](1-\alpha)(1-\beta) + \hat{A}^g, \tag{2.13}$$

and the stability condition is altered to

$$dK_{t+T}/dK_t = \prod_{s=t}^{T} (\alpha - \eta_{\tau s}[(K_s - \hat{A}^g)/K_s]) \leq 1. \tag{2.14}$$

In (2.14) $\eta_{\tau s}$ is the elasticity of the tax rate at time s with respect to the capital stock at time s. Assuming $\hat{A}^g$ is negative, then $\eta_{\tau s}$ is negative, making the stability condition less likely to be satisfied. Intuitively, an exogenous increase in capital at time t leads, in this case, to a reduction in required interest payments on government debt and to a higher level of the tax base at time t, which in this example is income. Hence, higher K_t means lower τ_t, which means more saving by the young in time t and, therefore, a larger value of capital at time $t+1$. A second potential cause of instability in this example is too large a ratio of government debt to capital.

Setting $K_{t+1} = K_t = K^*$ in (2.13) yields a nonlinear equation in the steady state capital stock. The solution to this equation may not be unique. Figure 2.2 plots equation (2.13), where $K_{t+1}^g(K_t)$ denotes the right-hand side of (2.13), under the assumption that there is one stable (point B) and one unstable (point C) steady state equilibrium (with positive capital). The function $K_{t+1}(K_t)$ from Figure 2.1, the case of no government, is also depicted. As described in detail in Chapter 3, government consumption and debt policies can crowd out capital formation, which, according to Figure 2.2, means that the K_{t+1} function with no government policy lies above that associated with the government policy of (2.13). Note that steady state capital is larger in the case of no government policy ($\hat{K} > K^*$). Although equation (2.13) describes the behavior of the two-period model given that the stock of debt $\hat{A}^g$ has already been accumulated and is not altered, it does not describe the economy's transition during the period this debt is accumulated.

The next section shows that the precise transition path from the no government steady state (point A in Figure 2.2) to the stable steady state with the specified long-run government policy (point B in Figure 2.2) depends critically on the timing and manner in which the level of debt $\hat{A}^g$ is accumulated. The discussion underscores the importance of analyzing fiscal policy transitions; analyses of fiscal policy's long-run outcome may provide little insight into short- and medium-run outcomes. Indeed, the short-run effects of particular fiscal policies can be exactly the opposite of their long-run effects.

B. Illustration of a dynamic fiscal policy transition – a temporary tax cut

A temporary tax-cut policy provides a good example of some of the issues involved in studying fiscal policy transitions. In this simple two-period life cycle model consider the case of a one-period tax cut that is deficit financed. Suppose that the economy is initially in a steady state in which there is no government debt and government consumption is financed by an income tax. The solution for the economy's initial steady state capital stock is obtained from

$$\hat{K} = \hat{K}^\alpha (1 - \hat{\tau})(1 - \alpha)(1 - \beta), \tag{2.15}$$

where $\hat{\tau}$ is the steady state income tax rate given by (2.12) under the assumption that $\hat{A}^g$ equals zero. If β equals 0.5 (half of lifetime earnings are consumed when young), α (capital's share of output) equals 0.3, and government consumption equals 15 percent of initial steady state output (which implies a value of 0.15 for $\hat{\tau}$), $\hat{K}$ equals 0.177, and the capital-output ratio, $\hat{K}^{1-\alpha}$, equals 0.297. This number may seem strange to those accustomed to thinking of capital–output ratios as being between 3 and 6, but the number makes sense once one realizes that a period in this two-period model corresponds to roughly 30 years in real time. Output in a two-period model is, therefore, roughly equivalent to output over a 30-

2 The two-period life cycle model

year period, and one must multiply the two-period capital–output ratio by 30 to arrive at a roughly equivalent annual figure. On an equivalent annual basis the two-period model's capital–output ratio is 8.91, which is larger than the ratios typically observed in Western economies.

Suppose that the government in this economy unexpectedly announces a one-period tax cut of one-third; that is, the government lowers the tax rate to 0.10 for one period. The government also announces that in the subsequent period and in each period thereafter it will set the income tax to balance its conventionally defined budget. That is, it will adjust income tax rates period by period to ensure that tax revenues equal expenditures on government consumption and interest payments on the official debt that was issued in the first period of the new policy transition. Stated differently, the government announces that following the tax cut it will maintain a constant level of debt. Since there is no population growth in this example, this policy also entails a constant per capita level of debt.

If the tax cut is announced at time $t=0$, the equation for the economy's capital stock at $t=1$ is

$$K_1 = \hat{K}^\alpha(1-0.10)(1-\alpha)(1-\beta) + A_1^g, \qquad (2.16)$$

where A_1^g is government net assets at time 1. Since the government issues debt at time 0 to offset the decline in its revenues, A_1^g is negative. The formula for A_1^g is

$$A_1^g = \hat{G} - 0.10\hat{Y}, \qquad (2.17)$$

where $\hat{Y}$ is the initial steady state level of income, and $\hat{G}$ is the constant level of government consumption (equal to $0.15\hat{Y}$). For $t \geq 2$ the economy's capital stock is determined by equation (2.13) with $\hat{A}^g = A_1^g$. During this part of the transition the income tax rate is endogenous, equaling the rate required to maintain budget balance in each period.

Table 2.1 presents the values of the economy's capital stock, debt, income, wage rate, and interest rate during the tax-cut policy transition. The new long-run capital stock is 0.097; that is, the tax-cut/debt policy "crowds out" 46 percent of the economy's capital stock. The ratio of the long-run (across steady states) reduction in the steady state capital stock to the long-run stock of debt accumulated by this policy is 2.7. This may seem large for a one-period tax cut, but recall that one period in this model is roughly 30 years. Certainly a policy that cuts tax rates by one-third for 30 years can be expected to have significant effects in a life cycle model. Table 2.1 indicates that less than one-fourth of the total crowding out of capital occurs during the first period that the tax cut is in place. By the beginning of period 3, roughly three-quarters of the eventual crowding

Table 2.1. *The transition arising from a one-period tax cut*

Period	Capital	Debt	Income	Wage	Interest rate
0	0.177	0.000	0.595	0.416	1.008
1	0.158	0.030	0.574	0.402	1.093
2	0.129	0.030	0.541	0.378	1.260
3	0.115	0.030	0.523	0.366	1.362
10	0.097	0.030	0.497	0.348	1.532
20	0.097	0.030	0.496	0.347	1.540
∞	0.097	0.030	0.496	0.347	1.540

out has occurred. This example previews the findings of Chapter 6, which indicate that crowding out can be a very slow process.

The policy also has important effects on income and factor prices. Both income and the wage rate are reduced in the long run by 17 percent, and the interest rate rises from 1.008 to 1.540. On an annualized basis this is an increase from an interest rate of 2.35 percent to 3.16 percent. The tax rate required to balance the conventionally defined long-run budget is 27 percent, which is almost twice its initial value.

The crowding out process can also be understood by referring to the national income account identity that stipulates that the change in the capital stock equals income minus total (private plus government) consumption. The decline in the capital stock between period 0 and period 1 reflects the increase in the consumption of the initial young and old generations. In the absence of the tax cut, the young and old generation at $t=0$ would have consumed 0.177 and 0.329, respectively. When the income tax is reduced, the young at $t=0$ now consume 0.187, and the old consume 0.338. The increase in the economy's period 0 consumption is 0.019, which is precisely the decline in the capital stock between period 0 and 1.

C. Deficiencies of the two-period model

Although the two-period model is a useful teaching aid, it obviously provides little or no insight into economic outcomes within a period that corresponds roughly to 30 years. In addition, certain assumptions made in the two-period model, such as complete retirement in the second period, are incompatible with other features of a more realistic model (for example, interest rate changes may alter the present value of lifetime labor earnings. Summers, 1981a, stresses this point.)

2 The two-period life cycle model

The simple two-period models described here yield first-order nonlinear difference equations in capital that can easily be used to calculate the economy's transition path. However, even the solution of a two-period model can be made complicated by small changes in the structure of the model. Suppose, for example, that in the model described above individuals work in their second as well as their first period. Then consumption of the young at time t depends on the present value of lifetime labor earnings, which, in turn, depends on the wage, interest rate, and income tax rate that will prevail at time $t+1$. These variables depend on the capital stock at $t+1$, K_{t+1}. In this model, the right-hand side of equations such as (2.13) would involve nonlinear functions of K_{t+1}, and the solutions to such problems would require numerical computation. Since the computer must be used to solve any but the simplest two-period problems and since such models provide only limited insight into short-run changes, a large-scale computer simulation model is needed to study the dynamics of fiscal policy.

CHAPTER 3

Modeling the economy

Now that the theory of life cycle behavior has been reviewed using the 2-period life cycle model, we are in a position to look at the more realistic 55-period life cycle simulation model. This model consists of three sectors: a household sector, a production sector, and a government sector. For each sector, there is a system of nonlinear equations relating endogenous behavioral variables (e.g., consumption, labor supply, etc.) to predetermined economic variables and taste and technological parameters. By jointly solving the equations of the sectors, we can obtain a solution for the equilibrium path of the economy.

A. Household behavior

At any given time the household sector comprises 55 overlapping generations of adults. Each year one generation dies and another takes its place. It is useful to think of these "new" adults as being 21 years old with an expected age of death of 75 years. As with other aspects of uncertainty found in the real world, lifetime uncertainty is not considered in this model.

Individual tastes are assumed to be identical, with differences in behavior being generated entirely by differences in economic opportunities. Since all individuals in an age cohort are assumed to be identical, all differences in economic opportunities are cross-cohort differences. The assumption that a single member is representative of each generation makes it possible to describe the aggregate behavior of members of a generation by the behavior of a single member.

Except where demographic questions are of central importance, the model does not include children and explicit family structure, and the rate of population growth is fixed at some constant annual rate, denoted by n.[1] Unless otherwise indicated, n is set equal to 0.01.

Households in the model make lifetime decisions about consumption and leisure on the basis of the life cycle model of behavior, leaving no bequests and receiving no inheritances. As noted in the introduction, evidence is mixed about how accurately this strict version of the life cycle

---

[1] These issues are discussed in Chapter 11.

3 Modeling the economy

model describes individual behavior, but it remains the best alternative for examining problems of the sort considered in this book.

1. Preferences

Each household is assumed to have preferences that can be represented by a utility function with current and future values of consumption and leisure as arguments. Leisure is measured as a fraction of the maximum amount of time an individual could work in a given year, taking values between zero and one.

We restrict preferences by requiring that the utility function be time-separable and of the nested, constant elasticity of substitution (CES) form. Time separability means that lifetime utility can be expressed as a function of individual functions of leisure and consumption in each period:

$$U(c, l) = U[u_1(c_1, l_1), \ldots, u_{55}(c_{55}, l_{55})], \tag{3.1}$$

where c_t and l_t are consumption and leisure in year t. It is also assumed here that the functions $u_t(\cdot)$ do not vary over time, so that $u_t(\cdot) \equiv u(\cdot)$. The nested CES form further restricts both functions, $u(\cdot)$ and $U(\cdot)$. The annual function takes the form

$$u_t = [c_t^{(1-1/\rho)} + \alpha l_t^{(1-1/\rho)}]^{1/(1-1/\rho)}, \tag{3.2}$$

while the lifetime function is written

$$U = 1/(1-1/\gamma) \sum_{t=1}^{55} (1+\delta)^{-(t-1)} u_t^{(1-1/\gamma)}, \tag{3.3}$$

where ρ, α, γ, and δ are taste parameters that permit a wide range of individual behavior to be represented by this general specification of preferences. Each is associated with a different aspect of individual tastes.

The parameter ρ determines how responsive an individual's annual labor supply is to that year's wage rate. As was first shown by Arrow et al. (1961), the elasticity of substitution between c_t and l_t in expression (3.2) is constant and equal to ρ. That is, the percentage change in the ratio of l to c with respect to a percentage change in the wage rate always equals ρ. The term α represents the intensity of household preferences for leisure relative to consumption. The greater is α, the less labor the household will supply in order to obtain consumption goods, preferring a greater amount of leisure instead. Were α equal to zero, households would choose to have no leisure, and the result would be a fixed labor supply assumption, as in some other models.

In expression (3.3), δ is a discount rate, often referred to as the "pure" rate of time preference. It indicates the degree to which, other things being equal, the household would prefer leisure and consumption in an earlier rather than later year. The larger is δ, the more of its lifetime resources a household will spend early in its life and the less it will save. The remaining taste parameter, γ, can be shown to equal the household's intertemporal elasticity of substitution between consumption in different years. The elasticity of substitution determines the percentage change in the ratio of any two years' consumption with respect to a percentage change in the relative price of consumption in the two years. The size of γ governs the responsiveness of households to changes in the incentive to save.

Although this is an extremely general utility function, it does impose certain constraints on preferences. First, the degree of substitutability of commodities across time and within any year is fixed by the constant elasticities of substitution, ρ and γ. Second, the intertemporal elasticity of substitution, γ, expresses the degree of substitutability of leisure, as well as consumption, across different years. Hence, one cannot consider preferences in which leisure is either less or more substitutable over time than consumption. Finally, time separability means that individual decisions at any time depend only on the future; past levels of consumption and leisure will bear on a household's preferred behavior only insofar as they alter the household's current net worth. Given the paucity of empirical evidence about individual preferences, it is not possible to identify precisely all of the preference parameters even of the present model. There is little reason, therefore, to resort to a more general, and more complicated, model.

The values used for different parameters of the household utility function, together with those characterizing firm behavior, are discussed in Chapter 4.

2. *The household budget constraint*

At each date, the household decides how much to work and how much to consume. The excess of after-tax earnings from labor and capital income is saved and added to the household's stock of assets. Because the household has a lifetime horizon, it makes its current choice as part of a lifetime plan for consumption and labor supply in each future year, deciding on the path for labor and consumption over time that maximizes its utility function (3.3) subject to the lifetime budget constraint that it leave no debts.

No other budget-related constraints are placed on the household. Such constraints could include a requirement that the household never, rather than just not at death, be in a position of net indebtedness. Such a con-

3 Modeling the economy

straint would make more sense in a model with uncertain lifetime or individual bankruptcy, where repayment of debts could be avoided through death or default. There is some indirect evidence that at least a small portion of the population faces such a "liquidity" constraint, in that aggregate consumption appears to be somewhat more sensitive to contemporaneous increases in income than would be predicted by the life cycle model with lifetime planning horizons (Hall and Mishkin, 1981; Flavin, 1981). Whether this represents liquidity constraints or myopic behavior has not been established.[2] However, this does not appear to be an important omission given the other abstractions from reality and our emphasis on medium- and long-run behavior of the economy.

Formally, the household chooses only its current level of consumption and leisure in each year, along with its planned consumption and leisure in future years. Given that households are assumed to have perfect foresight, however, each year's current decision will be consistent with previously made plans. Therefore we can consider the entire path of consumption and leisure as having resulted from a single optimization decision at the date of the household's "birth," when it has no previously accumulated assets.[3]

In the absence of taxation and social security, the household's budget constraint depends only on current and future values of interest rates and wage rates. The requirement that the present value of lifetime consumption not exceed the present value of lifetime earnings is, in this case,

$$\sum_{t=1}^{55} \prod_{s=1}^{t} [1+r_s]^{-1} [w_t e_t (1-l_t) - c_t] \geq 0, \tag{3.4}$$

where r_t is the interest rate in period t, w_t is the standardized wage rate in year t (the wage rate of a new adult), and e_t is an adjustment factor to allow for the fact that the household may earn more or less per hour in year t because of differences in skill levels among households of different ages. One may think of the vector **e**, composed of values of e_t for all t, as the household's "human capital" profile, reflecting its change in earning capacity over time. It is taken as fixed from the household's viewpoint.

In addition to this overall budget constraint, it is reasonable to impose the requirement that labor supply can never be negative; that is, if the

---

[2] For a different approach to the detection of such constraints from household saving behavior, see Mariger (1986).
[3] The one exception to this rule is a government policy change that is not anticipated. Here, household behavior before and after the change result from two separate optimization decisions, the first in the household's first year and the second the year that the policy change occurs (or is announced). For the second optimization decision, the household will generally have assets that it accumulated up to that date. This is discussed further in Chapter 4.

household would choose to demand more than one unit of leisure in a given period (there is nothing in the decision problem specified so far to prevent this), the individual must "retire" for that year, supplying zero labor. This is represented by the inequality constraints,

$$l_t \leq 1 \quad \text{for all } t. \tag{3.5}$$

3. Choice of consumption and leisure

For expositional purposes, let us consider first how households behave in their consumption and labor supply decisions in the absence of government policy. Maximization of the utility function (3.3) subject to the budget constraint (3.4) and the retirement constraints (3.5) yields first-order conditions for consumption and leisure in each year that must be satisfied by the optimum values of consumption and leisure:

$$(1+\delta)^{-(t-1)}\Omega_t c_t^{-1/\rho} = \lambda \left[\prod_{s=2}^{t}(1+r_s)^{-1}\right] \tag{3.6a}$$

$$(1+\delta)^{-(t-1)}\Omega_t \alpha l_t^{-1/\rho} = \lambda \left[\prod_{s=2}^{t}(1+r_s)^{-1}\right] w_t^*, \tag{3.6b}$$

where λ is the shadow price of the lifetime budget constraint and represents the utility value of an additional unit of income, in present value, and the terms Ω and w^* are defined by

$$\Omega_t = [c_t^{(1-1/\rho)} + \alpha l_t^{(1-1/\rho)}]^{[(1/\rho - 1/\gamma)/(1-1/\rho)]} \tag{3.7}$$

$$w_t^* = w_t e_t + \mu_t, \tag{3.8}$$

where μ_t is the shadow wage in year t. This term differs from zero if and only if the individual chooses to retire in year t and represents the excess over the effective wage per unit of leisure foregone, $w_t e_t$, that the individual would require to leave retirement and supply a positive amount of labor. The term w_t^* is normally referred to as the individual's "reservation" wage.

The combination of conditions (3.6a) and (3.6b) yields an expression relating contemporaneous leisure and consumption:

$$l_t = (w_t^*/\alpha)^{-\rho} c_t \tag{3.9}$$

from which it is evident how the terms ρ and α influence the labor-leisure tradeoff. If ρ is held fixed, an increase in α increases l_t/c_t. If α is held fixed, the percentage change in l_t/c_t with respect to a change in the effective price of leisure, w_t^*, equals ρ.

Substitution of (3.9) into (3.7) provides an expression for Ω_t in terms of c_t; given this formula, (3.6a) yields an equation expressing the evolution of consumption over time for the household:

3 Modeling the economy

$$c_t = [(1+r_t)/(1+\delta)]^\gamma [v_t/v_{t-1}] c_{t-1}, \qquad (3.10)$$

where

$$v_t = [1 + \alpha\rho w_t^{*(1-\rho)}]^{[(\rho-\gamma)/(1-\rho)]}. \qquad (3.11)$$

The interpretation of (3.10) is complicated by the presence of the term v_t/v_{t-1}, which involves the effective wages w^* in both periods. In simpler models with fixed labor supply, corresponding here to the case where $\alpha = 0$, this ratio equals one and has no effect on the growth rate of consumption. In this special case, (3.10) says that consumption will grow over time if the interest rate r exceeds the pure rate of time preference δ. The rate of this growth depends on γ; the percentage change in the ratio of c_t to c_{t-1} in response to a percentage change in $(1+r)$, the relative price of consumption in the two years, equals γ, the intertemporal elasticity of substitution.

When α is nonzero, this result still holds if w^* does not vary over time. In that case, leisure and consumption grow at the same rate. More generally, however, if w^* does vary over time, the simultaneous effects of intratemporal and intertemporal substitution are at work. For example, wage growth over the life cycle does two things. It causes an increase through time in consumption, relative to leisure, but also a decline through time in leisure, as the household shifts its labor supply from earlier years to take advantage of the higher wage. The size of the first effect is governed by ρ; the size of the second by γ. If $\rho = \gamma$, these effects exactly cancel, and v always equals one. If $\rho > \gamma$, the first effect is larger, and consumption grows faster if wages grow. If $\rho < \gamma$, the intertemporal substitution effect dominates and consumption grows more slowly.

The transition equation for leisure following from (3.9) and (3.10) is

$$l_t = [(1+r_t)/(1+\delta)]^\gamma [v_t/v_{t-1}]^{-\rho} (w_t^*/w_{t-1}^*)^{-\rho} l_{t-1}, \qquad (3.12)$$

from which it can be shown that leisure grows more slowly when there is wage growth.

It is important to remember that equations (3.10) and (3.12) determine the shape of the consumption and leisure profiles, but not their absolute levels. In general, there is no analytic solution for the actual values of c and l, which must be determined numerically.[4]

---

[4] To attempt such a solution in this type of model, one would normally apply (3.10) successively to obtain an expression for c_t in terms of c_1. Use of (3.9) then allows the expression of l_t in terms of c_1 as well. Combining these expressions with the budget constraint, (3.4), then yields an equation in c_1 in terms of fixed parameters. However, when retirement is present, there are other endogenous variables in this resulting expression: the multipliers μ. Hence, one still does not have a closed form solution for c_1. When progressive taxes are present, this problem is compounded by the endogeneity of tax rates.

B. The impact of taxation on household behavior

Taxation will affect the household by altering both the absolute resources it has at its disposal and the relative prices of leisure and consumption in different years; it has both income and substitution effects. It is the latter, of course, that cause the distortions normally associated with taxation.

Different tax systems have different effects. Given the notation already introduced, these effects are easily summarized. The results presented below for the different tax systems are demonstrated in the appendix to this chapter. For convenience, we repeat the central equations governing household behavior before discussing the impact of taxation.

$$\sum_{t=1}^{55} \prod_{s=1}^{t} [1+r_s]^{-1} [w_t e_t (1-l_t) - c_t] \leq 0 \tag{3.4}$$

$$l_t \leq 1 \quad \text{for all } t. \tag{3.5}$$

$$(1+\delta)^{-(t-1)} \Omega_t c_t^{-1/\rho} = \lambda \left[\prod_{s=2}^{t} (1+r_s)^{-1} \right] \tag{3.6a}$$

$$(1+\delta)^{-(t-1)} \Omega_t \alpha l_t^{-1/\rho} = \lambda \left[\prod_{s=2}^{t} (1+r_s)^{-1} \right] w_t^* \tag{3.6b}$$

$$\Omega_t = [c_t^{(1-1/\rho)} + \alpha l_t^{(1-1/\rho)}]^{[(1/\rho - 1/\gamma)/(1-1/\rho)]} \tag{3.7}$$

$$w_t^* = w_t e_t + \mu_t \tag{3.8}$$

$$l_t = (w_t^*/\alpha)^{-\rho} c_t \tag{3.9}$$

$$c_t = [(1+r_t)/(1+\delta)]^\gamma [\nu_t/\nu_{t-1}] c_{t-1} \tag{3.10}$$

$$\nu_t = [1 + \alpha \rho w_t^{*(1-\rho)}]^{[(\rho-\gamma)/(1-\rho)]} \tag{3.11}$$

$$l_t = [(1+r_t)/(1+\delta)]^\gamma [\nu_t/\nu_{t-1}]^{-\rho} (w_t^*/w_{t-1}^*)^{-\rho} l_{t-1}. \tag{3.12}$$

1. *Income taxation*

Under a progressive income tax, there are two relevant tax rates in each year: the marginal tax rate on income (the tax on the last dollar earned), denoted by τ_t, and the average tax rate on income (total taxes divided by total income), denoted by $\bar{\tau}_t$. Expressions (3.4)–(3.12) still accurately describe behavior if a few alterations are made:

> The period t interest rate appropriate for discounting becomes $r_t(1-\bar{\tau}_t)$. This alters expressions (3.4) and (3.6).
>
> Given the use of the average tax rate in computing the after-tax discount rate, the shadow value of income appearing in (3.6) must be multiplied by the term

3 Modeling the economy

$$\theta_t = \prod_{s=t+1}^{55} [1+r_s(1-\tau_s)]/[1+r_s(1-\bar{\tau}_s)]$$

to correct for the fact that an increase in period t consumption reduces future income and future average tax rates.

The wage rate appropriate for the measurement of income in period t, in expression (3.4), becomes $w_t(1-\bar{\tau}_t)$.

The marginal wage rate w^*, defined in (3.8) and appearing in several other expressions, becomes $w_t e_t(1-\tau_t) + \mu_t$.

The marginal interest rate relevant to the transition equations (3.10) and (3.12) becomes $r_t(1-\tau_t)$.

When the income tax is a proportional one, the values of $\bar{\tau}$ and τ are the same in any given year. In this case, the adjustment simply calls for replacing the gross returns r and w with the net returns $r(1-\tau)$ and $w(1-\tau)$, with $\theta = 1$. When marginal and average tax rates differ, there are two different after-tax returns. The marginal after-tax returns matter for the determination of consumption-leisure, as in (3.9), and present-future tradeoffs, as in (3.10) and (3.12), while the average after-tax returns enter into the budget constraint.

A number of the effects of income taxation are immediately observable from these changes. First, since the net marginal wage is lower (given the gross wage w), expression (3.9) predicts a higher ratio of leisure to consumption in each year. Second, since the net marginal interest rate is lower (given r), expression (3.10) predicts a slower rate of growth in consumption. These changes in behavior will have complicated feedback effects on the economy through the production sector (changes in r and w) and the government sector (changes in τ and $\bar{\tau}$); thus the ultimate impact can be known only from solving the entire model.

2. Labor income or capital income taxation

An income tax includes both labor and capital income in its base. This is not an accurate description of what is officially called the "income tax" in most countries, because many items of income are excluded (intentionally or not) from the base. Moreover, many policy prescriptions call for the removal of all of a particular type of income from the tax base, for example, all capital income. Hence, it is important to consider income taxes that do not treat labor and capital income equally. We consider two such extreme examples: a labor income tax and a capital income tax. The expressions describing optimal behavior under each of these tax systems correspond to those for a progressive income tax where either the net returns to capital are fixed at r (the labor income tax) or the net returns to labor are fixed at w (the capital income tax).

34   **Dynamic fiscal policy**

3.   *Consumption taxation*

A progressive consumption tax is one based on the household's annual level of consumption, c_t. The tax would normally be levied on a tax exclusive base (i.e., on consumption expenditures net of tax, not gross of tax). The effect on expressions (3.4)–(3.12) is as follows:

> The average consumption tax rate enters into expression (3.4), and c_t is replaced by $c_t/(1+\bar{\tau}_t)$.
> The marginal consumption tax rate enters into the right-hand side of (3.6a), and λ is premultiplied by the term $(1+\tau_t)$. Just as w_t^* represents the price per unit of leisure in (3.6b), this new term in (3.6a) represents the price of consumption goods, inclusive of the consumption tax.
> This has the effect of reducing the effective marginal wage, since consumption goods cost more per dollar of income. Hence, in expressions (3.9) and (3.11), w_t^* is divided by $(1+\tau_t)$.
> The marginal price of consumption in different periods, $(1+\tau)$, affects the rate of consumption growth. In expression (3.10), the term $(1+r_t)/(1+\delta)$ is multiplied by the ratio $(1+\tau_{t-1})/(1+\tau_t)$. Thus if the marginal consumption tax rises over time, consumption will grow less quickly.

As should be evident, a consumption tax, like an income tax, affects both the labor–leisure and savings decisions. However, in the special case where the tax is proportional at a constant rate, the consumption taxes do not enter directly into expression (3.10), except through the terms ν_t and ν_{t-1}. In this case, a consumption tax and a labor income tax both distort only the labor–leisure choice, through a reduction in the effective marginal wage.

4.   *Social security*

The social security system levies payroll taxes on individual households and gives them retirement benefits. There are a number of ways to treat these taxes and benefits. At one extreme, one could simply view the payroll taxes as "forced saving" by households and the benefits as a return to such saving. In a model without liquidity constraints, such as the present one, this would have no effect on the ultimate behavior of the household, which would simply offset the forced saving by its own dissaving.

At the other extreme, one could treat the benefits and payroll taxes as being unrelated, with the taxes having a potentially distortionary effect on labor supply. However, neither of these polar extremes correctly describes the social security system in the United States, where benefits and

3 Modeling the economy

taxes are tied together in an imperfect and complicated way. The method of dealing with social security from the household's perspective is discussed in Chapter 10.

C. Firm behavior

1. *The production function*

The model has a single production sector that is assumed to behave competitively, using capital and labor subject to a constant-returns-to-scale production function. Capital is assumed to be homogeneous and nondepreciating, while labor differs only in its efficiency. That is, all forms of labor are perfect substitutes, but individuals of different ages supply different amounts of some standard measure of labor input per unit of leisure foregone. This amount is the term e_t for age cohort t, introduced above.

The production function is assumed to be of the constant elasticity of substitution form

$$Y_t = A[\epsilon K_t^{(1-1/\sigma)} + (1-\epsilon)L_t^{(1-1/\sigma)}]^{[1/(1-1/\sigma)]}, \tag{3.13}$$

where Y_t, K_t, and L_t are output, capital, and labor at time t, A is a scaling constant, ϵ is a parameter measuring the intensity of use of capital in production, and σ is the elasticity of substitution in production, representing the percentage change in the ratio of K to L with respect to a percentage change in the wage rental ratio, w/r.

Throughout the simulations presented in the following chapters we assume A to be constant over time and thereby rule out the possibility of technological change. It is generally impossible to include such change without also assuming a continuous change in tastes; otherwise the result would be either an increasing or decreasing trend in labor force participation, which would lead in the long run to an absurd result.[5]

2. *The demand for labor*

The model incorporates the assumption that firms can adjust the amount of labor employed costlessly. Combined with the previously stated assumption of competitive behavior, this leads to the standard result that, in equilibrium, the gross (of taxes) wage in period t, w_t, must equal the marginal product of labor. Given the form of the production function, this leads to the equation

---

[5] To see this problem, note from equation (3.9) that as wages grow over time, the consumption–leisure ratio will trend continuously unless $\rho = 1$, which corresponds to the special Cobb–Douglas case where consumption is a constant fraction of potential labor income.

$$w_t = (1-\epsilon)A[\epsilon K_t^{(1-1/\sigma)} + (1-\epsilon)L_t^{(1-1/\sigma)}]^{1/(\sigma-1)}L_t^{-1/\sigma}, \qquad (3.14)$$

which expresses the wage as a function of the stocks of capital and labor in the same year.

3. The investment decision

Many economic models treat capital symmetrically with labor in the firm's decision process and assume that capital can be adjusted costlessly to a new desired level. In some cases, we make this assumption in our own analysis, in which case the firm sets the marginal product of capital equal to the interest rate, r:

$$r_t = \epsilon A[\epsilon K_t^{(1-1/\sigma)} + (1-\epsilon)L_t^{(1-1/\sigma)}]^{1/(\sigma-1)}K_t^{-1/\sigma}. \qquad (3.15)$$

Equations (3.14) and (3.15) together give the wage rate and interest rate as functions of the stocks of capital and labor.

This seems to be a much less accurate description of the actual conditions governing investment than it is of those governing work force decisions. Although it makes for much simpler analysis, it is not always an innocuous assumption to impose, particularly when the short-run effects of policy are at issue.

4. Adjustment costs and "q"

Many theoretical alternatives are more consistent with the observed lags in the investment process. One that is particularly tractable is based on the "q" theory of investment. As first envisaged by Tobin (1969), this theory predicts that firms will invest when the stock market value of their assets exceeds the cost of replacement.

As subsequently shown by Abel (1979), this behavior pattern is consistent with the firm's convex costs of installing new capital goods, in addition to the price of the goods themselves. Were no such adjustment costs present, firms would find it optimal to invest so much in each year that the gap between the market value and the replacement cost of capital goods would be driven to zero. With respect to adjustment costs, the high levels of investment that this policy would sometimes require would cause the firm to incur unacceptably large additional expenses. The firm would thus be motivated to "smooth" its investment over time. With this smoothing or "partial adjustment," behavior comes the possibility that a firm's market value will, from time to time, vary from the replacement cost of its assets, being higher in periods of strong investment and lower in periods of weak investment.

3 Modeling the economy

Subsequent work by other authors has clarified the conditions required for the firm's market value to be an accurate indicator of the incentive to invest (Hayashi, 1982) and the alterations necessary to the model in the presence of taxes (Summers, 1981b). We model investment according to the developments in this literature.

Each firm is assumed to face adjustment costs that are quadratic in investment. The total cost of new investment goods in year t is

$$C(I_t) = [1 + .5b(I_t/K_t)]I_t, \qquad (3.16)$$

where b is some technologically determined parameter. The second term in square brackets represents the additional installation costs. This yields a marginal cost of investment of $[1 + b(I_t/K_t)]$, which increases linearly with I_t. Since this form of the adjustment cost function leads to investment paths that are identical for firms of different sizes except for their scale, a firm's value must bear a fixed relationship to the size of its capital stock. This value, in turn, must equal the marginal cost of capital goods, since new and old capital goods must be of equal future profitability (Hayashi, 1982). Note that when I_t is positive the marginal cost of investment (the market value of capital) exceeds the replacement cost, and when I_t is negative the marginal cost of investment is less than the replacement cost.

5. Taxation and market value

In the presence of taxation, however, the marginal cost of investment goods to the firm must be calculated in after-tax terms. This requires two adjustments to our model. First, the costs of adjustment, as an expense, should be tax deductible. This makes the marginal adjustment cost, after tax, equal to $b(1 - \tau_t)(I_t/K_t)$ in year t, where τ_t is the marginal tax rate faced by the firm. In addition, there may be investment subsidies that reduce the firm's out-of-pocket cost still further. In the United States, these generally take two forms: investment tax credits and accelerated depreciation allowances. In each case, the firm receives a reduction in taxes either immediately or soon after it purchases an asset; this reduction effectively reduces its price.

In the model, we represent investment incentives of this type by assuming that firms are allowed to deduct a fraction, z, of their new investment purchases (exclusive of adjustment costs, which are already fully expensed). This means that the net cost of such goods to the firm is $(1 - z\tau_t)I_t$. Hence, at time t the total marginal cost of investment, which equals the value of the firm, is

$$q_t = [(1 - z\tau_t) + (1 - \tau_t)b(I_t/K_t)]. \qquad (3.17)$$

Note that, even absent adjustment costs, q_t will not equal one. The reason is that although old and new capital goods are equally productive, their different tax treatments (old capital will receive no additional investment incentives) must be reflected in the price of the firm's existing capital stock.[6]

6. The relationship of real and financial variables

Just as a firm's market value will vary from capital stock replacement cost because of adjustment costs and investment incentives, so, too, the interest rate will vary from the marginal product of capital. In behaving competitively, firms should purchase more capital until the last unit yields a rate of return equal to the interest rate. When capital's market value within the firm varies over time, such capital gains and losses form a part of the return to capital.

This total rate of return, based on the after-tax marginal cost of investment goods (which equals q), must equal the interest rate:

$$r_t = (mpk_t + q_{t+1} - q_t)/q_t, \qquad (3.18)$$

where mpk_t is the marginal product of capital defined in expression (3.15) and q_t is as defined in (3.17). This equation and (3.17) show that the interest rate will equal the marginal product of capital when there are neither adjustment costs nor capital gains arising because of reductions between t and $t+1$ in the term τz. Adjustment costs work in the opposite direction, raising q and the required marginal product of capital. During periods of strong investment, when q is especially high and expected to fall, this anticipated capital loss raises the required marginal product of capital still further.

D. Government behavior

The government in this model raises taxes to pay for its own spending on goods and services. Because we focus on fiscal issues, we ignore the indirect effects that this spending has on consumer behavior and assume simply that government consumption grows at the same rate as the population. In addition, there is a separate social security system, modeled after the one found at present in the United States. This system has its own tax instrument, the payroll tax, and faces the requirement that it be self-financing over time. Although the U.S. unified federal budget now

---

[6] For further discussion of the tax adjustment of q in the United States, see Summers (1981b). For historical calculations of the size of the tax discount associated with investment incentives, see Auerbach (1983a).

3 Modeling the economy

includes both general and social security revenues and expenditures, this self-financing requirement still remains in force.

1. The government budget constraint

Nothing in the model or in the real world requires the government's budget to be in balance in any given year. As long as the government is free to issue debt, the difference between spending and taxes simply results in an equal increase in the amount of outstanding government debt. This may be written

$$D_{t+1} - D_t = G_t + r_t D_t - T_t, \qquad (3.19)$$

where D_t is the stock of outstanding debt at the beginning of year t, G_t is government spending on goods and services in year t, $r_t D_t$ is spending on debt service in year t, and T_t is net tax collections in year t. Note that common measures of the level of the budget and government spending include not only spending on goods and services, but also debt service and transfer payments. In (3.19) transfer payments are subtracted from gross tax receipts to obtain the net tax figure.

Successive application of expression (3.19) for time periods 0 to N yields

$$\sum_{t=0}^{N} \left[\prod_{s=0}^{t} (1+r_s)^{-1} \right] T_t = \sum_{t=0}^{N} \left[\prod_{s=0}^{t} (1+r_s)^{-1} \right] G_t + D_0 - \prod_{t=0}^{N} (1+r_t)^{-1} D_N. \qquad (3.20)$$

If debt cannot grow as fast or faster than the interest rate indefinitely, the last term in this expression must converge to zero as N becomes large. This must happen, in the long run, unless the economy's growth rate exceeds the rate of interest, a condition never satisfied in the long run in our model. Thus, the government budget constraint in (3.20) reduces to the requirement that the present value of tax collections (over an infinite horizon) must equal the present value of government spending on goods and services plus the initial stock of government debt:

$$\sum_{t=0}^{\infty} \left[\prod_{s=0}^{t} (1+r_s)^{-1} \right] T_t = \sum_{t=0}^{\infty} \left[\prod_{s=0}^{t} (1+r_s)^{-1} \right] G_t + D_0. \qquad (3.21)$$

It should be stressed that this is not an assumption, but a result only of the requirement that the growth rate of government debt be bounded above by the interest rate. An immediate implication is that there are restrictions on the feasibility of certain changes in fiscal policy that involve changes in revenue or expenditures. For example, normally there cannot be such a thing as a "permanent" income tax cut, for this would introduce an imbalance to the equality, in present value, of taxes and spending plus initial debt. Income tax cuts may be of long duration, but must eventually bring forth compensating tax increases.[7] Even if the government does not increase taxes directly, some compensating effect must take place, be it a renunciation of the federal debt or an increase in the "inflation tax" (Sargent and Wallace, 1981). Since neither of these avenues is open in our model, the government must offset tax cuts in one year with tax increases in another or with current or future reductions in government consumption. Which taxes will be increased and in what year is, in reality, uncertain. In the model, however, we assume that the government's future policy compensations are announced and known.

Since there are many possible compensating future responses to a current tax cut or other current government policy, one cannot sensibly talk about a current policy's effect on today's economic behavior without specifying and simultaneously discussing compensating future policies. The reason is simply that today's economic behavior depends on future expected as well as current policies. Thus, there is no single answer to the question How will current saving respond to a reduction in capital income taxes? The answer depends strongly on whether this cut is paid for by increases in future taxes on labor income, future taxes on capital income, or current taxes on labor income.

2. *The instruments of government policy*

In formulating fiscal policy subject to the intertemporal budget constraint described in (3.21), the government in our model has at its disposal progressive taxes on consumption, all income, capital income, and labor income. The debt that it issues when the budget is not in balance is short-term debt, of one year's maturity. In some simulations the compensating changes that the government undertakes to satisfy its intertemporal budget constraint will also be required to satisfy additional, short-run constraints, such as year-by-year budget balance.

A typical fiscal policy experiment consists of specifying the change in policy that is desired along with the source from which the compensating change must occur. For example, one could specify a 20 percent reduction in the income tax for five years, followed thereafter by an increase in the income tax sufficient to satisfy expression (3.21). The deficit, rather than a particular tax instrument, may also be used as the direct policy tool. One could specify a 10 percent increase in the current annual deficit

---

[7] An exception to this rule occurs when the economy is in such a distorted equilibrium as the result of high marginal tax rates that lowering tax rates does not lower revenue. Empirical evidence suggests that such "Laffer curve" considerations are unimportant (see Fullerton, 1982).

3 Modeling the economy

for five years, and concurrent tax rates would automatically adjust to yield this result.

3. *The social security system*

The social security system is kept logically separate in the model because of its historical legal and financial separation from other government operations, at least in the United States. Payroll taxes are assessed independently of whatever other taxes on labor income may exist, and benefits are paid for by payroll taxes.

As in reality, the system's net cash flow (tax collections less benefits) is not required to be nonnegative in any given year; the only stipulation is that a present value budget constraint like the one in (3.21) be satisfied. Many of the subsequent social security simulations, however, are conducted assuming annual social security budget balance. It has been the policy of the U.S. social security system to maintain its accumulated trust fund at a very low level in comparison with that of its annual gross cash flow.

E. Equilibrium under perfect foresight

In the static general equilibrium models discussed in Chapter 1, a general equilibrium solution is one in which the behavior of each sector of the economy is consistent with the prices that are established, and markets clear. The concept of equilibrium is no different in our model, except that the behavior of households, firms, and the government must be consistent not only with current prices, but also with future ones.

Household labor supply and consumption must be optimal, given the entire future path of interest rates, wage rates, and tax rates. Firm investment decisions must adequately reflect the future behavior of interest rates and the stock market. The government's projected path of tax schedules must satisfy its intertemporal budget constraint. Given the behavior of each sector, markets for labor and capital must clear.

Because of the assumption of perfect foresight (the same would be true even with a limited degree of foresight), the behavior of the economy today depends on conditions in the future. One cannot compute a "separate" equilibrium for a given year without a complete characterization of future economic developments. Hence, the solution method must treat the present and future together, so that the products of different years correspond to those of different markets in the traditional large-scale static models. The exact methodology used is the subject of the next chapter.

Dynamic fiscal policy

Appendix: Effect of taxation on household behavior

This appendix demonstrates how household behavior, as described by expressions (3.4) to (3.12) in the text, is affected by taxation.

Progressive income taxation

Under progressive income taxation, the household budget constraint (3.4) becomes

$$\sum_{t=1}^{55} \left\{ \prod_{s=2}^{t} [1+r_s(1-\bar{\tau}_s)] \right\}^{-1} [w_t e_t(1-l_t)(1-\bar{\tau}_t) - c_t] \geq 0, \quad (3A.1)$$

where $\bar{\tau}_t$ is the average income tax rate in year t. Letting λ be the Lagrange multiplier associated with this constraint, and μ_t the multiplier of the retirement constraint (3.5) in year t, one obtains the following first-order condition for the maximization of the utility function (3.3) with respect to c_t:

$$(1+\delta)^{-(t-1)} \Omega_t c_t^{-1/\rho} = \lambda \left(\left\{ \prod_{s=2}^{t} [1+r_s(1-\bar{\tau}_s)] \right\}^{-1} - J_t \right), \quad (3A.2)$$

where Ω_t is as defined in (3.7), and J_t is the indirect effect of c_t on the budget constraint through changes in the average tax rates $\bar{\tau}_{t+1}, \ldots, \bar{\tau}_{55}$. Letting M_s, $s > t$, be the partial derivative of the budget constraint with respect to $\bar{\tau}_t$, we have

$$J_t = \sum_{s=t+1}^{55} M_s \frac{\partial \bar{\tau}_s}{\partial c_t}, \quad (3A.3)$$

where

$$M_s = \left[\frac{r_s}{1+r_s(1-\bar{\tau}_{ys})} \right]$$

$$\cdot \sum_{q=s}^{55} \left\{ \prod_{z=2}^{q} [1+r_z(1-\bar{\tau}_z)] \right\}^{-1} [(1-\bar{\tau}_q) w_q e_q (1-l_q) - c_q]$$

$$- \left\{ \prod_{z=2}^{s} [1+r_z(1-\bar{\tau}_z)] \right\}^{-1} w_s e_s (1-l_s). \quad (3A.4)$$

Note that assets at the beginning of year s must equal the present value of planned consumption less planned earnings over the years s through 55. That is,

$$A_s = \sum_{x=s}^{55} \left\{ \prod_{z=s}^{x} [1+r_z(1-\bar{\tau}_z)] \right\}^{-1} [(1-\bar{\tau}_x) w_x e_x (1-l_x) - c_x]. \quad (3A.5)$$

We can simplify (3A.4):

3 Modeling the economy

$$M_s = -\left\{\prod_{z=2}^{s}[1+r_z(1-\bar{\tau}_z)]\right\}^{-1}[w_s e_s(1-l_s)+r_s A_s]$$

$$= -\left\{\prod_{z=2}^{s}[1+r_z(1-\bar{\tau}_z)]\right\}^{-1} y_s. \tag{3A.6}$$

If $T_Y(\cdot)$ is the progressive income tax function, then $\bar{\tau}_z = T_Y(y_s)/y_s$ and $\tau_s = T_Y'(y_s)$. Thus

$$\frac{d\bar{\tau}_s}{dc_t} = \left[\frac{T_Y'(y_s)}{y_s} - \frac{T_Y(y_s)}{y_s^2}\right]\frac{dy_s}{dc_t} = (\tau_s - \bar{\tau}_s)\cdot\frac{1}{y_s}\frac{dy_s}{dc_t}. \tag{3A.7}$$

Thus, from (3A.6) and (3A.7),

$$M_s \frac{d\bar{\tau}_s}{dc_t} = -\left\{\prod_{z=2}^{s}[1+r_z(q-\bar{\tau}_z)]\right\}^{-1}(\tau_s - \bar{\tau}_s)\frac{dy_s}{dc_t}. \tag{3A.8}$$

Since l is held fixed,

$$\frac{dy_s}{dc_t} = r_s \frac{dA_s}{dc_t}. \tag{3A.9}$$

By definition,

$$A_s = A_{s-1}[1+r_s(1-\bar{\tau}_{s-1})]+w_{s-1}e_{s-1}(1-l_{s-1})(1-\bar{\tau}_{s-1})-c_{s-1}. \tag{3A.10}$$

Thus,

$$\frac{dA_s}{dc_t} = \begin{bmatrix}[1+r_{s-1}(1-\bar{\tau}_{s-1})]\dfrac{dA_{s-1}}{dc_t} - y_{s-1}\dfrac{d\bar{\tau}_{s-1}}{dc_t} & s>t \\ -1 & s=t.\end{bmatrix} \tag{3A.11}$$

Using (3A.7) and (3A.9) to solve for $d\bar{\tau}_{s-1}/dc_t$ in terms of dA_{s-1}/dc_t, we may rewrite (3A.11) as

$$\frac{dA_s}{dc_t} = \begin{bmatrix}[1+r_{s-1}(1-\tau_{s-1})]\dfrac{dA_{s-1}}{dc_t} & s>t \\ -1 & s=t\end{bmatrix} \tag{3A.12}$$

which, solved recursively, yields

$$\frac{dA_s}{dc_t} = -\prod_{z=t+1}^{s-1}[1+r_z(1-\tau_z)] \tag{3A.13}$$

and, using (3A.8) and (3A.9),

$$M_s \frac{d\bar{\tau}_s}{dc_t} = \left\{\prod_{z=2}^{s}[1+r_z(1-\bar{\tau}_z)]\right\}^{-1}(\tau_s - \bar{\tau}_s)r_s\left\{\prod_{z=t+1}^{s-1}[1+r_z(1-\tau_z)]\right\}$$

$$= \left\{\prod_{z=2}^{t}[1+r_z(1-\bar{\tau}_z)]\right\}^{-1}\left\{\prod_{z=t+1}^{s-1}\frac{1+r_z(1-\tau_z)}{1+r_z(1-\bar{\tau}_z)}\right\}$$

44   Dynamic fiscal policy

$$\cdot \left\{ \frac{[1+r_s(1-\bar{\tau}_s)]-[1+r_s(1-\tau_s)]}{1+r_s(1-\tau_s)} \right\}$$

$$= \left\{ \prod_{z=t+1}^{t} [1+r_z(1-\bar{\tau}_z)] \right\}^{-1} [Q_{s-1}-Q_s], \quad (3A.14)$$

where

$$Q_s = \sum_{z=t+1}^{s} \frac{1+r_z(1-\tau_z)}{1+r_z(1+\bar{\tau}_z)}. \quad (3A.15)$$

Thus, from (3A.3)

$$J_t = \left\{ \prod_{z=2}^{t} [1+r_z(1-\bar{\tau}_z)] \right\}^{-1} [(Q_t - Q_{t+1})$$

$$+ (Q_{t+1} - Q_{t+2}) + \cdots + (Q_{54} - Q_{55})]$$

$$= \left\{ \prod_{z=2}^{t} [1+r_z(1-\bar{\tau}_z)] \right\}^{-1} [Q_t - Q_{55}]$$

$$= \left\{ \prod_{z=2}^{t} [1+r_z(1-\bar{\tau}_z)] \right\}^{-1} \left\{ 1 - \prod_{z=t+1}^{55} \left[\frac{1+r_z(1-\tau_z)}{1+r_z(1-\bar{\tau}_z)} \right] \right\}. \quad (3A.16)$$

Thus, (3A.2) may be rewritten (compare to 3.6a in the text)

$$(1+\delta)^{-(t-1)} \Omega_t c_t^{-1/\rho} = \lambda \left\{ \prod_{s=2}^{t} [1+r_s(1-\bar{\tau}_s)] \right\}^{-1} \theta_t, \quad (3A.17)$$

where

$$\theta_t = \prod_{s=t+1}^{55} \frac{1+r_s(1-\tau_s)}{1+r_s(1-\bar{\tau}_s)}. \quad (3A.18)$$

The first-order condition with respect to l_t, arrived at in similar fashion (compare to 3.6b), is

$$(1+\delta)^{-(t-1)} \Omega_t \alpha l_t^{-1/\rho} = \lambda \left\{ \prod_{s=2}^{t} [1+r_s(1-\bar{\tau}_s)] \right\}^{-1} \theta_t (W_t e_t + \mu_t). \quad (3A.19)$$

The remaining effects of the income tax follow directly from these equations.

Analysis of the effects of progressive taxation of labor or capital income separately follows in a straightforward way, with either the marginal and average tax rates on capital or those on labor being set equal to zero.

Progressive consumption taxation

Here, the budget constraint (3.4) becomes

$$\sum_{t=1}^{55} \left[\prod_{s=2}^{t} (1+r_s) \right]^{-1} [w_t e_t (1-l_t) - c_t (1+\bar{\tau}_{c_t})] \geq 0, \quad (3A.20)$$

3 Modeling the economy

where $\bar{\tau}_t$ is the average consumption tax rate in year t. Maximizing the associated Lagrangian with respect to c_t yields (compare with 3.6a)

$$(1+\delta)^{-(t-1)}\Omega_t c_t^{-1/\rho} = \lambda \left[\prod_{s=2}^{t}(1+r_s)\right]^{-1}\left[(1+\bar{\tau}_t)+c_t\frac{d\bar{\tau}_t}{dc_t}\right]$$

$$= \lambda \left[\prod_{s=2}^{t}(1+r_s)\right]^{-1}(1+\tau_t), \tag{3A.21}$$

using the definitions of τ_t and $\bar{\tau}_t$. The first-order condition for l_t (compare with 3.6b) is

$$(1+\delta)^{-(t-1)}\Omega_t \alpha l_t^{-1/\rho} = \lambda \left[\prod_{s=2}^{t}(1+r_s)\right]^{-1}[w_t e_t + \mu_t]. \tag{3A.22}$$

Dividing (3A.22) by (3A.20) and substituting the result into (3A.21) yields

$$(1+\delta)^{-(t-1)}c_t^{-1/\gamma}v_t^{-1/\gamma} = \lambda \left[\prod_{s=2}^{t}(1+r_s)\right]^{-1}(1+\tau_t), \tag{3A.23}$$

where v_t is as defined in (3.11).

Combining (3A.23) for successive value of t yields

$$c_t = \{[(1+r_t)/(1+\delta)][(1+\tau_{t-1})/(1+\tau_t)]\}^{\gamma}[v_t/v_{t-1}]c_{t-1} \tag{3A.24}$$

(compare with 3.10).

CHAPTER 4

Simulation methodology

The general equilibrium economic model described in Chapter 3 forms the basis for all the simulation results presented in this book. This chapter examines the choice of parameter values and the method of solving for the quantities and prices that characterize the perfect foresight equilibrium.

A. Solution method

The calculation of the equilibrium path of the economy, given a particular parameterization, typically proceeds in three stages: (1) solving for the long-run steady state of the economy before the assumed change in fiscal policy begins, (2) solving for the long-run steady state to which the economy eventually converges after the policy takes effect, and (3) solving for the transition path that the economy takes between these two steady states.

The perfect foresight assumption is important only in this third stage, since in either of the long-run steady states economic variables are constant from one year to the next; any plausible assumption about the formation of expectations would lead individuals to have correct foresight in such situations. The transition begins when information about the policy change becomes available. One should visualize this as an unanticipated change in the fiscal policy regime.

Households and firms have perfect foresight in both old and new policy regimes, but do not anticipate the policy change. The policy change may take the form of immediate changes in fiscal variables or of immediate announcements of future changes in fiscal variables. In the case of preannounced policies, the transition also begins in year 1 (the year always used to index the beginning of the transition), although there is no change in fiscal policy until several years later; that is, since households and firms have perfect foresight about the future switch in regime, in preannounced policy changes the transition begins as soon as the future policy is announced.

The iteration techniques used in each of the three stages of the solution are basically the same, although the actual procedure is more complicated when one is solving for the transition path because economic variables are changing over time.

4 Simulation methodology

1. *The initial steady state*

Solution for the equilibrium of the economy in the initial steady state amounts to solving a complicated system of nonlinear equations based on the behavior of households, firms, and the government, as outlined in Chapter 3. The solution is obtained using an iterative technique often referred to in the literature as the Gauss–Seidel method.

The algorithm starts with guesses of a subset of the endogenous variables and initially treats these variables as exogenous in some of the equations of the system in which they appear. This simplification makes the resulting system easier to solve for the endogenous variables, including the variables for which guesses were made. When the solution for these "guessed" variables equals the guesses themselves, a true solution to the full system has been found. Otherwise, the "solution" is not consistent with the values of the guessed endogenous variables, and new guesses are tried, typically a combination of the two sets of values from the previous iteration.

A schematic representation of the algorithm is given in Figure 4.1. Beginning with guesses about the aggregate capital stock, K, total labor supply, L, the age-specific shadow wages, μ, the payroll tax, ϕ, the vector of social security wealth, **SSW**, and the vectors of age-specific marginal and average tax rates, τ and $\bar{\tau}$, we use (3.14) and (3.15) to calculate the wage and interest rates consistent with the factor supplies. When combined with the tax rate, shadow wage, and social security wealth guesses, this allows us to solve for optimal household behavior using, for example, (3.4) to (3.12).

The individual labor supply decisions that result tell us whether our shadow wage guesses were accurate, and aggregation of labor supply over individuals gives a new estimate of the total supply of labor and the level of social security payroll taxes needed to pay for promised benefits. Using individual consumption decisions and knowledge of after-tax labor earnings and after-tax interest rates we can calculate accumulated savings at each age. Adding up the savings of all age groups provides a new guess of total private assets. Subtracting the assumed level of public debt yields a new guess for the capital stock. The level of assumed government revenue, combined with the new estimates of individual behavior, gives us new estimates of how high tax rates must be set to achieve this revenue requirement.

Typically, 10–20 iterations are required to achieve convergence to a solution for the initial steady state.

2. *The final steady state*

The policy change considered in a simulation may be one of two types. The first type of policy change is such that we can solve for the new steady

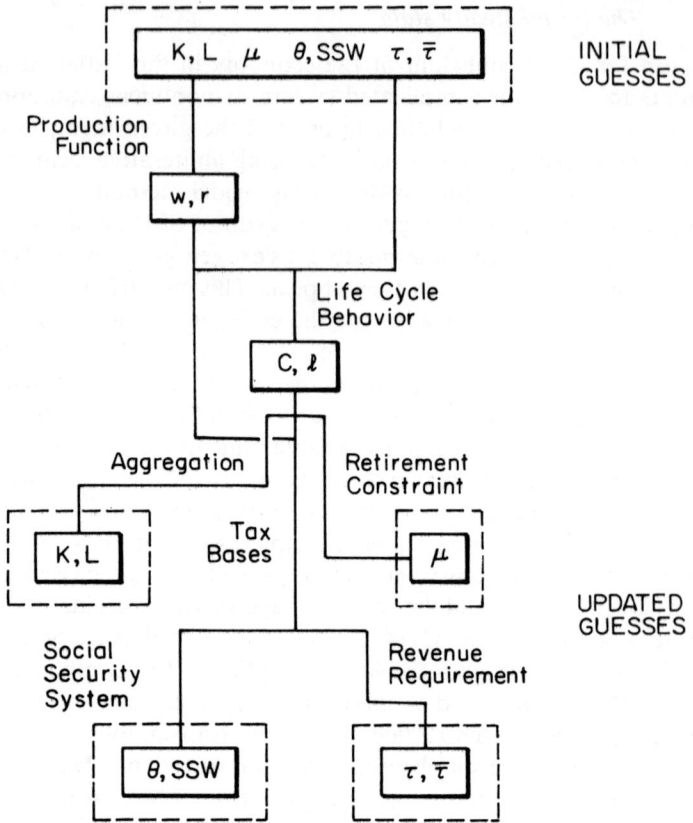

Figure 4.1. The model and its solution.

state without knowledge of the precise transition path. The second type of policy change requires solving for the final steady state together with the transition path.

An example of the first kind would be a switch from an income tax to a consumption tax. Here, we would specify that all revenue in the final steady state must come from consumption taxes. An example of the second kind would be a five-year tax cut, during which national debt is accumulated, followed by a one-time income tax increase sufficient to preserve the level of debt per capita at its existing level. In this case, the new higher tax rate required in the new steady state depends on the amount of debt issued along the economy's transition path. Hence, we cannot know the new steady state level of debt until we have solved for the economy's

4 Simulation methodology

transition path. In such circumstances, we solve for the final steady state and transition path simultaneously.

Aside from this complication, solution for the final steady state proceeds exactly as for the initial steady state.

3. *The transition*

The approach used to solve for the economy's equilibrium transition path is similar to that used to calculate the initial and, where possible, final steady states. There are several complications, however. First, because the economy undergoes a transition in which conditions change over time, it is necessary to solve explicitly for behavior in each year. Moreover, because households and firms are assumed to take into account future prices in determining their behavior, it is necessary to solve simultaneously for equilibrium in all transition years.

This is done in the following way. The simulation model provides the economy with 150 years to reach a new steady state. After 150 years, the model constrains all prices, tax rates, and shadow wages to be constant. If the final steady state has already been calculated, it is used to provide the values of these variables. Otherwise, they are solved together with those for the years 1-150. The choice of 150 years is arbitrary, but is intended to provide enough time so that the economy will settle down by itself well before it is "forced" to in year 150. Thus, the constraint requiring that the number of years in the transition do not exceed 150 is not binding. The same path would result if 140 or 160 years were assumed, but not if a substantially shorter period, such as 30 years, were used, for in that time the economy typically is still adjusting.[1]

---

[1] An issue that arises in calculating the transition path is whether it is unique. Previous analyses with overlapping generations models (e.g., Calvo, 1978a; Kehoe and Levine, 1985) have provided examples in which there is a continuum of transition paths to the new equilibrium.

The nonuniqueness problem arises if there are not enough boundary conditions (initial conditions plus the requirement of convergence to a steady state) to determine the transition path. It occurs in cases where there are more stable roots to the linearized version of the system in the neighborhood of the final steady state equilibrium than there are initial conditions. The requirement of convergence eliminates only the unstable roots (those outside the unit circle) from the solution, leaving, in some cases, a continuum of feasible paths that satisfy the initial conditions. (If there are fewer stable roots than initial conditions, then no convergent solution exists, but this problem does not arise here.)

Although we have not explicitly calculated the roots of a linearized version of our own model to ascertain whether this problem might be present, such analysis has been conducted for a similar model by Laitner (1984). He found the transition path to be determinate, and the number of stable roots equal to the number of initial conditions (which, in this model, were the relevant past values of the capital stock). This result, along with our own findings that, in practice, the solution calculated by our model does not depend on the initial guesses chosen for the transition path, strongly suggests that indeterminacy in our model is not a problem.

As with the steady states, a Gauss–Seidel iteration algorithm is employed, but here the problem is 150 times larger since the equilibrium of the economy in each of the 150 years is solved simultaneously. Aside from this greater complexity, a final difference in solving for the transition path as opposed to the initial steady state is that individuals alive at the time the policy is adopted must be treated differently. Whereas individuals born after the transition begins know what economic conditions will confront them, those born before the beginning of the transition behave up to the time of the change in government policy as if the old steady state would continue forever. At the time of the announcement of a new policy to be instituted either immediately or in the near future, existing cohorts are "born again"; they behave like members of a new generation, but have a shorter life expectancy and their initial assets result from prior accumulation.

B. Parameterization of the model

To solve the model, we must choose values for the preference parameters, δ, α, ρ, and γ, the production elasticity, ϵ, the production scaling constant, A, the adjustment cost term, b, and the human capital vector, **e**. Some of these parameters (such as γ and **e**) have been precisely estimated in several empirical studies. This is not the case for the others, however, and indirect methods must be used to obtain values for certain parameters.

1. Household preferences

a. *Intertemporal elasticity of substitution* (γ): Although most studies of this parameter have not included leisure in the utility function, the estimates of γ do not appear to be particularly sensitive to this simplification. Most studies, regardless of methodology, have consistently found values of γ to lie within a reasonably narrow range.

Among those who have focused only on consumption, Weber (1970) estimated γ to lie between 0.13 and 0.41, but in a later study (Weber, 1975) found a higher range, between 0.56 and 0.75. More recently, several studies have derived their estimates from models of optimal household portfolio behavior under uncertainty. Grossman and Shiller (1981) found γ to range from 0.07 to 0.35, Mankiw (1981, 1985) recorded values of 0.25 and 0.37, respectively, Summers (1982) reports about 0.33, and Hall (1981) found values generally below 0.1. In contrast, Hansen and Singleton (1983) and Mankiw, Rotemberg, and Summers (1985) obtained estimates above 1.

4 Simulation methodology

In an early study that accounted for both leisure and consumption, Ghez and Becker (1975) estimated γ to be at most 0.28. More recently, MaCurdy (1981) obtained estimates ranging between 0.10 and 0.45. In the light of this evidence, we choose a value of $\gamma = 0.25$ for our baseline simulations.

b. *Intratemporal elasticity of substitution* (ρ): There is far less direct empirical evidence concerning the value of ρ. Ghez and Becker (1975), for example, found an aggregate value of $\rho = 0.83$. With respect to the contemporaneous wage, much evidence is available on the labor supply elasticities of both men and women, and "standard" values for the uncompensated elasticity close to zero for men and equal to at least one for married women (Heckman 1974, Rosen 1976, Hausman 1981). However, the translation of these elasticities into estimates of ρ depends on the degree to which the underlying wage changes are permanent or temporary and whether they are anticipated or not.

The more temporary the wage change, the smaller the income effect that is included in the estimated labor supply response. Likewise, the further in advance that the wage change is anticipated, the more the household will have an opportunity to make prior saving adjustments, such as saving less in response to anticipated wage increases. This offset will reduce the income effect on labor supply occurring after the wage change, because the effect is being spread over a longer planning horizon. As Auerbach, Kotlikoff, and Skinner (1983) have shown, a wide range of values of ρ is consistent with estimated wage elasticities.[2] Our chosen base case value of ρ equal to 0.8 falls near the center of this range and is approximately equal to the direct estimate of Ghez and Becker (1975).[3]

c. *The pure rate of time preference* (δ): There is scant evidence of the appropriate value of δ. We choose a value of 0.015 largely because, given other parameters, it leads to a realistic consumption profile and labor supply decision and, for reasonable tax parameters and levels of government consumption, yields an amount of aggregate capital consistent with observed U.S. capital–output ratios. A higher value of δ would lead to less saving, while the opposite would be true for lower values.

---

[2] See MaCurdy (1981) for a related discussion.

[3] One recent study that does explicitly treat the dynamic labor-consumption decision is MaCurdy (1983), who estimates parameters of a utility function that, though intertemporally separable, has a different form from that of (3.3). However, given his reported substitution effects for hours and consumption with respect to the contemporaneous after-tax wage and the sample means for these variables plus the monthly labor endowment, it is possible to estimate the value of ρ at the sample means. This yields an estimate of $\rho = 1.96$ for a sample of prime-age males! This estimate of ρ appears to be quite different from those of most previous researchers.

d. *The leisure preference parameter* (α): This parameter, too, has received little attention in empirical investigation. We seek a value for it which will result in realistic levels of labor supply. If $\alpha = 0$, households will work the maximum number of hours in every year. For $\alpha = 1.5$, our chosen value, prime-age workers in typical simulations work approximately 40 percent of the time, or, if we base our calculations on a full-time labor endowment of 5,000 hours per year, they work 2,000 hours per year, or 40 hours per week.

2. Production parameters

For the production sector, values are required for the parameters σ, e, ϵ, and A and b.

a. *Human capital profile* (e): The vector **e** determines relative wages by age. The profile used is based on estimates obtained by Welch (1979) from a cross-sectional regression of weekly labor earnings of full-time workers on personal variables including experience and experience squared.[4] The resulting wage profile peaks at adult age 30 (which the reader should think of as an actual age of about 50), and wages at that age are 45 percent higher than at age 1 (21). The wage at age 55 (75) is 22 percent lower than the wage at age 1.

b. *Elasticity of substitution* (σ): There has been considerable research into the elasticity of substitution between capital and labor in U.S. manufacturing (Nerlove, 1967; Berndt and Christensen, 1973), with the usual finding of values of 1 or slightly less. For our basic parameterization, we set $\sigma = 1$, thereby assuming a Cobb–Douglas production function.

c. *Capital intensity parameter* (ϵ): It is well-known that for a Cobb–Douglas production function, factor shares are constant, and the capital share in income equals the capital-intensity parameter, ϵ. Using the historical share of capital in national income in the U.S., we set $\epsilon = 0.25$.

d. *Production function constant* (A): This parameter depends on the units chosen for output. It should be a hundred times larger if output is measured in cents rather than dollars. Thus, we are free to choose A, choosing the output units at the same time. It is convenient to choose a value that leads to a wage rate per one-year-old adult of exactly 1.0 in

---

[4] The equation used is $e_t = 4.47 + 0.033t - 0.00067t$, where t is the individual's number of years of experience, corresponding to adult age in our specification.

4 Simulation methodology

our basic income tax equilibrium, with a proportional income tax of 15 percent. This requires a value of $A = .892657593$, which we used throughout.

e. *Marginal adjustment cost parameter* (b): In most of our simulations, we ignore adjustment costs, setting $b = 0$. When adjustment costs are included, a value of $b = 10$ is chosen. This value stands at the low end of some estimates (e.g., Summers, 1981b; Abel and Blanchard, 1986; or Poterba and Summers, 1983). However, all these estimates were derived from regressions of investment on calculated values of q that, for a number of reasons described in the studies, may have been inaccurate. Hence, it seems reasonable that the measured response of investment to q has been understated and the size of the parameter b overstated by such estimates.

3. Government behavior

a. *Fiscal policy:* As mentioned above, the base case assumed for government fiscal policy is an income tax of 15 percent. This choice represents a compromise made necessary by the simplicity of the model compared to the real world. On the one hand, U.S. federal government spending on goods and services (excluding investment goods) absorbs about 10 percent of the national product. On the other hand, the spending of all levels of the U.S. government on goods and services is about one-quarter of the national product.[5] Although the income tax pays for most spending on goods and services by the federal government, this is not the case for state and local governments. In 1984, the receipts from individual and corporate income taxes at all levels equaled 17.7 percent of national income. This is probably closest to the parameter we are seeking, and hence the value used, 15 percent, appears quite reasonable in terms of overall revenue.

At the same time, the actual tax system, particularly at the federal level, is characterized by a tax base that is much narrower than national income, and hence by much higher marginal tax rates than would be suggested by these revenue percentages. The effect of this base narrowing is one of the issues explored in the simulations presented below.

In our base case steady state there is no initial government debt, but the effects of accumulating government debt are considered in detail in Chapter 6.

---

[5] *Economic Report of the President, 1985,* Tables B-1 and B-21.

b. *The social security system:* In some sets of simulations the social security system is omitted to maintain as much clarity as possible in evaluating what may already be fairly complicated policies. Where the social security system is included, the basic assumption is that benefits are based on an average of past earnings comparable to the average indexed monthly earnings (AIME) actually used in the United States with a "replacement rate" – the ratio of actual benefits to this earnings average – patterned on typical replacement rates in the United States. Because of the complexity of these calculations, further discussion is deferred until the social security system first appears in the simulations in Chapter 10.

C.   Conclusions

Modern computing technology makes it relatively easy to solve models as complicated as the one described in Chapter 3. However, the choice of appropriate parameter values is not always straightforward. It is here that economics begins and computer science ends. But rather than resort to oversimplified models that don't require such parameterization, it seems far more sensible to use the best available information in calibrating as realistic a model as possible.

The answer to uncertainties about the "correct" values of various parameters is sensitivity analysis, which tests the dependence of conclusions on the choice of parameters by simulating the same policy under a range of parameter estimates. As it does in this study, sensitivity analysis should form an important part of any numerical simulation analysis.

CHAPTER 5

Tax reform – choice of the tax base

The proper choice of tax bases is a central question in tax reform. The choice has important implications for the course of saving and economic growth, the distribution of welfare across generations, and the level of economic efficiency in the economy. This chapter considers each of these issues in relation to four proportional taxes: an income tax, a consumption tax, a labor income tax, and a capital income tax.

In recent years, there has been much discussion (e.g., Pechman, ed., 1980, 1985; Bradford and others, 1984; Bradford, 1986; Institute for Fiscal Studies, 1978; Hall and Rabuska 1983) about the implementation of a consumption tax and its merits relative to an income tax. Whereas research in the past focused on issues such as simplicity and enforcement, which are not dealt with here, recent work has concentrated on the relatively favorable treatment of saving provided by a consumption tax. However, what has been termed "consumption tax treatment" by others more closely resembles a labor income tax. This distinction has important implications for questions about the desirability of switching to a consumption tax. Section A of this chapter distinguishes among the four tax bases examined here.

Since deficit finance and changes in the level of government consumption are covered in Chapter 6, the assumptions of constant government consumption per capita and annual budget balance are maintained throughout this chapter. The requirement that the government annually collect a constant amount of revenue per capita provides a formula for determining annual tax rates along the transition paths associated with switching from an income tax to each of the alternative tax bases.

A. Key points

Nominal vs. effective tax bases: In assessing the results of this chapter, one should bear in mind that although nominal and effective tax bases are equivalent in the simulations reported below, effective tax bases of actual economies can be substantially different from their nominal tax bases. This point can be illustrated by an economy with a personal income tax plus a subsidy to capital at the business level of equal value. In such an economy the subsidy to capital at the business level cancels the tax on capital income at the personal level, and the result is an effective labor income tax. Chapter 9 places special emphasis on the distinction between effective and nominal income and consumption tax bases. It is shown that the perhaps seemingly incidental addition of investment expensing to an income tax structure effectively transforms the income tax to a consumption tax.

Sensitivity analysis: Another point to consider about the outcome of any simulation is the sensitivity of the result to the choice of parameters. In conducting sensitivity analysis it is important to consider not simply the marginal impact of changing one parameter while holding others at base case values, but also what happens when several parameters are assigned values different from those of the base case. This is necessary because the outcomes of the simulation model are nonlinear functions of the model's parameters. The sensitivity analysis conducted below examines a wide range of parameter values.

Welfare changes vs. efficiency: Although the model described in Chapter 3 is well suited to studying the effects of tax base changes on the welfare of different generations, one cannot simply add up such changes in welfare to assess the potential efficiency gains or losses from tax reform. By efficiency we mean Pareto efficiency. In this context, Pareto efficiency is a situation in which no generation can gain without some other generation being made worse off. Tax reforms that improve the welfare of some generations while reducing that of others may, in conjunction with the redistribution from winning to losing generations, offer the prospect of Pareto improvements; but one cannot assess the potential efficiency gain without actually implementing the intergenerational redistribution.

To distinguish potential efficiency gains from changes in the welfare of different generations that are possibly offsetting we introduce an additional government institution, the Lump Sum Redistribution Authority (LSRA). The LSRA transfers resources across generations through lump sum taxes and transfer payments. Since this additional fiscal institution does not engage in consumption, we require that it break even in present value; that is, the present value of its tax receipts must equal the present value of its transfer payments.

Announcement effects: As described below, shifting tax bases has important substitution as well as income effects. In the short run,

5 Tax reform – choice of tax base

these substitution effects are either greatly enhanced or greatly reduced by preannouncing a future change in tax regimes. Since the agents in this model have perfect foresight, such preannounced changes in the future course of tax rates will lead to immediate substitution responses. Thus, announcing today that a consumption tax will be imposed in two years leads to an immediate substitution of current for future consumption to take advantage of the temporarily low relative price of current consumption. This chapter considers both the saving and efficiency aspects of early announcements of policy changes.

Principal findings: The principal findings in this chapter are as follows:

> The consumption tax base generates significantly more long-run capital formation than either the wage tax or the income tax. Capital formation under the wage tax typically exceeds that under the income tax. The size of the long-run capital stock under a pure capital income tax is much smaller than under the income tax.
> Proportional consumption taxation appears to be significantly more efficient than proportional income taxation. In contrast, the transition from a proportional income tax to a proportional wage tax typically generates an efficiency loss despite the fact that the proportional wage tax, like the consumption tax, does not distort saving decisions.
> The rankings of the four tax bases with respect to their effects on savings and efficiency are insensitive to reasonable variations in parameter values.
> Policies that potentially raise the long-run level of capital per worker, such as shifting from an income tax to a wage tax, may nonetheless imply a lower level of long-run economic welfare and reduce economic efficiency.
> The short-run response to certain announced future changes in the tax base can be exactly opposite to those motivating the switch in tax bases.

B. Conceptual issues

1. *Income and substitution effects from switching tax bases*

The structural tax policies considered in this chapter have one feature in common: namely, they compensate the private sector for the removal of the proportional income tax by imposing an alternative proportional tax. Since these policies involve no changes in the timing and level of the government's direct absorption of resources, they leave unchanged, in the aggregate, the private sector's intertemporal consumption and leisure possibility frontier. If it so chooses, the private sector can consume as much and work as little in the new tax regime as it does in the old. Such a response clearly leaves the private sector in the aggregate with the same collective resources to finance its own as well as the government's unaltered time path of government consumption.

Although there is no change in the private sector's aggregate intertemporal possibilities frontier, the structural tax policies studied here induce the private sector to choose a different point on that frontier. These policies alter the relative prices of consumption and leisure faced by different generations over their lifetimes. They also directly redistribute income across generations. The income and substitution effects arising from these price changes and from more direct intergenerational redistribution account for changes in the position on the possibilities frontier chosen by the private sector.

a. *Income effects:* Since the tax policies considered here are compensated, there is no overall income effect for the private sector, and the income effects arising from these policies are the result of redistribution between generations and not of an overall change in private sector resources. The key question concerning the net impact of these income effects is whether the redistribution is toward or away from younger generations. As stressed in Chapter 2, older generations have, ceteris paribus, larger marginal propensities to consume goods and leisure than younger generations. This is a reflection of their shorter remaining years of life. For generations not yet born the marginal propensity to consume is obviously zero. Hence, redistribution from older to younger generations will typically lower aggregate consumption and raise aggregate labor supply. Consequently, aggregate savings will rise.

One can illustrate the source of these income effects by considering a switch from wage to consumption taxation in the highly stylized two-period model of Chapter 2. For simplicity, ignore general equilibrium changes in pre-tax factor earnings, and assume that agents work only in their first period and consume only in their second period. In this model, since leisure is not a choice variable, both the wage and consumption taxes effectively represent lump sum taxes (if we ignore changes through time in consumption tax rates).

In the case of a wage tax, young workers experience a loss in lifetime resources of $\tau_w W$, where τ_w is the wage tax rate and W is first-period

5 Tax reform – choice of tax base

labor earnings. In the case of a consumption tax, the workers experience an effective reduction in their lifetime incomes of $\tau_c W/(1+\tau_c)$, where τ_c is the consumption tax rate; that is, since workers must pay $(1+\tau_c)$ to purchase consumption in period two under the consumption tax, the present value of their lifetime consumption falls from W to $W/1+\tau_c$. Equations (5.1) and (5.2) give the lifetime budget constraints for the cases of wage and consumption taxation, respectively:

$$C_2/(1+r) = W(1-\tau_w) \tag{5.1}$$

$$C_2(1+\tau_c)/(1+r) = W. \tag{5.2}$$

If $1/(1+\tau_c) = (1-\tau_w)$, the two budget constraints are identical. However, this need not be the case. Under the wage tax, τ_w is determined by the government's annual budget balance constraint:

$$\tau_w W = G, \tag{5.3}$$

while under the consumption tax τ_c is determined by the constraint

$$\tau_c C_2 = G. \tag{5.4}$$

For the case of a wage tax, (5.1) and (5.3) imply the budget constraint

$$C_2/(1+r) = W - G. \tag{5.5}$$

The corresponding constraint for the consumption tax based on (5.2) and (5.4) is

$$C_2/(1+r) = W - G/(1+r). \tag{5.6}$$

When we compare (5.5) and (5.6), it is clear that switching from wage to consumption taxation increases the lifetime consumption opportunities of young workers, that is $1/(1+\tau_c) > (1-\tau_w)$; intuitively, although young workers still have to pay G to the government over their lifetime, under the consumption tax the payment is not due until the second period and thus has a lower present value. The reduction in the present value of lifetime taxes occurs not only for the first generation of workers alive at the time of the tax change, but for all subsequent generations as well.

This gain to the initial young and to subsequent generations is paid for by a loss to the initial generation of elderly who, having paid G once in the form of wage taxes when young, are forced to pay G again in their last period of life in the form of consumption taxes. Note that the present value gain to the initial young generation and to each subsequent generation (ignoring general equilibrium changes in w and r) equals $rG/(1+r)$. The sum in present values of these gains over all those benefiting from the policy is G, which is exactly the loss to the initial generation of elderly. Thus, as stressed by Summers (1981a) in his insightful article about structural tax change, changing the timing of a tax payment over the life cycle can significantly alter the burden of taxation across generations and, thus, the intergenerational distribution of resources.

In comparison with the income tax, an immediate switch to consumption taxation or capital income taxation shifts the tax burden toward the initial generation of elderly. In contrast, switching the tax base from income to wage taxation shifts the tax burden toward initial young generations as well as subsequent generations from the initial generation of elderly alive at the time of the regime switch; i.e., eliminating the income tax eliminates taxes on the capital income of the initial elderly generation.

b. *Substitution effects:* Switching tax regimes can also lead to significant substitution effects. To illustrate the role of substitution effects, let us abstract from the income effects just described and examine a switch from a wage to a capital income tax under the assumption that the present value of taxes is not altered by changing tax structures. This is a compensated tax change since the removal of the wage tax is compensated by the imposition of the capital income tax. Consider again the two-period model of Chapter 2 with consumption in both periods. Figure 5.1 illustrates the partial equilibrium effect of such a (present value) compensated tax change. The slopes of lines 1 and 2 equal $1+r$, where r is the before-tax interest rate. The slope of line 4 is $1+r(1-\tau_r)$, where τ_r is the capital income tax rate.

Point A is the equilibrium under wage taxation, while point B corresponds to the equilibrium under a capital income tax. The government collects the same present value, G, in taxes under both tax structures, and private consumption occurs along the same budget frontier, line 2; since the increase in capital income taxation is compensated by a decline in lump sum taxation, the consumer ends up consuming on her initial budget frontier. Under smooth convex indifference curves, private consumption in period 1 unambiguously rises from C_1^* to C_1^{**}. (Note that if the private sector had maintained its initial consumption bundle, the government's capital income tax rate would have been lower by the difference in the slopes of lines 3 and 4 divided by r.) The policy depicted in Figure 5.1 – by raising consumption of young workers and leaving, by assumption, the budget opportunities and thus the consumption of the elderly generation unchanged – implies an unambiguous decline in national saving.

In contrast to the saving effect of a compensated capital income tax, that of a compensated tax on labor earnings in a model with variable labor supply may be ambiguous. For example, suppose labor supply is variable in both periods of a two-period model; then the compensated labor income tax will lead to an increase in leisure as well as a decline in

5 Tax reform – choice of tax base

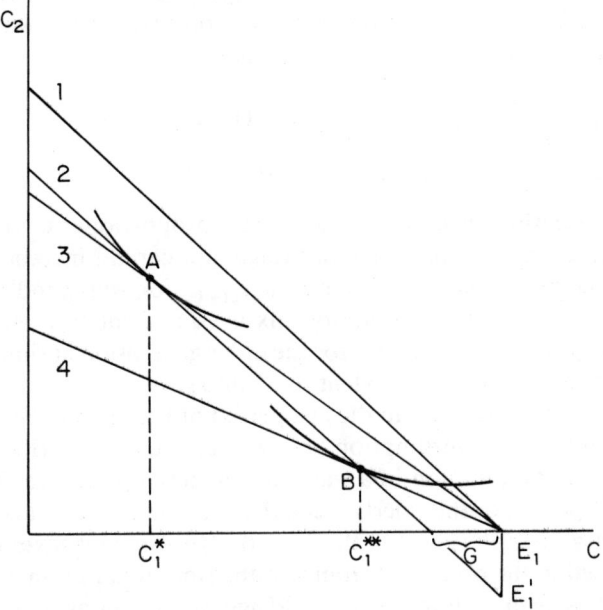

Figure 5.1. The savings effect of a compensated switch from wage to capital income taxation.

consumption in both periods. If the reduction in first-period consumption equals the decline in first-period labor earnings, the compensated labor income tax will have no impact on savings in the two-period model. If, on the other hand, labor supply occurs only in the first period and the worker is retired in the second period, then the compensated wage tax will lower first-period saving, which equals the two-period model's capital stock. The reason is that workers will substitute away from future as well as current consumption in response to the labor income tax. Since the decline in first-period labor earnings equals the decline in the present value of first- plus second-period consumption, first-period earnings fall by more than first-period consumption.

2. Comparing tax structures

The effects of changing the tax base can be better understood by examining the relationship among tax bases. Equation (5.7) gives the lifetime budget constraint for a young agent at time t in the simple two-period model with labor supplied inelastically and only in the first period. Equation

(5.8) gives the budget constraint for an old agent at time t. Each of the four taxes – the income tax, τ_y; the consumption tax, τ_c; the wage tax, τ_w; and the capital income tax, τ_r – are included.

$$C_{1t}(1+\tau_{ct}) + \frac{C_{2t+1}(1+\tau_{ct+1})}{1+r_{t+1}(1-\tau_{yt+1}-\tau_{rt+1})} = W_t(1-\tau_{wt}-\tau_{yt}) \tag{5.7}$$

$$C_{2t}(1+\tau_{ct}) = A_t[1+r_t(1-\tau_{rt}-\tau_{yt})]. \tag{5.8}$$

From these equations it is easy to see that a proportional income tax is equivalent to equal-rate proportional wage and capital income taxes. Another tax equivalency occurs if τ_{ct} equals τ_{ct+1}. For young individuals at time t in this case, the consumption tax is equivalent to a wage tax levied at rate $\tau_{ct}/(1+\tau_{ct})$. However, for the older generation at time t, imposing a consumption tax is equivalent to a lump sum tax on their assets; since these assets must be spent in the last period of life, part of the elderly's assets is spent on the consumption tax. Hence, one can describe a consumption tax as a combination of a wage tax and a lump sum wealth tax.

From the perspective of the elderly, capital income and income taxes also represent effective wealth taxes. In this case the government taxes the income (as opposed to the principal) from wealth. Since wealth is in inelastic supply once it has been accumulated for old age, such taxes are equivalent to lump sum taxes from the perspective of the elderly. As is well known, lump sum taxes do not distort economic choices. Hence, the lump sum tax feature of consumption taxes, capital income taxes, and income taxes is important in determining the relative efficiency of the four tax regimes.

Another important point is that changes through time in the tax rates of a given tax base can transform the tax from one effective tax base to another. Take the case of increases through time in the consumption tax rate. By dividing both sides of (5.7) by $(1+\tau_{ct})$ one can see that such a policy raises the relative price of second-period consumption. Hence, a rising consumption tax rate acts, in part, like a capital income tax. If the model were augmented to include first- and second-period variable labor supply, then a wage tax that increases through time would also alter relative intertemporal prices; in this case the price of future leisure would fall relative to the price of current leisure, inducing a substitution of current for future labor supply.

3. *Distinguishing efficiency from redistribution: The Lump Sum Redistribution Authority*

The LSRA is a hypothetical construct used to measure the pure efficiency gains from tax reform. The LSRA is modeled as a separate, self-financing government agency that uses lump sum taxes and transfers to keep cohorts

5 Tax reform – choice of tax base

born before a specified date at their status quo level of utility and to raise the utility of all cohorts born after this date by a uniform amount. Equalization of the utility of those born after a certain date, a policy first analyzed in a two-period setting by Phelps and Riley (1978), seems to be a reasonable way of characterizing the infinite set of welfare paths the LSRA could generate.

The simulation model was adapted to solve for the economy's general equilibrium transition path consistent with the behavior of the standard government fiscal authority as well as the lump sum tax-transfer activity of the LSRA. Thus, for example, household consumption decisions under a consumption tax transition take into account the LSRA lump sum taxes and transfers. It is also important to note that the equilibrium path of consumption tax rates will differ from that generated in the absence of the LSRA, since changes in the behavior of households will necessitate modifications in the tax schedule imposed by the main government authority.

The LSRA faces a budget constraint requiring that its lump sum taxes and transfers sum to zero in present value. At any point in time, the LSRA holds net assets that may be positive or negative, but that equal the present value of its net future payments. These net assets are added to those held by the private sector to determine the economy's total stock of capital.

Lump sum taxes and transfers are collected and paid in year one (the first year of the transition) for all existing cohorts and in the first year of economic life for all subsequent cohorts. Equation (5.9) expresses the LSRA budget constraint, where v_i is the lump sum tax (negative, if a transfer) paid by members of generations born in year i, and n is the economy's population growth rate. The two parts of the expression in (5.9) correspond to the net taxes collected from existing and future cohorts, respectively.

$$\sum_{i=-53}^{0} (1+n)^i v_i + \sum_{i=1}^{\infty} (1+n)^i \left[\prod_{j=1}^{i} (1+r_j)^{-1} \right] v_i = 0. \tag{5.9}$$

When the LSRA is included in the simulation, the method of simulation is essentially the same as that previously used. However, the budget constraints of existing and future cohorts now include the terms v_i, and updated guesses of these must be made in each iteration step along with those of factor prices, tax rates, and shadow wages. In the first iteration of the simulation, all v_i's are given preliminary values of zero. In the course of each iteration, the model produces new estimates of the path of this vector **v**. A weighted average of the initial guess and this computed path generates a guess for the next iteration.

The calculation of **v** in each step is described in detail in the appendix to this chapter. It is important to remember that the vector **v** is included

Table 5.1. *The base case steady state*

Capital stock	95.1	Private consumption	20.70
Labor supply	19.1	Capital–output ratio	3.73
Wage	1.000	National saving rate	3.73%
Pre-tax interest rate	6.70%	Income tax rate	15%
National income	25.47	Social security tax rate	0%
Government consumption	3.82	Social security replacement rate	0%

in the full general equilibrium solution of the model. Thus, policies leading to large transfers to older cohorts (as will be the case for a consumption tax) will lead to an accumulation of debt by the LSRA and hence will crowd out some of the increase in capital that occurs in the basic simulation.

C. Simulation results

1. The initial steady state

Table 5.1 presents the simulated initial steady state values of the base case economy. The base case income tax rate is 15 percent; the base case capital–labor ratio is 5.0; the base case wage is 1, reflecting our choice of the coefficient A in the production function in (3.13); and the base case pretax return to capital is 6.7 percent. The economy's saving rate of 3.73 percent is substantially below the comparable U.S. rate of saving out of NNP, which has averaged 7.93 percent since 1950. On the other hand, the wealth-to-income ratio of the base case economy is 3.7, which is not far from the current U.S. wealth-to-income ratio of roughly 3.5.

Were we to assume a larger population growth rate than the 1 percent assumed here, the simulated saving rate would be closer to that observed in the United States. On the other hand, including social security as well as the dependency of children in the model significantly reduces the simulated saving rate as well as the simulated wealth-to-income ratio (see Chapters 10 and 11). The relatively low saving rate and ratio of wealth to income of this latter economy vis-à-vis the U.S. rate reflects the difficulty of explaining U.S. wealth accumulation solely on the basis of the zero bequest life cycle model unless one makes unrealistic assumptions concerning the shapes of age earning and age consumption profiles (Kotlikoff and Summers, 1981).

The shapes of age–earnings and age–consumption profiles of the base case economy are, however, fairly realistic; Figure 5.2 depicts these profiles. Note that by age 53 (age 73 if age 21 is used as the initial age of labor

5 Tax reform – choice of tax base

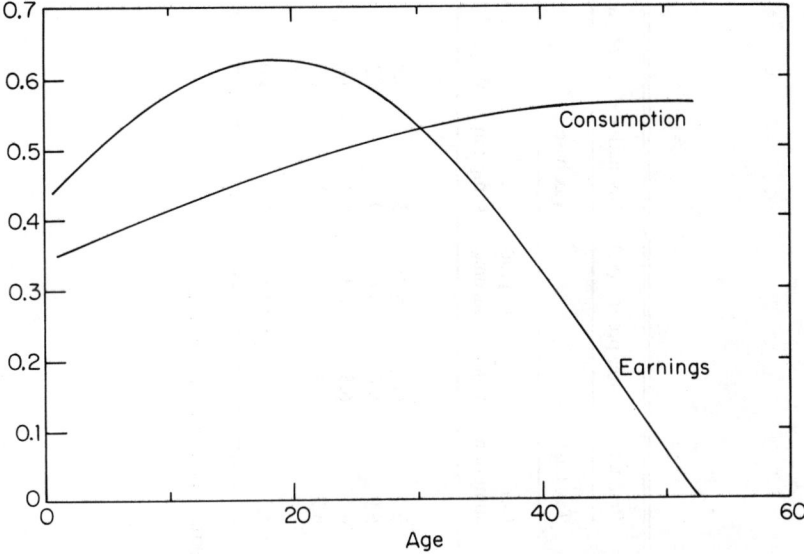

Figure 5.2. Age-earnings and age-consumption profiles in the base case steady state.

force entry) workers are fully retired. Partial retirement occurs much earlier in the life cycle, however. Labor supply is 0.46 (out of a time endowment of 1) at age 5 (age 25 in real time); it falls gradually to 0.41 by age 25 (age 45 in real time), and more rapidly thereafter. At age 45 (age 65 in real time) labor supply is only 0.18, less than one-third of the initial age zero value. If we take real nonsleeping time to be roughly 100 hours per week, then these labor supplies correspond to 46 hours per week at age 26, 41 hours per week at age 45, and 18 hours per week at age 65.

2.   Structural tax change

Table 5.2 displays the large impact structural tax policies can have on an economy's saving rate and related variables. Relative to the initial income tax regime, long-run saving rates are 19 percent larger under a consumption tax, 8 percent larger under a wage tax, and 32 percent smaller under a capital income tax. Changes in the economy's saving rate during the transition period are even more dramatic; in the first year after the switch to consumption taxation, the saving rate rises to 9.3 percent from an initial value of 3.7. In the case of the capital income tax, there is a negative 2.9 percent saving rate in the first year of the transition, and saving rates remain negative for more than a decade. The United States has occa-

Table 5.2. *Structural tax change*

Year of transition	Capital–labor ratio				Wage rate, pre-tax				Real interest rate, pre-tax (%)				Net national saving rate (%)			
	Tax base		Con-sumption	Wage	Capital income	Tax base		Con-sumption	Wage	Capital income	Tax base		Con-sumption	Wage	Capital income
	Con-sumption	Wage	Capital income				Con-sumption	Wage				Con-sumption	Wage			
Initial steady state	5.0	5.0	5.0	1.00	1.00	1.00	6.7	6.7	6.7	3.7	3.7	3.7
1	4.8	5.1	4.8	0.99	1.00	0.99	6.9	6.6	6.8	9.3	5.3	-2.9
5	5.1	5.1	4.4	1.01	1.01	0.97	6.5	6.5	7.3	8.2	5.0	-1.9
10	5.4	5.2	4.1	1.02	1.01	0.95	6.3	6.4	7.7	7.2	4.7	-1.0
50	6.2	5.4	3.0	1.05	1.02	0.88	5.7	6.3	9.7	4.5	4.0	2.0
150	6.2	5.4	2.9	1.06	1.02	0.87	5.7	6.3	10.1	4.4	4.0	2.5

Note: Switch from 15% proportional income tax to specified proportional tax regimes. Base case parameters.

5 Tax reform – choice of tax base

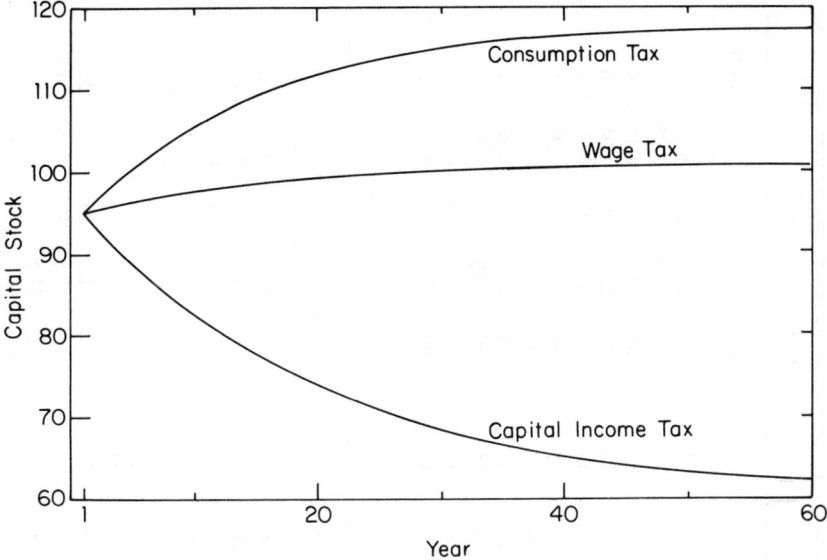

Figure 5.3. The impact on capital formation of tax reform.

sionally experienced such large swings in saving rates, although they have been neither solely nor primarily a reflection of changes in fiscal policy.

The capital deepening associated with switching from the 15 percent income tax to consumption and wage taxation generates long-run pre-tax wage rates that are 6 percent and 2 percent larger, respectively, than their initial values. In the case of capital income taxation, the long-run wage rate is 13 percent smaller than in the initial equilibrium. The capital accumulation paths for each of these transitions are shown in Table 5.2 and graphed in Figure 5.3. The long-run pre-tax real interest rate declines by 1 percent or less under consumption or wage taxation, but it rises 3.4 percentage points under capital income taxation. Long-run tax rates are 17.6 percent under a consumption tax, 20.1 percent under a wage tax, and 62.7 percent under a capital income tax. The much larger rate required under capital income taxation reflects the fact that capital income is a much smaller tax base than total income, labor income, or consumption.

3. *Sensitivity analysis*

a. *Parameter values:* The sensitivity of these results to alternative choices of parameter values is examined in the Tables 5.3 and 5.4. Table 5.3

Table 5.3. *Structural tax reform – steady state sensitivity analysis*

Parameters					Income tax							Consumption tax					
Gamma	Rho	Sigma	Delta	Alpha	K	L	Y	w	r (%)	τ_y (%)		K	L	Y	w	r (%)	τ_c (%)
0.25	0.80	1.00	0.015	1.5	95	19.1	25	1.00	7	15		118	19.0	27	1.06	6	18
0.10	0.80	1.00	0.015	1.5	45	19.3	21	0.82	12	15		55	19.1	22	0.87	11	17
0.50	0.80	1.00	0.015	1.5	148	19.2	29	1.11	5	15		183	19.1	30	1.18	4	18
0.25	0.30	1.00	0.015	1.5	100	21.7	28	0.98	7	15		124	21.5	30	1.04	6	18
0.25	1.50	1.00	0.015	1.5	89	16.6	22	1.02	6	15		111	16.9	24	1.07	5	17
0.25	0.80	0.80	0.015	1.5	80	19.9	24	0.99	6	15		95	20.0	25	1.02	5	18
0.25	0.80	1.25	0.015	1.5	113	18.0	27	1.02	8	15		145	17.7	29	1.10	7	17
0.25	0.80	1.00	0.050	1.5	55	19.2	22	0.87	10	15		68	19.1	23	0.92	9	17
0.25	0.80	1.00	−0.030	1.5	202	19.3	31	1.20	4	15		250	19.2	33	1.27	3	18
0.25	0.80	1.00	0.015	0.5	114	30.6	38	0.93	8	15		140	30.4	40	0.98	7	17
0.25	0.80	1.00	0.015	3.0	80	13.1	18	1.05	6	15		99	12.9	19	1.11	5	18

Parameters					Wage tax							Capital income tax					
Gamma	Rho	Sigma	Delta	Alpha	K	L	Y	w	r (%)	τ_w (%)		K	L	Y	w	r (%)	τ_r (%)
0.25	0.80	1.00	0.015	1.5	101	18.6	25	1.02	6	20		60	20.9	24	0.87	10	63
0.10	0.80	1.00	0.015	1.5	46	18.7	21	0.84	11	20		34	21.1	21	0.75	16	60
0.50	0.80	1.00	0.015	1.5	159	18.7	29	1.14	4	20		84	20.9	26	0.95	8	65
0.25	0.30	1.00	0.015	1.5	107	21.3	28	1.00	7	20		63	23.4	27	0.86	11	64
0.25	1.50	1.00	0.015	1.5	93	15.9	22	1.04	6	20		57	18.2	22	0.89	9	62
0.25	0.80	0.80	0.015	1.5	85	19.6	24	1.00	5	18		44	21.5	23	0.82	11	73
0.25	0.80	1.25	0.015	1.5	118	17.3	27	1.04	7	23		87	19.8	27	0.93	9	49
0.25	0.80	1.00	0.050	1.5	61	18.6	22	0.90	9	20		24	21.5	20	0.69	20	68
0.25	0.80	1.00	−0.030	1.5	201	18.9	31	1.21	4	20		188	20.6	32	1.16	4	58
0.25	0.80	1.00	0.015	0.5	121	29.9	38	0.95	8	20		72	32.5	35	0.82	12	64
0.25	0.80	1.00	0.015	3.0	85	12.7	18	1.08	5	20		51	14.4	18	0.92	7	63

Table 5.4. *Steady state changes in the capital stock and factor returns (parameters)*

					DK/K (%)			Dw/w (%)			Dr/r (%)		
Gamma	Rho	Sigma	Delta	Alpha	Cons	Wage	CapInc	Cons	Wage	CapInc	Cons	Wage	CapInc
0.25	0.80	1.00	0.015	1.5	24	6	−37	6	2	−13	−14	−14	43
0.10	0.80	1.00	0.015	1.5	22	2	−24	6	2	−8	−8	−8	33
0.50	0.80	1.00	0.015	1.5	24	7	−43	6	3	−17	−20	−20	60
0.25	0.30	1.00	0.015	1.5	24	7	−37	6	2	−12	−14	0	57
0.25	1.50	1.00	0.015	1.5	25	4	−36	5	2	−13	−17	0	50
0.25	0.80	0.80	0.015	1.5	19	6	−45	4	2	−16	−17	−17	83
0.25	0.80	1.25	0.015	1.5	28	4	−23	8	2	−9	−13	−13	13
0.25	0.80	1.00	0.050	1.5	24	11	−56	6	3	−21	−10	−10	100
0.25	0.80	1.00	−0.030	1.5	24	0	−7	6	1	−3	−25	0	0
0.25	0.80	1.00	0.015	0.5	23	6	−37	5	2	−12	−13	0	50
0.25	0.80	1.00	0.015	3.0	24	6	−36	6	3	−12	−17	−17	17

presents the long-run (across steady state) levels of the capital stock, labor supply, wage rate, pre-tax interest rate, and tax rates under the four tax structures for a range of parameter values. Table 5.5 summarizes some of the information in Table 5.4; it presents percentage changes in the long-run capital stock and factor prices associated with switching from a 15 percent proportional income tax structure to an equal annual revenue consumption, wage, or capital income tax. In considering these tables one should bear in mind that for each set of parameter values the level of government consumption equals 15 percent of the level of income in the income tax simulation using those parameters. Hence, as one moves down the rows in these tables the absolute amount of government consumption differs, although it is always 15 percent of the level of income in the income tax steady for the row-specific parameters.

As Table 5.3 indicates, the size of the steady state stock of capital is quite sensitive to the choice of certain preference parameters. For example, in the income tax base case, raising γ from 0.10 to 0.50 generates more than a threefold increase in the stock of capital. The direction of change is intuitive since larger values of γ imply steeper age–consumption profiles. Variations in the time preference rate, δ, can also significantly alter the long-run stock of savings; lowering the time-preference rate (reducing the degree of consumption impatience) from 0.015 to −0.030 implies more than a doubling of steady state capital under income tax finance. However, a −0.030 time-preference rate implies a rapid and highly unrealistic rate of growth of consumption with age.

In contrast to the supply of capital, the steady state aggregate labor supply is relatively unresponsive to these changes in γ and δ. It is, however, quite sensitive to the choice of ρ, the static elasticity of substitution between consumption and leisure, and the choice of the term α, the leisure utility share. Under income tax finance, raising ρ from −0.03 to 0.015 implies, ceteribus paribus, a reduction in aggregate labor supply of close to one-quarter, while raising alpha from 0.5 to 3.0 reduces aggregate labor supply by more than one-half.

Although aggregate factor supplies and factor prices may be sensitive to parameter specification, especially if one is willing to entertain parameter values that produce unrealistic age–consumption profiles and labor supplies, the qualitative effects of structural tax reform may be relatively insensitive to the precise choice of parameters (see Table 5.4). For example, switching from 15 percent proportional income taxation to equal revenue consumption taxation across all 11 sets of parameters in Table 5.3 raises the steady state stock of capital by at least 19 percent. The largest increase in the 11 cases is 28 percent. If one ignores the extreme values for the time-preference rate, δ, in Table 5.4, the increase in long-run capital

Table 5.5. Sensitivity analysis of structural tax reform: consideration of nonlinearities

				DK/K (%)			Dw/w (%)			Dr/r (%)		
Gamma	Rho	Sigma	Delta	Alpha	Cons	Wage	CapInc	Cons	Wage	CapInc	Cons	Wage	CapInc
0.10	1.50	0.80	0.015	1.5	23	5	−28	5	1	−11	−11	0	56
0.50	0.30	1.25	0.015	1.5	28	5	−24	8	2	−9	−17	0	17
0.10	0.30	0.80	0.015	1.5	20	2	−27	5	1	−10	−17	0	42
0.50	1.50	1.25	0.015	1.5	32	4	−24	8	3	−9	−17	−17	17
0.10	1.50	1.25	0.015	0.5	30	2	−21	4	0	−7	−11	0	22

formation when switching from income to wage taxation ranges from 2 percent to 7 percent, and the reduction in capital when switching to capital income taxation ranges from −23 percent to −43 percent.

The corresponding changes in factor prices arising from structural tax reform also exhibit far less sensitivity than might be suggested by the sensitivity of the levels of long-run factor supplies to parameter choice. If we ignore extreme time-preference rates, the long-run increase in the wage ranges from 4 to 8 percent in the case of consumption taxation, from 2 to 3 percent in the case of wage taxation, and from −8 and −16 percent in the case of capital income taxation. The range of percentage changes in the pre-tax interest rate can be much larger than percentage changes in the wage (per efficiency unit) even if extreme values for the time-preference rate are excluded. For example, when σ equals 0.80 and other parameters take base case values, switching to capital income taxation produces an 83 percent increase in the pre-tax interest rate; in contrast, the increase is only 13 percent if one assumes a value of σ equal to 1.25.

Table 5.5 presents simultaneous variations in parameters from their base case values that illustrate the nonlinear interactions in the relationship between the economic variables of Table 5.3 and the parameters. For the sets of parameters in Table 5.5 the increase in the steady state capital stock from switching to consumption taxation ranges from 23 percent to 32 percent; the increase from switching to wage taxation ranges from 2 percent to 5 percent, and the decrease from switching to capital income taxation ranges from −21 percent to −28 percent. These ranges either fall within the range of results in Table 5.3 or are not greatly different from those ranges. Hence, these combinations of alternative parameters do not alter the three central messages of Table 5.4 that, over a broad range of parameter values and starting from a 15 percent income tax steady state:

> Switching to consumption taxation significantly increases long-run capital formation.
> Switching to wage taxation produces a modest increase in long-run capital formation.
> Switching to capital income taxation significantly reduces long-run capital formation.

b. *The scale of taxation:* Another type of potential nonlinearity and important issue of sensitivity analysis relates to the level of the tax rate. As is well known, the extent of economic inefficiency associated with distortionary taxation rises approximately with the square of the tax rate. Hence, an economy with a 30 percent income tax will experience much more than double the efficiency losses that an economy with a 15 percent

5 Tax reform – choice of tax base

Table 5.6. *Sensitivity analysis of structural tax reform: level of initial steady state income tax rate (percent)*

Income tax rate	DK/K			Dw/w			Dr/r		
	Cons	Wage	CapInc	Cons	Wage	CapInc	Cons	Wage	CapInc
15	24	6	−37	6	2	−13	−14	−14	43
20	34	8	n.a.	8	3	n.a.	−14	−14	n.a.
30	61	11	n.a.	13	4	n.a.	−25	−13	n.a.
45	118	−2	n.a.	22	3	n.a.	−45	−9	n.a.

n.a. Not available.

income tax will experience. Since certain tax structures are more efficient than others (see the discussion later in this section), the extent of these differences will be magnified the larger the level of government consumption that must be financed by distortionary taxes. In addition to changing the degree of economic efficiency, increases in the level of tax-financed government consumption have direct implications for national savings that depend on the tax structure used to finance the additional government consumption. This issue is discussed in Chapter 6. It is useful to point out here, however, that comparisons of tax structures may be quite sensitive to the assumed scale of government consumption.

Table 5.6 examines how the scale of government consumption and, thus, the scale of taxation alter steady state comparisons of tax structures. Base case parameters are assumed in Table 5.6, which compares changes in capital stocks and factor prices associated with switching from income tax regimes with 15, 20, 30, and 45 percent tax rates. There are no entries for switching to capital income taxation when the initial income tax exceeds 15 percent. Our method for finding an equilibrium steady state does not converge for these cases; intuitively, the capital income tax base is not large enough to finance such a large scale of government consumption; there is a general equilibrium Laffer curve relating capital income tax revenues to the capital income tax rate, and the revenue required in the simulations in question exceeds the maximum point on this Laffer curve.

The comparisons of income, wage, and consumption tax bases shown in Table 5.6 are quite interesting. They show that the extent to which the choice of the tax structure alters long-run capital formation and factor returns is highly sensitive to the scale of government consumption being financed. In switching from income to consumption taxation, the increase in long-run capital formation is 24 percent when the level of income taxation is 20 percent in the initial income tax steady state; in contrast, the increase is 118 percent when the initial steady state features a 45 percent income tax rate! When income and wage taxation are compared, the impression given in Table 5.3 that wage taxation implies somewhat more capital formation changes dramatically if the initial income tax steady state tax rate is 45 percent. In this case switching to wage taxation lowers the long-run level of capital by 2 percent!

Increases in government consumption "crowd in" capital formation when consumption tax finance is being used (see Chapter 6). The opposite is true when the income tax is used to finance increased government consumption. This difference in crowding in and crowding out from increased government consumption under the two tax structures explains the dramatic difference between the figures of 24 percent and 118 percent in Table 5.6. The explanation for the wage tax results appears to reflect the relative inefficiency of wage taxation relative to income taxation. In the wage tax steady state corresponding to the 45 percent income tax steady state, the wage tax rate is 67 percent. This very high tax on labor supply suggests a much more severely distorted labor supply choice than in the case of a 45 percent income tax. Indeed, in the wage tax steady state, labor supply is 14 percent smaller than in the income tax steady state. Lower life cycle labor supply means lower life cycle earnings and less life cycle savings. Although life cycle savings are 2 percent smaller as a result of switching from 45 percent income taxation to equal revenue wage taxation, the wage tax steady state capital–labor ratio is larger because of the 14 percent decline in steady state labor supply. Hence, wages rise and interest rates fall in this as well as the other wage tax simulations.

D. Welfare effects of structural tax reform

Changes in after-tax prices of factors and goods obviously alter the utility levels of each cohort alive at the time of the tax change or born thereafter. One measure of these utility differences is the equivalent percentage increase in full lifetime resources (assets plus the present value of earnings based on working full time) needed in the original income tax regime to produce each cohort's realized level of utility under the specified alternative tax regimes. For cohorts living in the new long-run equilibrium under consumption, wage, and capital income tax regimes, the equivalent variations are 2.32 percent, −0.90 percent, and −1.14 percent. These figures are smaller than the long-run changes in wage rates indicated in Table 5.2 because they encompass the additional amount of both lifetime leisure and consumption that could hypothetically be afforded in the old

5 Tax reform – choice of tax base

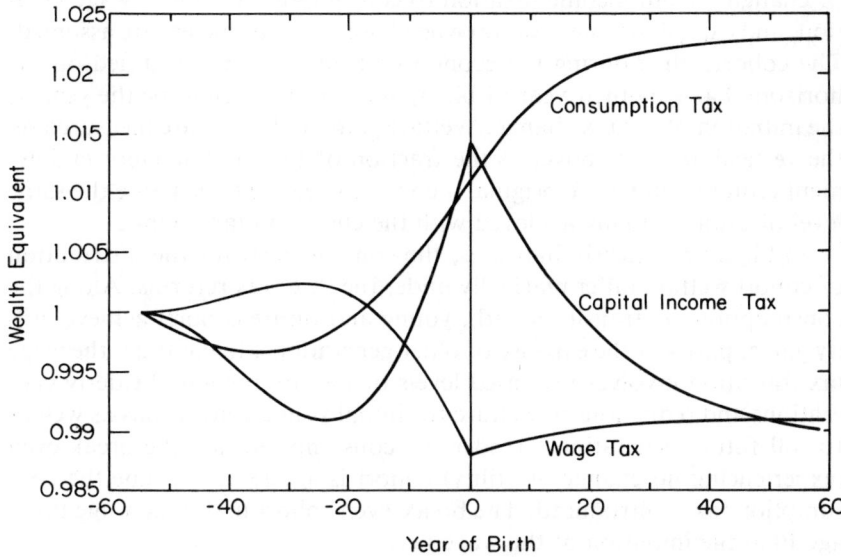

Figure 5.4. The welfare effects of tax reform.

steady state. Stated differently, since 51 percent of lifetime resources are spent on leisure in the initial steady state, a 1 percent increase in full-time resources would permit a 2.04 (1/0.49) percent increase in lifetime consumption if leisure is held constant.

One perhaps surprising feature of these numbers is that steady state utility is lower under wage taxation than under income taxation despite an 8 percent increase in capital intensity. The before-tax wage rises to 1.02 from an initial value of 1, but the after-tax wage is 0.80 in the wage tax steady state compared with 0.85 under the income tax. In addition, the long-run after-tax interest rate, which determines prices of future consumption and leisure, is only 0.61 percentage points greater in the wage taxation steady state. Despite the larger capital stock in the wage tax steady state, aggregate steady state consumption is lower, in part because of the smaller aggregate supply of labor induced by the increased wage tax.

Analysis of changes in steady state welfare indicates that the impact of tax reform on the welfare of generations alive after the transition to the new steady state is complete. Although the long-run welfare effects are important, much of the concern about the welfare effects of structural tax change centers on the impact on generations alive during the transition to the new steady state. Figure 5.4 presents the effects on cohort welfare of changing from income taxation to consumption taxation, wage taxation, and capital income taxation when base case parameters are assumed. The cohorts alive during the economy's transition are identified on the horizontal axis by their year of birth, and zero is taken to be the year of the initiation of the tax change. Welfare gains and losses are measured on the vertical axis, as above, as the fraction of full lifetime labor endowment required under the original income tax regime to generate the same level of utility actually achieved with the change in tax regime.

As Figure 5.4 clearly indicates, the consequences for the distribution of cohort welfare differ markedly under the three tax reforms. Along the consumption tax transition path, young and future cohorts achieve utility gains, partly at the expense of older generations. In contrast, the wage tax transition involves increased levels of welfare for initial elderly generations and reductions in welfare for initial young generations as well as for all future generations. Under the consumption tax, the break-even (experiencing no change in utility) cohort is age 13 at the time the consumption tax is introduced. The break-even cohort under the wage tax is age 10 at the initiation of the wage tax.

In the case of the capital income tax, the initial elderly are made worse off as are all those born 23 years or more after the tax change. The generations experiencing a welfare gain from switching to the capital income tax structure are all those cohorts below age 3 (age 23 if age 20 is the age of adulthood) when the policy change is made and those cohorts born before year 23.

The shapes of these curves is easily understood. Under the consumption tax, elderly generations are faced with a much heavier tax burden than they would have experienced under the income tax. For these older cohorts, labor earnings are small, and consumption is financed by depleting accumulated savings. Since the elderly are dissaving, their consumption exceeds their income, and they are particularly hard hit by switching from income to consumption taxation. Young and future generations gain from a switch to consumption taxation because older generations are forced to bear a larger proportion of the present value of government consumption expenditures. In contrast, under the wage tax the burden of taxation is shifted away from older generations and transferred to initial young and future generations. The change to capital income taxation, like the change to consumption taxation, shifts the tax burden onto initial older generations; but the associated reduction over time in the capital stock and therefore the wage implies a lower level of welfare for generations born after year 22. Initial young generations and those born prior to year 23 gain from the reduction in their lifetime tax burden, but are not greatly affected by the transition effects on wages because the wage

5 Tax reform – choice of tax base

Table 5.7. *Efficiency gains or losses from switching from income to wage taxation*

Parameters			Income tax in initial income tax steady state	Efficiency gain or loss (wealth equivalent, %)
Gamma	Rho	Sigma		
0.25	0.80	1.00	0.15	−0.25
			0.25	−1.18
0.10	0.80	1.00	0.15	−0.70
			0.25	−3.42
0.50	0.80	1.00	0.15	−0.10
			0.25	−0.46
0.25	0.30	1.00	0.15	0.03
			0.25	0.06
0.25	1.50	1.00	0.15	−0.55
			0.25	−2.89
0.25	0.80	0.80	0.15	−0.11
			0.25	−0.54
0.25	0.80	1.25	0.15	−0.58
			0.25	−2.69

Note: Table assumes base case values for alpha and delta.

changes slowly through the transition; although it is ultimately 13 percent lower than its initial value, it is only 5 percent lower after the first 10 years of the transition.

E. The relative efficiency of alternative tax structures

1. *Base case results*

The results with respect to the welfare effects of alternative tax structures beg the question of whether policies that increase capital accumulation also increase economic efficiency. One approach explored by Auerbach and Kotlikoff (1983a) is to seek combinations of taxes that, when used in conjunction with deficit finance, raise the welfare of all cohorts to at least that enjoyed under the income tax. Such Pareto improving welfare paths do not, however, offer a single, precise measure of the efficiency gain (or loss) resulting from a tax change. Incorporating the LSRA in the simulation does provide such a measure. In the simulations on which Tables 5.7 and 5.8 are based, the LSRA uses its lump sum taxes and transfers to

78   Dynamic fiscal policy

Table 5.8. *Efficiency gains or losses from switching from income to consumption taxation*

Parameters			Income tax in initial income tax steady state	Efficiency gain or loss (wealth equivalent, %)
Gamma	Rho	Sigma		
0.25	0.80	1.00	0.15	0.29
			0.25	1.04
0.10	0.80	1.00	0.15	0.37
			0.25	1.29
0.50	0.80	1.00	0.15	0.28
			0.25	0.98
0.25	0.30	1.00	0.15	0.25
			0.25	0.92
0.25	1.50	1.00	0.15	0.36
			0.25	1.26
0.25	0.80	0.80	0.15	0.19
			0.25	0.75
0.25	0.80	1.25	0.15	0.45
			0.25	1.54

Note: Table assumes base case values for alpha and delta.

leave unchanged the welfare of all generations alive at the time of the change in tax regimes and to raise or lower uniformly the welfare of all future generations. These tables present efficiency gains or losses from dynamic tax reform measured as a wealth equivalent. They present the results for switching to wage and consumption taxation for a range of parameter values and initial income tax rates of 15 and 25 percent, respectively.

Tables 5.7 and 5.8 indicate efficiency gains from switching to consumption taxation and, with one exception, efficiency losses from switching to wage taxation. The efficiency changes are considerably larger in absolute value when an initial 25 percent income tax rather than a 15 percent income tax is assumed. This reflects the fact that economic distortions rise with the square of tax rates.

When base case parameters are assumed, the efficiency gain in switching from a 15 percent income tax to an equal revenue consumption tax is equivalent to raising full-time resources in the initial steady state by 0.29 percent for each generation born after the tax structure is changed. If an initial income tax of 25 percent is assumed, the efficiency gain is 1.04 percent. If the LSRA maintains unchanged the welfare of all initial

5 Tax reform – choice of tax base

cohorts as well as those born in the first 20 years after the tax switch, the efficiency gains available to all cohorts born after the first 20 years of the transition are 0.80 percent in the case of an initial 15 percent income tax and 3.10 percent in the case of an initial 25 percent income tax.

As the discussion of equations (5.7) and (5.8) makes clear, the consumption tax combines a distortionary wage tax and a nondistortionary lump sum tax on existing wealth. Individuals who have already accumulated wealth at the time the consumption tax is unexpectedly introduced have no way of avoiding paying consumption taxes when they spend this wealth. Since their consumption out of wealth is a completely inelastic form of behavior, taxing this behavior is nondistortionary. Of course, individuals can try to avoid the consumption tax by working less, but for a large segment of society – namely, the elderly – this is not a particularly important option, since they are, to a large extent, already retired. The greater the revenues from the implicit lump sum tax on wealth imposed by the consumption tax, the smaller the revenue that must be obtained from the distortionary wage tax component of the consumption tax. Hence, in comparison with switching from income to only wage taxation, switching from income taxation produces a smaller effective tax rate on labor supply.

Since full-time resources are spent on both consumption and leisure, it may be instructive to express these gains in terms of the percentage increase in lifetime consumption that could be financed. In the 15 percent income tax initial steady state the present value of lifetime consumption represents only 49 percent of the present value of full lifetime resources; hence, the efficiency gain provided to all cohorts born after the change in tax structure is 0.59 (0.29/0.49) percent of initial steady state lifetime consumption under a 15 percent initial income tax. It is 1.86 percent (1.04/0.56) under a 25 percent initial income tax. The efficiency gain can also be expressed in relation to annual GNP. Raising the full-time resources of each successive new generation in the initial 15 percent income tax steady state by 0.29 percent is equivalent to a perpetual increase in GNP of 0.20 percent.

The efficiency loss in switching to wage taxation from the 15 percent income tax steady state is 0.25 percent of the present value of full lifetime resources (0.51 percent of the present value of lifetime consumption). Starting with a 25 percent income tax, the efficiency loss is 1.18 percent of full lifetime resources (2.11 percent of lifetime consumption). In contrast to the consumption tax, which is more efficient than the income tax because it is effectively equivalent to a lump sum tax on wealth plus a distortionary tax on labor supply, the wage tax regime has no such implicit lump sum tax. Hence, in the wage tax regime the amount of revenue that must be collected by taxing labor supply and the distortions of labor supply are larger than under the consumption tax regime.

Given the implicit lump sum tax embedded in the consumption tax, it is not surprising that the consumption tax is more efficient than either the income or the wage tax. It is perhaps surprising, however, that the income tax, at least in the base case, is more efficient than the wage tax. After all, the income tax distorts two margins of choice, namely, the intertemporal tradeoff between current and future consumption and current and future leisure and the static tradeoff between consumption and leisure at a point in time. In contrast, the wage tax distorts only the static consumption–leisure margin of choice.

Although it does distort an additional margin of choice, the income tax distorts these two choices at a lower tax rate than the wage tax, which distorts a single margin of choice, that is, under the income tax labor supply is taxed at a 15 percent rate, while it is taxed at 20 percent under the wage tax. Hence, the income tax appears to be more efficient because it spreads out the distortions over two choices, in contrast to the wage tax, which concentrates all its distortion on a single choice margin. Hence, the finding here of more efficient income than wage taxation is in accord with the general second-best proposition that it is better to tax more than fewer commodities. Of course, the theory of the second best provides more precise tax-setting prescriptions that depend on the relative complementarity of the arguments of the utility function. According to Auerbach, Kotlikoff, and Skinner (1983), second-best theory does not suggest that income taxation will always be more efficient than wage taxation (indeed, Table 5.7 presents a case in which it is less efficient); rather, the relative efficiency of the two taxes will depend on the particular structure of preferences.

A second reason for the relative efficiency of the income tax emphasized by Chamley (1981) compared with the wage tax is that there is a small element of lump sum taxation in the income tax. Consider the taxation of capital income under the income tax. At any point in time the capital stock is fixed and, if we ignore labor supply changes, the marginal product of capital and therefore capital income are fixed. Hence, the immediate period tax on capital income is a lump sum tax. In the switch to wage taxation from income taxation the economy foregoes this lump sum tax on capital income.

As for the capital income tax, the LSRA transition to this tax structure starting with a 15 percent income tax is infeasible, at least for the base case parameters. The capital income tax base is too small to generate the same amount of revenues as in the 15 percent income tax rate initial steady state. However, switching to capital income taxation with the LSRA is feasible if the initial income tax is 10 percent. In this case

5 Tax reform – choice of tax base

the welfare loss in switching from income to capital income taxation is 2.15 percent of full-time resources. Despite the increase in effective lump sum taxation associated with switching solely to capital income taxation, the increase in intertemporal distortion under the capital income tax makes this tax structure far less efficient than an income tax.

It is instructive to compare the steady state welfare changes described in the previous section with these efficiency effects. In switching from 15 percent income taxation to consumption taxation, the non-LSRA steady state welfare gain is 2.32 percent, which is eight times larger than the corresponding LSRA efficiency gain of 0.29 percent. Similarly, in switching to wage taxation from an initial 15 percent income tax, the non-LSRA steady state welfare loss is 0.90 percent, 3.6 times larger in absolute value than the corresponding LSRA efficiency loss of 0.25 percent.

The difference in these numbers clearly reflects the differences in intergenerational redistribution under the non-LSRA and LSRA policies. In the non-LSRA transition to consumption taxation, initial elderly generations suffer reductions in their welfare, which benefit future generations. Indeed, the lion's share of the long-run welfare gain to future generations in switching to consumption taxation is attributable to the policy's intergenerational redistribution rather than to its improvement in economic efficiency. In the case of switching to wage taxation, the 0.90 percent long-run welfare loss in the non-LSRA transition is 3.6 times larger than the LSRA efficiency loss because the non-LSRA transition involves a redistribution to initial elderly generations at the expense of future generations; such redistribution to the initial elderly is ruled out in the LSRA simulations.

2. *Efficiency gains – sensitivity analysis*

Tables 5.7 and 5.8 consider the sensitivity of the base case wage and consumption tax LSRA efficiency calculations to the choice of γ, the intertemporal elasticity of substitution; ρ, the intratemporal elasticity of substitution between goods and leisure; and σ, the elasticity of substitution in production between capital and labor. In general, the wage tax efficiency gains appear more sensitive to the choice of parameter values than the consumption tax efficiency gains. This is not surprising, since the consumption tax represents a combination of a wage tax and a lump sum tax, and the gains to switching to partial lump sum taxation remain even when one is considering parameter values that imply behavioral responses quite similar to income and wage taxation.

Larger values of γ entail greater inefficiency associated with intertemporal distortions and, thus, smaller reductions in efficiency from switching to wage taxation. In the case of a 25 percent initial income tax the efficiency loss from switching to wage taxation is 3.42 percent of full-time resources when γ equals 0.10; it is only 0.46 percent when γ equals 0.50. These percentage differences may suggest larger absolute differences than is the case. As indicated in Table 5.3, the wage rate and interest rate are larger and smaller, respectively, when γ equals 0.50 than when it equals 0.10. Hence, the present value of full-time resources is larger when γ equals 0.50 than when it equals 0.10.

In the case of switching to consumption taxation from 25 percent income taxation, the efficiency gain declines from 1.29 percent when γ equals 0.10 to 0.98 percent when γ equals 0.50. However, since the present value of full-time resources almost triples when γ rises from 0.10 to 0.50, the efficiency gain in absolute value is larger when γ equals 0.50 than when it equals 0.10.

Larger values of ρ, the elasticity of substitution between consumption and leisure, imply larger percentage efficiency losses in switching to wage taxation. Starting from the 25 percent income tax steady state, there is a 6 percent efficiency gain in adopting wage taxation when ρ equals 0.30 and other base case parameters are assumed; when ρ equals 1.50 there is a 2.89 percent efficiency loss. In contrast, larger values of ρ imply, ceteris paribus, greater (percentage as well as absolute) efficiency gains from switching to consumption taxation. These results are intuitively plausible; smaller values of ρ are associated with less serious distortions of the labor supply decision for a given tax on labor income. This leads to smaller efficiency losses under wage taxation and smaller efficiency gains from switching to consumption taxation.

As σ approaches zero, capital and labor approach perfect complementarity in production; in the limit, for σ equal to zero, taxing capital is equivalent to taxing labor since there is a single composite input. Since the distinction between taxing capital and labor vanishes as σ declines, the efficiency losses in switching to wage from income taxation decline with a decline in σ. The reduced substitution in production associated with a drop in σ also means that the income tax will cause less distortion and, therefore, the (percentage as well as absolute) gain in switching to partial lump sum taxation under a consumption taxation will be smaller.

F. Announcement effects

1. Impact on short-run saving

Early announcement of future policy changes can significantly alter economic behavior in periods prior to the implementation of the new policy. Given the time required to formulate and enact new tax legislation,

5 Tax reform – choice of tax base

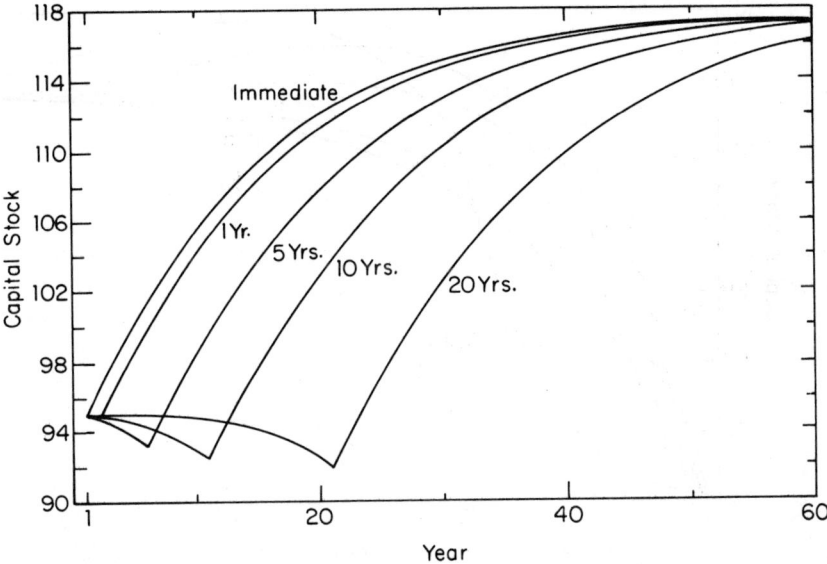

Figure 5.5. The effects on capital formation of preannounced switches to consumption taxation.

announcement effects are a serious concern. Indeed, simulating the early announcement of a policy designed to stimulate savings, such as switching to a consumption tax, indicates potentially dramatic declines in national saving in the period prior to the enactment of the new policy.

Consider first the effect in year zero of announcements of a complete switch from a 15 percent income tax to consumption taxation starting immediately, or in 5, 10 or 20 years. Whereas the national saving rate jumps from 3.73 percent to 9.27 percent if the consumption tax is implemented immediately, the short-run (year 1) saving rate falls to 1.93 percent in response to information that the consumption tax switch will occur in year 2. Clearly the near-term prospect of high consumption tax rates significantly lowers the price of current consumption relative to the price of consumption after the switch to consumption taxation; that is, announcing today that high consumption tax rates are to be imposed in a few years is similar to imposing a stiff short-term capital income tax. The short-run response of households to this policy is to increase significantly the level of private consumption.

Figure 5.5 depicts the effects on the capital stock of preannounced switches to consumption taxation. The labels on the curves indicate the number of years in advance that the tax change is announced. In the case

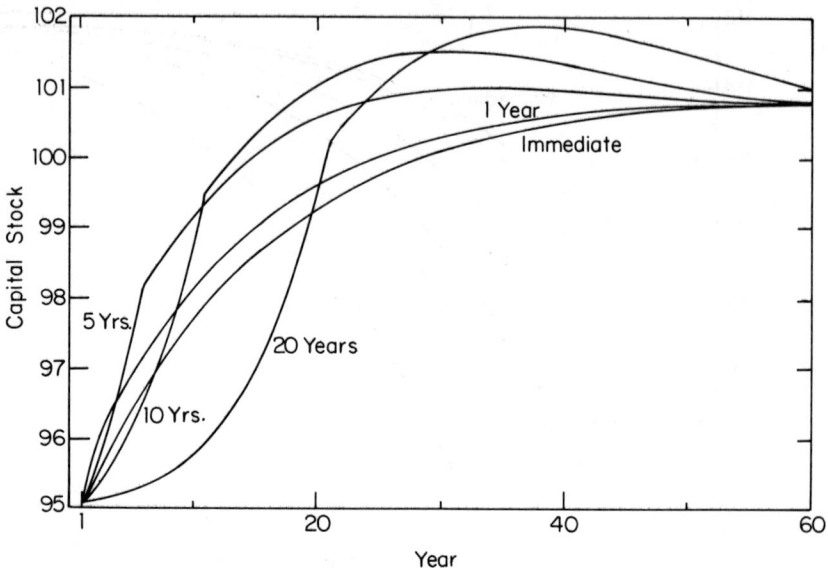

Figure 5.6. The effects on capital formation of preannounced switches to wage taxation.

of the 20-year preannounced switch to consumption taxation, the capital stock gradually falls from its initial (year 1) value of 95 to 92 in year 21, when the consumption tax is instituted. Slightly smaller reductions in capital occur by years 11 and 6 in the 10-year and 5-year preannounced switches to consumption taxation.

With regard to short-term saving rates, announcing future wage taxation has the opposite effect of announcing future consumption taxation. Here the promise of lower rates of capital income taxation in the near future reduces the relative prices of future consumption and leisure, leading to a substitution of future for current consumption and leisure and an increase in short-term saving rates. For example, if a shift to wage taxation is announced five years in advance, the national saving rate immediately rises from 3.73 percent to 5.57 percent.

Figure 5.6 depicts the effect of early wage tax announcements on capital formation. In the case of a 5-year preannounced switch, the capital stock in year 6, when the switch occurs, has already increased by almost half of the ultimate increase. Hence, much of the policy's impact on savings occurs before the policy is actually instituted. The 10- and 20-year preannouncement paths of capital illustrate this as well; they also show that the stock of capital can overshoot its ultimate value.

5 Tax reform – choice of tax base

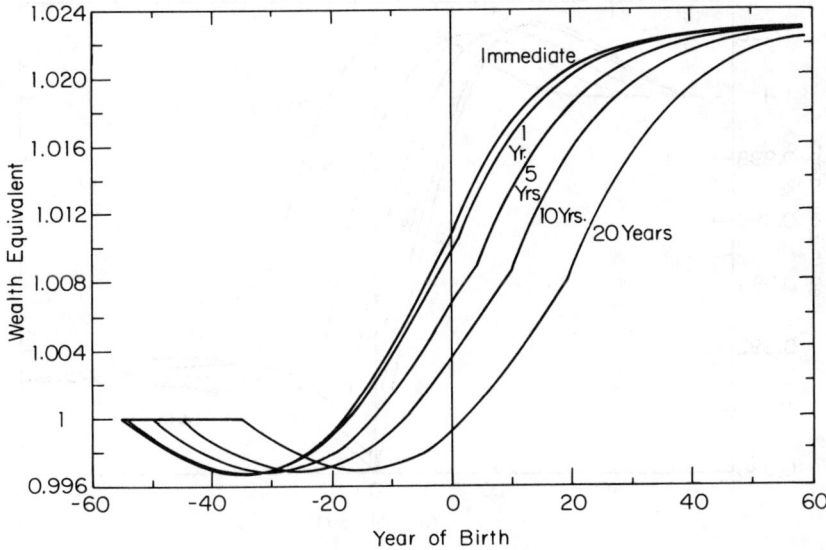

Figure 5.7. The welfare effects of preannounced switches to consumption taxation.

The announcement effects in both Figures 5.5 and 5.6 indicate that economic behavior changes less in the short term the further the date of policy implementation is in the future. Yet policy changes that will not occur for 10 years can still change saving rates in year zero by more than 20 percent.

2. *Welfare effects*

The welfare implications of preannouncing the switch to consumption and wage taxation are diagrammed in Figures 5.7 and 5.8, respectively. More distant implementation of the consumption tax relieves initial elderly cohorts of the heavy taxation of their retirement consumption. In contrast, initial young cohorts are hurt by a delay in the switch to a consumption tax. For these generations the short-run crowding out of capital means lower wages during some if not all of their remaining working years. The gains to future generations are also reduced by a delay in the implementation of consumption taxation. Again, the initial crowding out of capital in anticipation of the consumption tax means a smaller stock of capital during the economy's transition path than would have occurred under immediate implementation.

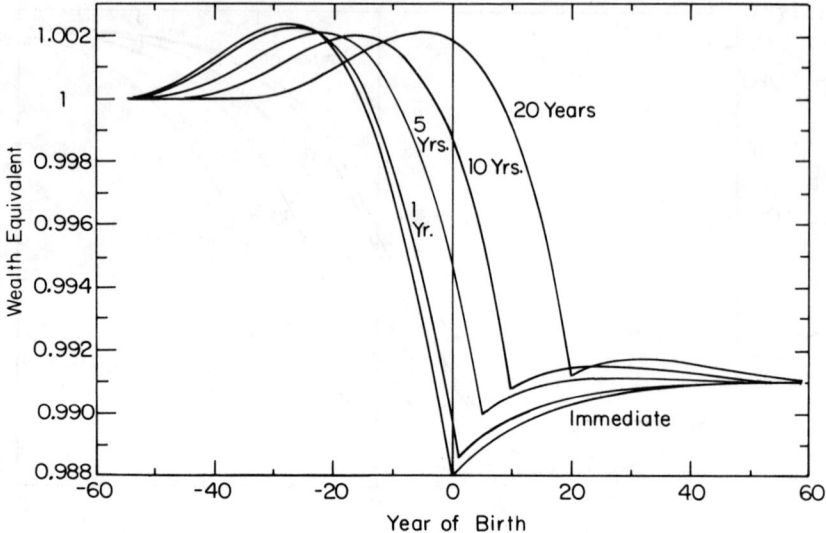

Figure 5.8. The welfare effects of preannounced switches to wage taxation.

Young and future generations benefit from the delay in implementing the wage tax. Delaying the tax switch still induces immediate additional capital formation, which spells higher wages for these cohorts, but the government also collects more revenue in the short run from the initial elderly. Hence, the taxation of younger and future generations can be reduced, in present value, by the additional amount of revenue collected from retirees in the short run.

3. *Efficiency implications of early policy announcements*

Preannouncing structural tax reforms can also greatly reduce if not reverse the potential efficiency gains from such reforms. Consider a preannounced shift from a 15 percent income tax to a consumption tax. Whereas the efficiency gain from switching immediately to a consumption tax is 0.29 percent (see Table 5.8), the gain is only 0.024 percent if the switch is announced 5 years in advance. If the switch is announced 20 years in advance there is an efficiency loss of -0.18 percent. If the initial income tax steady state features a 25 percent tax rate, announcing the switch to consumption taxation 5 years in advance results in a -0.024 percent efficiency loss, while announcing the switch 20 years in advance leads to

5 Tax reform – choice of tax base

a -1.00 percent efficiency loss. These figures should be compared with the corresponding 1.04 percent efficiency gain from enacting the policy immediately.

Clearly, delaying the switch to consumption taxation exacerbates intertemporal distortions. Hence, we have the paradoxical result that applying the right medicine (the consumption tax) too late can actually make the patient (the economy) worse off.

Appendix: LSRA transfers

Because the utility function described in (3.3) is homothetic, increases in individual wealth, given fixed prices, bring about proportional increases in the vectors **c** and **l**. Thus, to solve for the additional resources needed by an individual born after time zero to attain a utility level $\hat{u}$, we solve for ϕ such that

$$\left(\frac{1}{1-1/\gamma}\right) \sum_{t=1}^{55} (1+\delta)^{-(t-1)} \{[(1+\phi)c_t]^{(1-1/\rho)} + \alpha[(1+\phi)l_t]^{(1-1/\rho)}\}^{[(1-1/\gamma)/(1-1/\rho)]} = \hat{u} \quad (5A.1)$$

$$\phi = \left(\frac{\hat{u}}{\bar{u}}\right)^{1/(1-1/\gamma)} - 1, \quad (5A.2)$$

where $\bar{u}$ is the current level of utility being attained with a transfer level $\bar{v}_i$. The difference between $\bar{v}_i$ and the product of ϕ and the present value of full-time earnings yields a guess of the additional resources, Δv_i, that must be transferred to the individual to attain the utility level $\hat{u}$. Adding $\bar{\Delta} v_i$ to v_i gives us a function $v_i(\hat{u})$ of total transfers needed for utility level $\hat{u}$.

For individuals alive when the transition begins, the same procedure is followed using the utility subfunctions that apply over the remaining years of life. For individuals of cohorts $i < i^*$, $\hat{u}$ is set at the level that would have been enjoyed under the original tax regime, u_0. The present value, T, of all such transfers, $v_i(u_0)$, $i < i^*$, is then calculated. The value of u^* is chosen by requiring that the present value of *all* LSRA transfers is zero:

$$T + \sum_{i=i^*}^{\infty} \left[\prod_{j=0}^{i} (1+r_j)\right]^{-1} (1+n)^i v_i(u^*) = 0. \quad (5A.3)$$

This also yields solutions for $v_i(u^*)$, the new guesses for v_i, which are weighted with the old vector $\bar{v}$ to provide values for the next iteration.

CHAPTER 6

Deficits, government spending, and crowding out

In recent years the coincidence of large official budget deficits in several industrialized countries and exceptionally high short-term real interest rates has aroused considerable interest in the economics of deficit finance. Since 1980 U.S. official debt in the hands of the public has more than doubled. During the same period, the U.S. rate of saving out of net national production has averaged less than two-thirds the average saving rate of the prior 30 years. Part of the explanation for the recent low saving rates in the early 1980s was consumption smoothing in the face of the recession of 1981–2; but in the relatively prosperous years of 1984 and 1985 the saving rate has remained low. The 1985 saving rate of 4.4 percent is precisely half of the rate observed on the average in the 1950s.

Deficit finance is alleged to "crowd out" domestic saving, and, depending on the international mobility of investment, to "crowd out" domestic investment (capital formation) as well. According to the standard scenario, the reduction in the stock of capital relative to the supply of labor implies an increase in the factor price of capital relative to that of labor; real interest rates rise and real wages fall. The life cycle model of savings predicts precisely this combination of events with regard to deficit finance. Indeed, the life cycle model is the principal neoclassical model generating such predictions.

Since the predictions of the life cycle model appear to underlie much of the concern about deficit finance, it is important to examine closely those predictions. A related concern about government policy is the possible crowding out of capital formation by government consumption. Increases in government consumption may or may not be associated with increases in government deficits. Hence, it is important to examine balanced budget as well as deficit-financed increases in government consumption.

This chapter considers the impact on savings and capital formation of conventional deficit policies and balanced budget increases in government consumption. Conventional deficit policies considered are (1) short-term tax cuts holding government expenditures fixed and (2) increases in expenditures holding tax rates fixed in the short run. Since Chapter 10 examines changes in transfer expenditures, specifically social security transfers, changes in expenditures here are confined to changes in government

6 Deficits, government spending, and crowding out

consumption. The policies involving balanced budget increases in government consumption include (1) permanent increases in government consumption and (2) temporary increases in government consumption.

The seven important lessons of this chapter are as follows:

> Deficit finance and government consumption can significantly crowd out capital formation and lower the welfare of future generations.
>
> Tax cuts of short duration can lead to short-run *crowding in,* although substantial crowding out occurs in the long run. Hence, short-term changes in capital formation may provide little or no guide to the ultimate impact of deficit finance.
>
> Crowding out from deficit finance is a very slow process because it results from increased consumption spending over potentially long horizons.
>
> Deficit policies that lead to very sizable increases in long-term interest rates may involve no change or even declines in short-term interest rates.
>
> The inclusion of adjustment costs to the life cycle model has only a trivial affect on the time path of interest rates arising from a policy of deficit finance, despite its smoothing of the path of the capital stock.

A. Short-term tax-cut policies

1. *Theoretical issues*

a. *Intergenerational redistribution and its impact on saving:* As dictated by the government's intertemporal budget constraint (equation 3.20), short-term reductions in tax rates, when the time path of expenditures is fixed, eventually necessitate increases in tax rates to maintain intertemporal budget balance. Hence, the tax-cut policies considered here involve: (1) short-term reductions in income tax rates, (2) the issuance of government debt during the period of the tax cut to make up the shortfall in government revenues, and (3) at the cessation of the tax cut, increases in the income tax rate to balance the government's conventional budget such that government debt per capita no longer increases, but rather remains at its level as of the end of the tax cut.

With government consumption held constant, policies involving short-term cuts and long-term increases in income tax rates fundamentally involve government redistribution; in this case the redistribution is across generations, with initial older generations benefiting from the tax cuts because they will be either dead or partly or fully retired when tax rates are subsequentially increased. Hence they escape, to a large extent, the eventually higher tax rates. However, younger and future generations face the higher tax rates either over significant portions of their lives or over their entire lives.

This redistribution from younger and future generations to older generations produces an increase in total national consumption and a decline in national saving. The reason for this increase in national consumption is straightforward: older generations, with shorter remaining life spans, have larger marginal propensities to consume than younger generations and than future generations, whose marginal propensities to consume prior to being born are zero.

b. *Officially defined deficits as a measure of intergenerational redistribution – a word of caution:* As argued in Chapter 7, many government policies that redistribute from young and future generations to older generations have no impact on the conventionally defined level of government debt. Indeed, the short-term tax-cut policies examined here could be conducted with no change in officially reported government debt. Hence, the level of officially reported government debt is not a sufficient statistic for the government's intergenerational transfer policy, nor is it even necessarily correlated with the extent of such redistribution. This point should be kept in mind in considering the simulations of this chapter; although the stock of official debt increases in these simulations, one could devise tax-transfer policies whose simultaneous implementation would arbitrarily alter the reported course of official debt but leave unchanged the real effects of the tax-cut policy. The true indicator of the government's intergenerational redistribution is not the size of its arbitrarily defined official liabilities, but the change in the lifetime budget constraints of current and future generations. The temporary tax-cut policies considered here clearly expand the budget opportunities of initial older generations and contract those of young and future generations.

c. *Short-term tax cuts in the presence of adjustment costs:* As indicated in equation (3.18), adjustment costs introduce an additional term involving capital gains in the equation relating the real interest rate to the marginal product of capital. Since the marginal product of capital at time t depends on the ratio of the stock of capital to the supply of labor at time t, and since one would not expect these factor supplies to change radically in the very short run, even in the case of major tax cuts, one would not expect significant increases in short-term real interest rates in the absence

6 Deficits, government spending, and crowding out

of adjustment costs. With adjustment costs, however, short-term tax cuts will be associated with an immediate change in q (stock values), reflecting the change in new investment and subsequent transitional changes. Eventually the value of q will return to its initial steady state value. Hence, during the tax-cut transition the real interest rate will exceed or be less than the marginal product of capital by a term involving capital gains or losses on equities arising during the transition. Short-term rates could, in principle, rise significantly above the initial steady state marginal product of capital in response to temporary tax cuts if such policies involve a transition path with sizable short-term capital gains (increases in q).

2. Simulation findings

a. *Income tax cuts in the absence of adjustment costs:* Table 6.1 presents the effects of cuts in the income tax rate lasting 5 and 20 years where no adjustment costs are assumed. Recall that the initial steady state proportional income tax rate is 15 percent. During the period of tax cuts the income tax rate is reduced to 10 percent, and government debt is endogenous, the new issue of debt being equal to the conventional budget deficit. At the end of the tax cut the income tax rate becomes endogenous, and per capita government debt is held constant thereafter.

As indicated in Table 6.1, the long-run income tax rates, τ_y, resulting from cutting income tax rates by one-third for 1, 5, and 20 years are 15.3, 16.6, and 30.4 percent, respectively. The long-run reduction in per capita capital, K, is 1.3 percent for the 1-year tax cut, 7.8 percent for the 5-year tax cut, and 49.1 percent for the 20-year tax cut. Per capita labor supply, L, falls by a trivial amount in the 1- and 5-year tax cuts, but by 5.1 percent for the 20-year tax cut, owing to the sharp decline in real wages.

The transition paths displayed in Table 6.1 reveal a number of important features of crowding out. First, the 1- and 5-year tax-cut policies exhibit *crowding in* prior to the year tax rates are increased. During this period, short-term (one-year) interest rates are *lower*, not higher, owing to the deficit policy. In the 1-year tax reduction, the simulated economy's saving rate rises by 32 percent in the first year of the transition. However, in the second year of this simulation, after taxes have been raised, the saving rate is 8 percent lower than its initial steady state value.

In contrast to the two shorter-term tax cuts, the 20-year tax cut exhibits immediate crowding out. The short-run differences in these simulations clearly reflect the predominance of substitution over income effects in the case of the short-period tax cuts and the converse for the 20-year tax cut;

Table 6.1. *Crowding out under alternative short-term income tax-cut policies*

Year	S/Y	τ_y	w	r	L	K
Initial steady state	0.037	0.150	1.000	0.067	19.10	95.1
1-year income tax cut						
1	0.049	0.100	0.991	0.069	19.80	95.1
2	0.034	0.152	1.002	0.067	19.04	95.4
3	0.034	0.152	1.001	0.067	19.04	95.3
4	0.035	0.152	1.001	0.067	19.04	95.3
5	0.035	0.152	1.001	0.067	19.04	95.3
10	0.036	0.153	1.000	0.067	19.05	94.9
30	0.037[a]	0.153	0.998	0.067	19.07	94.2
60	0.037[a]	0.153	0.997	0.068	19.08	93.9
90	0.037[a]	0.153	0.997	0.068	19.08	93.9
Final steady state	0.037[a]	0.153	0.997	0.068	19.08	93.9
5-year income tax cut						
1	0.045	0.100	0.992	0.069	19.74	95.1
2	0.044	0.100	0.992	0.068	19.73	95.3
3	0.044	0.100	0.993	0.068	19.71	95.5
4	0.042	0.100	0.994	0.068	19.70	95.7
5	0.042	0.100	0.994	0.068	19.69	95.8
10	0.025	0.164	1.003	0.066	18.80	94.6
30	0.031	0.166	0.983	0.069	18.92	90.3
60	0.035	0.166	0.983	0.070	18.99	88.4
90	0.035	0.166	0.983	0.070	18.99	88.2
Final steady state	0.035	0.166	0.987	0.070	18.99	88.2
20-year income tax cut						
1	0.034	0.100	0.994	0.068	19.58	95.1
2	0.033	0.100	0.994	0.068	19.56	95.0
3	0.031	0.100	0.994	0.068	19.55	94.9
4	0.030	0.100	0.994	0.068	19.53	94.8
5	0.029	0.100	0.993	0.068	19.51	94.6
10	0.023	0.100	0.991	0.068	19.45	93.3
30	−0.014	0.246	0.964	0.075	17.72	76.1
60	0.011	0.284	0.888	0.096	18.08	56.0
90	0.020	0.297	0.867	0.103	18.11	50.8
Final steady state	0.023	0.304	0.856	0.107	18.13	48.5

[a] This saving rate is below that in the initial steady state to the fourth decimal.

in the 1-year tax cut, all but the oldest generation alive in the first year will face higher tax rates through the rest of their lives. Young generations will face the higher tax rate for such a long period that their budget possibilities and levels of welfare will actually be reduced. Although the

6 Deficits, government spending, and crowding out

income effects experienced by most current age groups from the change in the time path of tax rate are trivial, if not negative, each age group has strong incentives to substitute future for current consumption and leisure in response to the brief rise in after-tax wage rates and returns to capital. A key lesson of these short tax-cut simulations is that policies that inevitably crowd out saving and investment can look quite effective in promoting capital formation if one evaluates such policies using only the first few years of information.

A second point illustrated by Table 6.1 is that crowding out is typically a slow and gradual process. Although the 20-year tax cut reduces the capital stock (per capita) by almost half its initial value, the reduction during the first 10 years of the policy is only 1.9 percent. Indeed, most of the reduction in capital formation occurs after the first 30 years of the policy's enactment. Crowding out, once it begins, is also slow for the tax cuts of shorter duration. For economies of the type described in the simulation model, economic deficits can have a barely discernible impact on the economy in any particular year, although their cumulative impact is dramatic. The reason is that, although long-term tax cuts may have substantial income effects leading to higher consumption, the increased consumption is spread over many years by the life cycle savers receiving the tax cuts.

Although temporary tax cuts may initially crowd in capital formation, there is no way to escape the long-run costs of short-run deficit finance. This is the third important lesson of these simulations and the standard life cycle intertemporal theory on which they are based. Although one might think that, having crowded in capital through short-term tax cuts, one could adopt a painless policy for eliminating the accumulated debt (or simply meeting repayment commitments), such is not the case when income taxes must be relied on. One cannot postpone indefinitely raising tax rates, and once these rates are raised, the stimulus to saving through substitution effects is reversed; in addition, the cross-generational income effects that are at the heart of the crowding-out process ultimately play a decisive role in reducing national saving. Consider those older initial households, which by and large escape (through retirement or death) the eventual tax increases. These elderly, in the case of short-run tax cuts, may delay consuming their increases in lifetime resources until tax rates are raised, but once these rates are raised, their planned increase in consumption from their expanded after-tax lifetime budgets proceeds pari passu.

Table 6.1 also indicates that the extent of crowding out is a nonlinear function of the duration of the tax cuts. The reduction in capital in the 20-year tax cut is 6.8 times that in the 5-year tax cut. This nonlinearity is not

94 Dynamic fiscal policy

Table 6.2. *The intergenerational welfare effects of short-term tax cuts: welfare changes*

Generation born in year	Tax cut			
	1-year	5-year		20-year
	nac	ac	nac	nac
−54	0.00001	0.00002	0.00001	0.00001
−45	0.00004	0.00017	0.00012	0.00011
−25	0.00018	0.00090	0.00117	0.00419
−10	0.00027	0.00141	0.00146	0.00845
0	0.00016	0.00089	0.00048	0.00757
25	−0.00179	−0.00898	−0.01053	−0.06666
50	−0.00215	−0.01131	−0.01251	−0.10659
150	−0.00222	−0.01275	−0.01285	−0.14447

Note: ac stands for adjustment costs, nac for no adjustment costs.

surprising given other well understood nonlinear features of neoclassical economies. One example is the long-established proposition that tax distortions rise with the square of the tax rate. Note that the increase in the income tax rate under the 20-year deficit policy is 9.6 times that under the 5-year deficit policy. Hence, the inefficiency in the former economy's final steady state is considerably greater than that of the latter, and much of the response to the much greater tax distortion appears to take the form of reduced savings.

The long-run welfare reduction associated with the 20-year tax-cut policy is quite significant (Table 6.2). Generations born in the new steady state experience a level of welfare that is 14.5 percent below that of generations in the initial steady state; the welfare reduction is measured as the fraction of lifetime resources one would need to take from a generation in the initial steady state to leave that generation with the new (lower) steady state level of welfare. The size of the welfare loss inflicted on future generations is, perhaps, more easily understood by observing that the long-run after-tax wage falls by 14 percent, whereas the after-tax return to capital rises by less than 1 percent.

Note that in the 20-year tax cut the before-tax return to capital rises considerably, from 6.7 percent to 10.7 percent in year 150, but also quite slowly; when first initiated, the policy raises 30-year yields by less than 1 percentage point. Intuitively, the change in pre-tax yields in this standard neoclassical growth model is slow because interest rates are deter-

6 Deficits, government spending, and crowding out

mined by pre-tax marginal returns to capital, which, in turn, depend on the ratio of the stock of capital to the economy's labor supply. Although there is some short-term variation in labor supply, the capital stock is fixed in the immediate period of a policy change and, as is expected of stock variables, changes rather slowly through time. As already mentioned, adding adjustment costs permits the interest rate and marginal product of capital to differ. However, as now described, specifying even fairly substantial adjustment costs has little impact on the course of simulated interest rates.

b. *Tax cuts in the presence of adjustment costs:* To determine how adjustment costs influence the crowding out transition path, we repeated the 5-year income tax cut assuming an adjustment cost parameter b equal to 10 (see equation 3.16). This value for b is reasonably large; it implies that 5 percent of gross steady state investment expenditures is spent on adjustment costs.

Table 6.3 compares 5-year tax cuts with and without adjustment costs. Initial crowding in occurs in both cases. With adjustment costs, the initial crowding in means an initial (year zero) increase in the value of q and a subsequent decline in q until the period of crowding out occurs. Once crowding out begins, q starts to rise back to its initial steady state value. Hence, in this simulation, initial short-term real interest rates drop even more with adjustment costs than with no adjustment costs.

Despite sizable adjustment costs, the results with and without adjustment costs are similar. In particular, the size of the differences in interest rates in any given year is quite small; although the initial (year zero) change in q at the time of the announcement of the tax cut is reasonably large (0.022) in comparison with the interest rate, the subsequent annual capital losses and gains are considerably smaller. For example, in the tenth year of the transition, the capital gain is only 0.0004.

Table 6.3 points to two other notable features of the adjustment cost economy. The initial steady state capital stock is 9.8 percent lower, and the real wage is 2.6 percent lower in the case of adjustment costs. Furthermore, Table 6.2 indicates that the addition of adjustment costs alters somewhat the intergenerational redistribution associated with the 5-year tax cut; the initial elderly, in the case of adjustment costs, benefit from the year zero increase in q. However, those who are middle-aged (e.g., born in -25) enjoy somewhat less of an increase in welfare from the policy. This is the group that benefits most from the tax cut's crowding in. Such crowding in is reduced almost to zero by the introduction of adjustment costs, which cause a smoothing of capital stock fluctuations.

Table 6.3. *Five-year income tax cut with and without adjustment costs*

Year	S/Y ac	S/Y nac	τ_y ac	τ_y nac	w ac	w nac	r ac	r nac	q ac	q nac	L ac	L nac	K ac	K nac
Initial steady state	0.034	0.037	0.150	0.150	0.974	1.000	0.067	0.067	1.085	1.000	19.15	19.10	85.8	95.1
1	0.036	0.046	0.100	0.100	0.967	0.992	0.067	0.069	1.097	1.000	19.71	19.74	85.8	95.1
2	0.036	0.045	0.100	0.100	0.967	0.993	0.066	0.068	1.096	1.000	19.70	19.73	85.8	95.3
3	0.035	0.044	0.100	0.100	0.967	0.993	0.067	0.068	1.094	1.000	19.69	19.71	85.9	95.5
4	0.034	0.043	0.100	0.100	0.968	0.994	0.067	0.068	1.093	1.000	19.68	19.70	85.9	95.7
5	0.033	0.026	0.100	0.100	0.968	0.994	0.067	0.068	1.092	1.000	19.68	19.69	86.0	95.8
10	0.027	0.028	0.164	0.164	0.976	1.003	0.068	0.066	1.067	1.000	18.91	18.80	85.3	94.6
30	0.029	0.032	0.165	0.166	0.967	0.989	0.070	0.069	1.073	1.000	18.96	18.92	82.6	90.3
60	0.031	0.036	0.166	0.166	0.960	0.983	0.070	0.070	1.080	1.000	19.02	18.99	80.6	88.4
90	0.031	0.036	0.166	0.166	0.958	0.983	0.071	0.070	1.082	1.000	19.03	18.99	80.0	88.2
Final steady state	0.032	0.036	0.166	0.166	0.958	0.983	0.071	0.070	1.085	1.000	19.04	18.99	79.7	88.2

Note: ac stands for adjustment costs, nac for no adjustment costs.

B. Balanced budget increases in government consumption

1. *Theoretical issues*

If it is assumed that government consumption does not enter into private utility functions (equation 3.3) or that the utility of government consumption is separable from the utility of private consumption and leisure, there is no direct effect of increased government consumption on private consumption or leisure choices. Hence, changes in government consumption affect private choices only indirectly by altering variables, particularly tax rates, entering private budgets. Increases in government consumption do, however, directly reduce national saving by raising total national consumption. Stated differently, in the national accounting identity, $S_t = Y_t - C_t - G_t$, and increased government consumption directly raises G_t while indirectly altering the time paths of Y_t and C_t.

In the case of increases in government consumption that are financed by contemporaneous increases in taxes, initial and, potentially, subsequent generations experience declines in their lifetime incomes as a result of the rise in taxes. In addition to these income effects, there may be important substitution effects determining the private consumption and labor supply responses to increased government consumption. Understanding the extent and direction of the private consumption and labor supply responses is important since these responses could offset or exacerbate the decline in national saving directly engendered by the increase in government consumption. These private responses depend, of course, on the size of the increase in government consumption and the associated size of tax increase. They also depend critically on (1) whether the increase in government consumption is temporary or permanent and (2) which tax base is used to generate the needed additional revenue.

When the increase in government consumption is expected to be of short duration, say five years, the additional taxes levied to finance this consumption are correctly viewed as temporary tax increases. The lesson of the debt-financed temporary tax-cut simulations is that substitution effects play a dominant role when the period of tax increase or decrease is fairly short. These substitution effects will lead the private sector to consume more and work less during the period of high taxes; Hence, they reinforce the government's direct action in lowering national saving.

Consider next the choice of tax base. Suppose additional government consumption is paid for by raising wage taxes. Then initial elderly generations, who are fully or partly retired, will suffer little or no decline in their remaining lifetime affordable consumption. In contrast, if a consumption tax is used, initial elderly generations will share in the burden of the additional tax. If the consumption tax is levied as an ad valorem tax on retail sales, the elderly, like others in the economy, experience the tax as a rise in consumer prices relative to their remaining present values of lifetime resources.

Since the elderly have larger marginal propensities to consume than do the young and middle-aged, spreading the tax rise over all generations through a consumption tax implies a much greater offsetting reduction in private consumption than levying the additional tax primarily on young and middle-aged workers through a wage tax. This was the source of the much larger efficiency gains found in switching to the consumption tax basis in comparison with the wage tax base (see Chapter 5). An income tax, while placing more of the tax burden on the initial elderly than a wage tax, still places most of its tax burden on middle-aged and younger generations. Hence, the private consumption response to increased government consumption financed by an income tax is similar to the response when a wage tax provides the additional financing.

These considerations involve the income effects of the additional taxation. Substitution effects are also different depending on the choice of tax base used to finance the government's marginal consumption expenditures. A proportional income tax, in contrast to a proportional consumption or a wage tax, distorts intertemporal prices of consumption and leisure both in the short and long runs. Proportional wage and consumption taxes distort intertemporal tradeoffs only during transition periods when tax rates are changing over time (see equations 3.10 and, as modified for a wage tax, 3A.24).

2. Simulation findings

In Table 6.4 the impact of a permanent 33 percent increase in government consumption is compared with a temporary increase of equal magnitude that lasts only five years. The increase in government consumption is financed in both simulations by increasing the income tax to its required yearly value for budget balance. The initial steady state is the same as in the preceding tables of this chapter. Since government consumption is initially 3.82, the increase in this variable is 1.27. A permanent increase of 1.27 in government consumption crowds out capital, in the long run by 7.4. Since consumption is a flow and capital is a stock, it may be more meaningful to compare the ratio of the change in investment to the change in consumption. This crowding out ratio, $\Delta I_t/\Delta G_t$, is given in

Table 6.4. *Crowding out from balanced budget increases in government consumption*

Year	Permanent increase					5-year increase				
	K	L	w	τ_y	$\Delta I/\Delta G$	K	L	w	τ_y	$\Delta I/\Delta G$
Initial steady state	95.1	19.1	1.000	0.150	n.a.	95.1	19.1	1.000	0.150	n.a.
1	95.1	19.1	1.001	0.201	−0.377	95.1	18.6	1.007	0.204	−0.892
2	94.6	19.0	1.000	0.201	−0.348	93.9	18.6	1.004	0.205	−0.896
3	94.1	19.0	0.998	0.201	−0.322	92.8	18.6	1.001	0.206	−0.918
4	93.7	19.1	0.997	0.201	−0.295	91.6	18.5	0.998	0.207	−0.948
5	93.3	19.1	0.996	0.201	−0.271	90.3	18.5	0.995	0.208	−0.991
6	92.9	19.1	0.994	0.201	−0.250	88.9	19.3	0.981	0.151	−0.299
10	91.6	19.1	0.990	0.202	−0.173	90.0	19.3	0.984	0.151	−0.287
30	88.5	19.3	0.980	0.202	−0.088	93.4	19.2	0.995	0.150	−0.249
60	87.8	19.3	0.978	0.202	−0.087	95.0	19.1	1.000	0.150	−0.103
90	87.7	19.3	0.977	0.202	−0.085	95.1	19.1	1.000	0.150	−0.006
Final steady state	87.7	19.3	0.977	0.202	−0.085	95.1	19.1	1.000	0.150	0.000

n.a. Not applicable.

Table 6.4. It corresponds to the difference between investment along the new transition path and that along the old path divided by the corresponding difference in government consumption.

Under the permanent increase in G, the crowding-out ratio is 38 cents per dollar increase in G in year 1; the ratio gradually declines along the transition path. It is −0.271 in year 5, −0.173 in year 10, −0.088 in year 30, and −0.085 in the long-run new steady state. The policy generates a 2.3 percent long-run reduction in the wage and a 25 percent increase in the income tax rate.

Short-run crowding out under the temporary increase in G policy is considerably larger than in the case of a permanent increase in F. The difference can be attributed to the substitution effects associated with the temporary increase in G policy. Since the budget is balanced each year in this simulation, individuals recognize at the initiation of the policy that tax rates are only temporarily high. They substitute toward leisure and consumption during the five-year period of high tax rates and away from

Table 6.5. *The choice of tax bases in financing balanced budget permanent increases in government consumption*

Year	Income tax				Wage tax					Consumption				
	K	L	w	τ_y	K	L	w	τ_y	τ_w	K	L	w	τ_y	τ_w
Initial steady state	95.1	19.1	1.000	0.150	95.1	19.1	1.000	0.15	0.000	95.1	19.1	1.000	0.15	0.000
1	95.1	19.1	0.996	0.201	95.1	18.9	1.030	0.15	0.069	95.1	19.3	0.998	0.15	0.064
5	93.3	19.1	0.990	0.201	93.5	19.0	0.998	0.15	0.069	95.2	19.3	0.998	0.15	0.064
10	91.6	19.1	0.978	0.202	92.6	19.4	0.995	0.15	0.070	95.2	19.3	0.998	0.15	0.064
60	87.8	19.3	0.977	0.202	90.0	19.1	0.986	0.15	0.070	95.4	19.2	0.999	0.15	0.064
Final steady state	87.7	19.3	0.977	0.202	89.9	19.1	0.986	0.15	0.070	95.4	19.2	0.999	0.15	0.064

6 Deficits, government spending, and crowding out

leisure and consumption after tax rates are increased. Hence, during the first few years of this simulation crowding out of investment is almost dollar for dollar. Eventually the economy returns to its initial steady state, although the path back is slow; in year 10 the capital stock is 6.3 percent lower than its initial and ultimate value. In contrast, when the increase in G is permanent, the year 10 capital stock is only 3.7 percent lower than initially, although it is ultimately 7.8 percent lower. The strong substitution effect associated with the temporary higher G policy is evident in the year 1 change in aggregate labor supply, which drops by 2.6 percent. When the increase in G is permanent, there is no significant change in initial labor supply.

Table 6.5 indicates how the choice of tax bases to finance increases in G alters the extent of crowding out. In the wage tax and consumption tax simulations the initial steady state with a 15 percent proportional income tax is the same as before, but the additional required revenue is raised from the two respective alternative taxes. In contrast to financing additional G through an income tax, use of the consumption tax actually leads to a minor amount of crowding in of capital. Part of the explanation is that much of this additional tax hits the initial elderly who have large marginal propensities to consume; and part is that the consumption tax involves, at least in the long run, no additional intertemporal distortion of the consumption–saving decision. When a wage tax is used to collect the additional revenue, the extent of crowding out of capital formation is similar to that arising when the income tax is used. That crowding out is slightly smaller with the wage tax than with the income tax appears to reflect the smaller distortion of the consumption–saving choice when the wage tax is used for marginal financing.

C. Deficit-financed increases in government consumption

Table 6.6 examines crowding out when the government's permanent increase in its consumption is deficit-financed for either 5 or 10 years. After these periods of debt accumulation the income tax is raised to maintain budget balance. Whereas long-run crowding out with no deficit is 7.8 percent, it is 15.0 percent in the 5-year debt policy and 25.0 percent in the 10-year debt policy. This is due to the additional consumption by older initial generations that is made possible by the lower tax rates associated with short-run deficits. Such an income effect was present under the "pure" deficit policies in which there were no concurrent changes in government spending. In addition, in the short run the deficits *reduce* crowding out via the substitution effects that are associated with the temporarily lower tax rates.

Table 6.6. *Crowding out from debt-financed permanent increases in government consumption*

Year	No debt finance			5-year debt finance			10-year debt finance		
	K	w	τ_y	K	w	τ_y	K	w	τ_y
Initial steady state	95.1	1.000	0.150	95.1	1.000	0.150	95.1	1.000	0.150
1	95.1	1.000	0.201	95.1	0.992	0.150	95.1	0.993	0.150
2	94.6	1.000	0.201	94.9	0.991	0.150	94.7	0.992	0.150
3	94.1	0.998	0.201	94.6	0.991	0.150	94.4	0.991	0.150
4	93.7	0.997	0.201	94.4	0.991	0.150	94.0	0.990	0.150
5	93.3	0.996	0.201	94.2	0.990	0.150	93.7	0.989	0.150
10	91.6	0.990	0.202	91.3	0.993	0.215	92.1	0.985	0.150
30	88.5	0.980	0.202	83.7	0.990	0.217	79.0	0.959	0.242
60	87.8	0.978	0.202	81.1	0.989	0.218	72.2	0.935	0.248
90	87.7	0.977	0.202	80.8	0.960	0.219	71.3	0.931	0.249
Final steady state	87.7	0.977	0.202	80.7	0.959	0.221	71.1	0.931	0.249

CHAPTER 7

Economic versus accounting definitions of deficit finance and the potential for fiscal illusion

This chapter argues that conventional measures of deficit finance provide little, if any, basis for assessing the extent of intergenerational redistribution by the government. Since such redistribution is at the heart of the concern about deficit finance, conventional deficit measures may cause alarm when alarm is not warranted and, conversely, may calm observers when alarm is most appropriate. The point here goes beyond recent and past debates about "correctly" measuring the deficit (see, e.g., Eisner and Pieper, 1983; and Buiter, 1983). The point is much more fundamental. It is that any definition of "deficits" is inherently arbitrary from an economic perspective.

Although economists typically discuss fiscal policy in terms of officially reported values of "taxes," "spending," and "deficits," the accounting definitions of these terms are themselves arbitrary. Stated differently, economic theory provides no guide as to whether certain government receipts should be labeled "taxes" and others "borrowing," or whether certain government outlays should be termed "spending" and others "repayment of loans." In neoclassical models with optimizing, forward-looking households such as the one presented here, household budget constraints depend on marginal prices and endowments and are independent of accounting conventions; that is, relabeling government receipts and outlays will not alter the marginal prices and net lifetime resources of households and therefore will not alter household consumption and labor supply decisions. From the perspective of these micro budget constraints, fiscal policies that are tight are often mislabeled loose and vice versa. The failure to discuss fiscal policy in terms of its ultimate impact on household budget constraints raises the potential for fiscal illusion.

That the labeling of particular government receipts and payments is arbitrary from an economic perspective can be understood by referring to equation (3.21), which is reproduced in equation (7.1):

$$\sum_{t=0}^{\infty} \frac{T_t}{\prod_{s=0}^{t}(1+r_s)} = \sum_{t=0}^{\infty} \frac{G_t}{\prod_{s=0}^{t}(1+r_s)} + D_0. \qquad (7.1)$$

Although equation (7.1) is perfectly valid in asserting that the present value of the government's receipts (T_t) equals the present value of its payments (G_t), economic theory does not require that the receipts corresponding to T_t be labeled "net taxes," or that the government's obligation to pay D_0 (in present value) to the public be labeled "official government debt." For example, rather than labeling the payment obligation represented by D_0 a "debt," the government could call it a "transfer payment"; similarly, it could label the left-hand side of (7.1) "government assets," rather than the present value of taxes.

The "pay-as-you-go" financing of the U.S. social security system provides an excellent example of the inherently arbitrary nature of government accounting and of the potential for fiscal illusion. The social security system represents the federal government's largest program of intergenerational transfers, yet none of what effectively constitutes enormous borrowing from current and future generations was officially recorded as deficits. Recent estimates by social security actuaries suggest an unfunded social security liability of $4 to $6 trillion owed to the current adult population. These liabilities, although they are not legally enforceable obligations and have different risk properties than official debt, swamp estimates of the government's current official net liabilities.[1] Indeed, official per capita U.S. net liabilities (D_0 above) measured at market value in real 1986 dollars are smaller than they were 40 years ago, because of considerable federal holdings of financial and tangible assets and sizable capital gains on nominal government liabilities accrued during the 1970s (Eisner and Pieper, 1983, 1985; *1982 Economic Report of the President,* Chapters 4 and 5).

Historically, the government could have made its hidden annual social security "deficits" explicit simply by sending each social security taxpayer a piece of paper indicating his or her projected claim to additional future benefits "purchased" with his or her annual payment of social security "taxes" (Chapter 10 illustrates this explicitly). Had the government recorded social security taxes as payments for social security bonds, the government would have reported deficits, inclusive of these bond issues, in excess of $300 billion in several of the past 20 years, and deficits in excess of $100 billion in most of the past 20 years. One imagines that

---

[1] Although the default risk may be smaller for official than for unofficial implicit liabilities, the real return to official liabilities may still be highly risky. In the United States, for example, official commitments to future nominal expenditures do not correspond to commitments to future real expenditures. During the 1970s the U.S. federal government accrued $365.5 billion, measured in 1980 dollars, in real capital gains on its official liabilities while never missing a nominal principal or interest payment. This default on the real value of official liabilities through inflation that may, in part, have been anticipated, is documented in the *Economic Report of the President, 1982,* Chapter 5.

7 Deficit finance and fiscal illusion

this alternative tally of government indebtedness would have engendered different estimates of concepts such as "*the* full employment deficit" and would have led to an array of different econometric findings. Economists, insensitive to the problem of fiscal illusion, may well have reached different conclusions about the degree of fiscal stimulus.

Presumably, such a redefinition of official government liabilities would raise the question of whether to classify other implicit commitments to future expenditures as government debt. If one is willing to label implicit promises to pay future retirement benefits official liabilities, why not include implicit expenditure commitments to maintain the national parks, to defend the country, or to provide minimum sustenance to the poor?

A heated debate about the appropriate definition of government debt would likely lead some exasperated officials to suggest that we eliminate deficit financing entirely and simply rely on taxation. These officials might also argue that one could switch from deficit to tax finance with no effect whatsoever on the economy. Under the assumption of this book's model, they would be quite correct. Rather than raise additional funds by issuing government securities, the government could simply levy a head tax per adult, promising to provide each adult in the following year a tax credit equal to the tax plus interest on the tax. If the adult died during the year, the payment would be made to his or her estate. Those too poor to pay the head tax or those aged 54 and about to die could borrow against next year's tax credit to obtain the required funds. The equality, in present value, between each household's head tax and its head tax credit leaves household budgets and therefore private behavior unaltered. However, since future tax credits, like future social security benefit payments, are not recorded in the current budget, this policy permits the government to report a smaller deficit.

An analysis of (7.1) indicates more precisely how shrewd accounting can eliminate the reporting of deficits without changing any real policy. Define a sequence of head taxes, $\bar{T}_t$, that may be negative or positive, but that sum in present value for each household and therefore for the aggregate economy to zero, by

$$\bar{T}_0 = D_0(1+r_0) + G_0 - T_0, \text{ and}$$

$$\bar{T}_t = G_t - T_t \quad \text{for } t > 0. \tag{7.2}$$

Condition (7.3) follows immediately from (7.1) and (7.2).

$$\sum_{t=0}^{\infty} \frac{\bar{T}_t}{\prod_{s=0}^{t}(1+r_s)} = 0. \tag{7.3}$$

Adding zero as defined by (7.3) to the left-hand side of (7.1) and letting $T_t^{**} \equiv T_t + \bar{T}_t$ produces

$$\sum_{t=0}^{\infty} \frac{T_t^{**}}{\prod_{s=0}^{t}(1+r_s)} = \sum_{t=0}^{\infty} \frac{G_t}{\prod_{s=0}^{t}(1+r_s)}, \qquad (7.4)$$

and for all $t > 0$,

$$T_t^{**} = G_t. \qquad (7.5)$$

According to (7.5) the government can now report zero debt and zero deficit in every year in the future while running exactly the same policy. The trick in going from (7.1) to (7.5) is simply to have the government label private sector loans to the government positive "taxes" and to classify government loan repayments as negative "taxes."

Starting from (7.5), the government could further modify its accounting practices and start reporting enormous "surpluses," although it again engages in no real policy change. In the game here the government imposes additional positive head taxes, $\bar{T}_t$, and positive head transfer payments, $\bar{E}_{t+1}$, related by

$$\bar{T}_t = \frac{\bar{E}_{t+1}}{1+r_{t+1}}. \qquad (7.6)$$

Provided the taxpayers at t are the transfer recipients at $t+1$, this policy has no effect on household budget constraints. The official surplus (a stock) at time t, S_t, for $t > 0$ is now reported as

$$S_t = \frac{S_{t-1}}{1+r_{t-1}} + \bar{T}_t + T_t^{**} - G_t - \bar{E}_t = \bar{T}_t, \qquad (7.7)$$

since $\bar{E}_t = S_{t-1}/(1+r_{t-1})$ by construction, and $T_t^{**} - E_t$ equals zero from (7.5). The government can potentially make T_t and, therefore its reported surplus at time t as large as the economy's stock of wealth at time t.[2]

The fact that economic theory does not distinguish positive taxes or negative spending from government borrowing and positive spending or

---

[2] The government, in this case, "owns" all wealth and invests it in the private sector each period, either directly through government firms or indirectly through government loans to private firms and individuals. For neutrality, the allocation of government direct and indirect investment must correspond to what would otherwise have arisen in the absence of the "surplus." In this example the government acts like the private sector's bank, since private sector wealth is simply funneled through the government's hands and invested back in the economy. The "taxes," T_t, are, in effect, loans to the government, and the "spending," $\bar{E}_t$, represents repayment of principal plus interest. Just as positive "taxes" may constitute private loans to the government, negative "taxes" may be equivalent to government loans to the private sector. For example, accelerated depreciation allowances and other investment incentives at the early stages of an investment prospect, coupled with positive taxation of investment returns at later stages, can, apart from their impact on marginal incentives, be viewed as government loans to the private sector. The repayment of these "loans" is paid in the form of capital income taxes.

7 Deficit finance and fiscal illusion

negative taxes from government debt service potentially permits the government to report essentially any level of debt and deficits it wants without affecting the economy. In addition to this freedom to manipulate the reporting of deficits, the government has essentially unlimited flexibility in altering the size of reported taxes and spending given the level of deficits it chooses to report. The government could, for example, declare a new set of taxes, $\bar{T}_t$, and transfers, $\bar{E}_t$, of equal value. If we assume that households paying these additional taxes receive an identical amount back in the form of additional spending and that any changes in marginal incentives (prices) associated with the new taxes are exactly offset by changes in marginal incentives (prices) associated with the new spending, economic activity will remain unchanged. Reducing the size of government taxes and spending with no real consequences is also in the power of government bookkeepers.[3]

Between 1960 and 1983, U.S. federal spending on transfer payments, including grants-in-aid to state and local governments, rose from 6 to 14 percent of GNP; this change led many to praise, many to decry, and others to study the "growth" in government. Seventy-five percent of federal transfer payments are direct payments to individuals; most federal transfers to state and local governments are ultimately paid to individuals in the form of medical, housing, and general welfare support.

In principle, the federal government could have incorporated all postwar transfer payments within the tax code in the form of special tax credits and deductions. Had the government embedded this growth in spending in the tax code as additional "tax expenditures," a term coined by Surrey (1973) and adopted in the Congressional Budget Act of 1974, reported federal spending would simply have consisted of federal government consumption. Federal consumption, excluding purchases of durable goods but including imputed rent on government assets, fell as a fraction of NNP in the postwar period, from 10 percent in the 1950s to 8 percent

---

[3] For example, a household's welfare and social security benefit payments, before any reduction for earnings, could be labeled lump sum tax credits; and the schedule of potential losses of these benefits because of labor earnings could be added to other marginal labor tax and subsidy schedules facing the household (more precisely specific household members) in year t to produce a total net labor earnings tax schedule. This schedule would then be applied to household j's actual earnings to calculate total taxes on labor earnings in year t by household j. Similarly, the government's year t payments of interest and principal on net official debt held by household j would be subtracted from other net intramarginal taxes to determine household j's total net lump sum tax in year t. Effective (net) capital income tax rate schedules confronting each household in each future year would be determined by comparing before-tax returns earned on a household's marginal investment with the after-tax (including corporate and personal tax) return received by that household (Auerbach and Jorgenson, 1980).

in 1982. One presumes that over this period this manner of displaying economic reality would have led many of those who praised, decried, and studied the growth in government to have decried, praised, and studied its decline.

The point here is certainly *not* to claim that there are no real economic effects from policies that are associated with changes in reported taxes, transfers, and official government debt. Indeed, Chapter 6 presented a number of simulations in which real crowding out was associated with increases in official government debt. The point is that the size and character of the effects of fiscal policy cannot be judged from the size of taxes, transfers, and deficits per se because these accounting entries can vary widely without having any effect whatsoever on economic activity. If fiscal policy is to be discussed without engaging in fiscal illusion, we must describe changes in the government's consumption, which affect the economy directly and government-induced changes in household budget constraints, which affect the economy indirectly.[4]

From this perspective, an economic rather than an accounting definition of debt policy is a policy that transfers resources from young and future generations to older generations. Once one adopts this definition, it is clear that a variety of policies beyond those studied in Chapter 6 generate *economic* deficits. Structural tax change (see Chapter 5) is an important mechanism by which governments can redistribute toward early generations. Recall the policy of switching from consumption to wage taxation. Such a policy shifts the tax burden from the current elderly, who are largely retired, to young and middle-aged workers as well as future generations. Although these latter generations escape consumption taxation, the present value of the wage taxes exceeds the present value of the consumption tax payments they would otherwise have paid. Hence, their lifetime tax burden is increased by the policy. Except for the nature and timing of tax distortions, structural tax changes of this kind are quite similar to economic deficits arising from short-term tax cuts or those arising from unfunded government retirement programs. Each of these policies makes an initial set of generations better off at the expense of later generations.

---

[4] For most fiscal programs the relationship between their provisions and these fundamental policy instruments is easily discerned. For other policies the connection is extremely subtle. Chapter 9, for example, describes how government investment incentives redistribute resources from older to younger cohorts, not through the explicit collection and transfer of resources, but by lowering stock market values. Another example, pointed out by Boskin (1982) is the government regulations governing the characteristics of particular commodities; a rule that mandates automobile seat belts in new cars is essentially equivalent to the government's levying a tax on the purchase of each automobile and spending (consuming) these revenues on safety belts for each new automobile.

7 Deficit finance and fiscal illusion

The switch from consumption to wage taxation leads to a 14.4 percent long-run decline in (per capita) capital stock of the simulated economy under base case parameter values (see Table 5.3). This is twice the percentage reduction in capital formation that arose from cutting income tax rates by one-third for five years (see Table 6.1).

Another subtle method by which governments run economic deficits and surpluses is altering investment incentives. Investment incentives, are defined here as tax provisions that discriminate in favor of newly produced capital (see Chapter 9). The connection between investment incentives and economic deficits revolves around the pricing of old capital. Since each unit of old capital is at a tax disadvantage relative to a unit of new capital (for which investment incentives are available), its price must be less than that of a new unit of capital by exactly the present value difference in tax treatment. Reductions in investment incentives reduce the tax disadvantage of old capital and produce capital gains on old capital. Since older and middle-aged generations are primary holders of capital at any point in time, reducing investment incentives transfers resources from younger generations (who now must pay more for old capital) to older generations.

A third example of economic deficits that do not show up on government books is unfunded social security. Chapter 10 describes the extent of crowding out that could arise from this method of intergenerational redistribution. The switch from proportional to progressive income taxation, a subject considered in Chapter 8, also constitutes, to some extent, an economic debt policy; in comparison with the effect of a proportional income tax, the burden of a progressive income tax falls more heavily on middle-aged and younger workers with higher current incomes but lower assets than older generations, which are partly or fully retired.

A. Summary

The central ideas of this chapter may be summarized as follows:

> Conventional budget deficits are an arbitrary accounting construct from the perspective of neoclassical economic models.
> The government can run the same real policy independent of the size of the budget deficit or surplus it reports.
> Government policy is best described in terms of its impact on household budget constraints and the level of government consumption.
> Many policies that represent significant economic debt (intergenerational transfer) policies – such as unfunded social security,

changes in the tax structure, and changes in investment incentives – may easily be overlooked by focusing on officially reported deficits.

The excessive focus on official budget deficits as measures of economic debt in the U.S. and other economies suggests widespread fiscal illusion.

CHAPTER 8

Progressive taxation

In earlier chapters, we discussed the economic effects of taxation by exploring a wide range of dynamic tax policies encompassing different tax bases and a variety of assumptions about government borrowing. Thus far, however, this analysis has failed to take into account one important aspect of actual tax systems: tax progressivity. Although progressivity may be defined in many ways, a progressive tax structure has at least the following two characteristics: (1) Average tax rates increase with the size of the tax base, and (2) marginal tax rates generally exceed average tax rates regardless of the size of the tax base. In terms of government objectives, one may view the efficiency cost associated with (2) as being the price for accomplishing distributional equity goals through (1).

An important question is how these costs and benefits compare in realistic tax systems. Much of the recent political push for reduced marginal tax rates, in the United States and elsewhere, has been fueled by arguments about the potential gains from reducing tax distortions. Implicit in such arguments is the view that these efficiency gains are large in relation to any reduction in equity that would be brought about by lowering marginal and, necessarily, average tax rates on the well-to-do.

Tax progressivity is also important in the choice of tax base. The analysis in Chapter 5 considered the effects of switching the tax base from the income tax prevalent in most developed countries to taxes on wages, consumption, or capital income. The focus there was on the intergenerational redistribution such changes might bring as well as the associated efficiency gains or losses. However, much of the debate over the choice of tax base has also involved questions of intragenerational equity. Distributional equity has been an important issue, for example, in the debate between proponents of the income tax and the consumption tax. Much of this discussion has been concerned with proportional taxation. It would be misleading, however, to compare one proportional tax system to another when the real choice is between progressive tax systems. The degree of progressivity needed to provide a particular extent of redistribution through the tax system may vary across tax systems, as may the efficiency cost of tax progressivity per se.

112   Dynamic fiscal policy

To explore these issues, this chapter extends a number of simulations described in the preceding chapters to progressive taxes. The results suggest that the degree of tax progressivity, given the tax base, is at least as important an issue as the choice of tax base itself.

This chapter's principal findings are

> Switching from progressive to proportional taxation can significantly increase long-run capital formation, depending on the tax base in question.
>
> Switching from progressive income to progressive consumption taxation generates a much larger long-run increase in capital than the switch from proportional income taxation to proportional consumption taxation.
>
> In the case of the consumption tax the intergenerational redistribution associated with increased progressivity has a positive impact on savings that offsets the tax's increased disincentive to save.
>
> The efficiency gain (loss) in switching from income taxation to consumption (wage) taxation is significantly larger if these taxes are progressive.

A.   Modeling progressive taxes

Perhaps the simplest way to introduce progressivity is via a linear tax, sometimes referred to in the income tax literature as the negative income tax.[1] A linear tax is a proportional tax augmented by a lump sum transfer of equal value to each taxpaying unit, sometimes called a demogrant. Thus, the marginal tax rate, τ, is constant, and the average tax rate is

$$\bar{\tau} = \tau - D/B, \tag{8.1}$$

where D is the demogrant and B is the tax base. Note that the average tax rate is always less than the marginal tax rate and that it increases in B. A second simple tax scheme is the flat rate tax, which adds to a proportional tax system an exemption level, say, E. Individuals then face a zero marginal tax rate for B less than E, and a tax at rate τ for B greater than or equal to E. This yields an average tax rate of zero for $B < E$ and, for $B > E$,

$$\bar{\tau} = \tau(B-E)/B = \tau - \tau E/B. \tag{8.2}$$

---

[1] It should be noted that negative income tax systems could also have more than one marginal rate. Such a scheme has been proposed by such an unlikely combination of economists as James Tobin and Milton Friedman, and was one of the less successful parts of the 1972 campaign platform of George McGovern, the Democratic presidential nominee.

8 Progressive taxation

Note that when $\tau E = D$, these two tax systems are the same except for the treatment of individuals with tax bases below E. Under the negative income tax they receive net transfers, whereas under the flat rate tax they neither pay taxes nor receive transfers.

Although single-rate tax systems have been proposed, actual tax systems are normally characterized by increasing marginal as well as average tax rates. In the United States at present the lowest positive marginal tax rate under the federal income tax is 15 percent, and the highest is 33 percent. In other countries marginal tax rates on certain types of income reach as high as 90 percent.

The rationale for increasing marginal taxation may be understood by considering expressions (8.1) and (8.2). Single-rate systems, while progressive, must, as the individual's tax base rises, impose an average tax rate that approaches asymptotically the single marginal rate. It can go no higher. Thus, at high levels of income, if one is considering an income tax, the tax is roughly proportional to income. Such a linear income tax can be as progressive as is desired if one compares the poor to the non-poor, but not if one compares different classes of individuals in the latter group. Only additional marginal rate categories help to increase progressivity.

To model this characteristic of "real world" progressive tax systems, we assume in the following simulations that the marginal tax rate takes the form

$$\tau = \psi + \pi B, \quad \pi > 0. \tag{8.3}$$

This yields an average tax rate at B of

$$\bar{\tau} = \psi + \pi B/2. \tag{8.4}$$

When $\pi = 0$, the tax system is proportional. One may make the tax system more progressive, holding revenue constant, by increasing π and decreasing ψ simultaneously.

B. The impact of progressive taxation on economic decisions

Since the average tax rate is less than the marginal tax rate when taxes are progressive, it seems clear that a progressive tax must be more distortionary and impose a greater efficiency loss than an equal yield proportional tax. In a single-individual static model this is immediate. If a given level of revenue is to be raised, a progressive tax cannot differ from its proportional counterpart with respect to the income effect it imposes. Only the substitution effect will be different, with the progressive tax imposing the greater distortion because, unlike its proportional tax counterpart, its marginal rate exceeds its average tax rate.

The same logic would apply if there were not one, but several identical individuals; but there would be no reason for progressive taxes in such a world. With the introduction of population heterogeneity, the results become less clear. On the whole, of course, marginal tax rates must still exceed average tax rates. However, some individuals (e.g., the poor) will face lower average and marginal tax rates under a progressive tax than they would under the proportional tax counterpart with equal aggregate revenue yield. In the simulated economy, although there is a single representative member per generation, different individuals at a point in time face different tax rates because of changes over the life cycle in an individual's tax liability, for example, in the level of one's taxable income. Although it seems highly likely that progressivity will decrease economic efficiency, simulations are needed to understand how these changes in lifetime tax rate patterns influence behavior and economic welfare.[2]

1. Simulation findings

Table 8.1 compares the steady states of the economy under six tax regimes, each of which collects the same revenue as that collected with a 15 percent proportional income tax. These tax regimes are a proportional income tax, a proportional labor income tax, a proportional consumption tax, and progressive taxes on the same three bases (income, wages, and consumption). In the case of progressive taxes, the term ψ (see equation 8.3) is set equal to two-thirds of the corresponding proportional tax rate, and the term π is determined by the equal revenue requirement.

Under all three tax regimes, progressivity leads to a narrowing of the aggregate tax base. This may be inferred directly from the first line of the table, which shows the need for a larger aggregate average tax rate under each case of progressive taxation. Under these regimes, national income, labor supply, and the capital stock all fall as the result of tax progressivity. Although marginal tax rates generally exceed the aggregate average tax rate for each progressive regime, the lifetime pattern of marginal tax rates differs across the three cases.

Figure 8.1 shows the steady state lifetime profiles of tax rates under each of the three progressive tax bases. The profiles, τ_w, τ_y, and τ_c indicate marginal tax rates under the wage tax, the increase tax, and the consumption tax, respectively. The $\bar{\tau}_w$, $\bar{\tau}_y$, and $\bar{\tau}_c$ profiles are the corresponding

[2] In a static model with individuals of different ability, Sandmo (1983) has shown that the optimal linear labor income tax will reduce aggregate labor supply more than an equal yield proportional tax.

8 Progressive taxation

Table 8.1. *Effects of progressive taxation – 15 percent proportional income tax revenue benchmark*

	Income tax		Consumption tax		Labor income tax	
	Proportional	Progressive	Proportional	Progressive	Proportional	Progressive
Average tax rate[a]	0.150	0.157	0.176	0.180	0.201	0.210
Marginal tax rate						
age 5	0.150	0.192	0.176	0.216	0.201	0.287
age 25	0.150	0.236	0.176	0.246	0.201	0.301
age 45	0.150	0.182	0.176	0.259	0.201	0.188
Capital stock	95.1	87.0	117.7	117.4	100.1	95.2
Labor supply	19.1	18.5	19.0	18.5	18.6	17.9
National income	25.5	24.4	26.7	26.2	25.3	24.2

[a] Aggregate average marginal tax rate.

average tax rates. Under the income tax the marginal rate peaks at middle age, after substantial assets accumulate and before labor earnings begin to decline. The labor income marginal tax rate also peaks in middle age, but falls off even more sharply as retirement approaches, since capital income is not included in the tax base; by age 45, the marginal tax rate is less than that under the proportional tax regime. In contrast, consumption tax rates increase throughout life.

If one had to rank the three regimes according to the size of the tax base reduction resulting from progressivity, the worst would be the income tax, with the labor income tax a close second. Despite its structural similarity to the labor income tax, the consumption tax imposes a smaller additional reduction in the tax base when it is made progressive.

At first, this result may seem surprising; as mentioned in Chapter 3, when the consumption tax becomes progressive and rates rise with age (as in the simulation given here), it distorts the intertemporal consumption choice as well as the labor-leisure tradeoff; that is, rising marginal consumption tax rates, like a capital income tax, raise the price of future consumption relative to current consumption. Hence, we might expect this additional distortion to lead to a substantial reduction in saving and

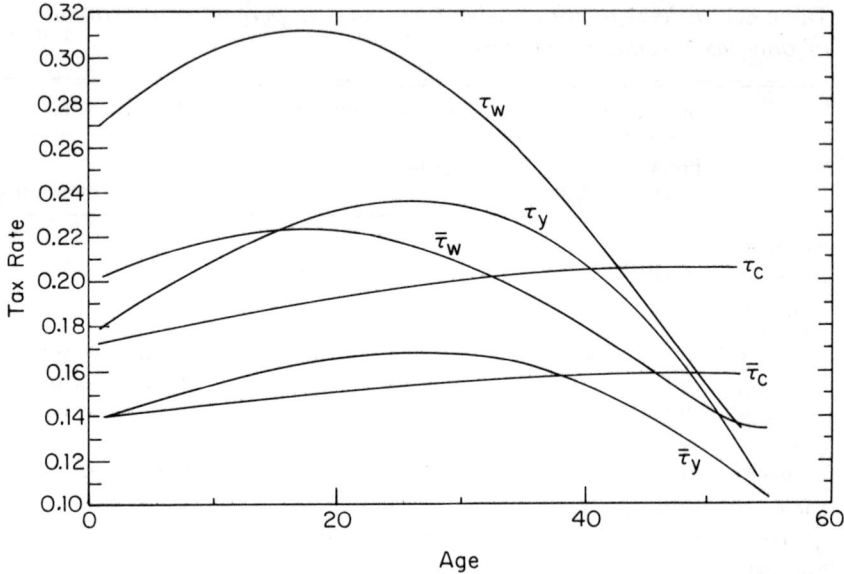

Figure 8.1. Lifetime profiles of marginal and average tax rates under different tax bases.

in the long-run capital stock. Yet the capital stock declines less with the move to progressivity under the consumption tax than under the labor income tax, which continues to leave the intertemporal consumption decision undistorted.

2. *Increased progressivity and intergenerational redistribution*

The explanations for the capital stock results of Table 8.1 are closely related to those governing the differential effects of the proportional consumption and labor income taxes (see Chapter 5). Recall that the capital stock under a consumption tax is much higher than under an equal yield labor income tax primarily because the transition from labor taxation to a consumption tax involves an intergenerational redistribution away from initial elderly generations, which suffer increased tax burdens, and to initial young and future generations, which enjoy reduced tax burdens. Given generational differences in marginal propensities to consume at a point in time, the income effects from this redistribution have an important role in raising savings. Another way to describe these effects is that for a typical individual, taxes occur much earlier in life under a wage tax than under a consumption tax. Given the same annual aggregate tax

8 Progressive taxation

revenue, the present value of taxes that each person must pay, and consequently the associated distortionary impact, will be higher under the proportional wage tax. Thus the level of economic activity, individual welfare, and the capital stock under the labor income tax will be lower than under the consumption tax.

The switch from progressive to proportional labor income taxation shifts the burden of taxation somewhat from initial older to initial middle-aged and younger generations as well as to future generations. Under the progressive wage tax, average tax rates start declining around age 20 (which corresponds to a "real" age of 40). Given the larger marginal propensity of the initial elderly to consume, this redistribution and its associated change in the timing of tax payments over the lifespan are, in part, responsible for the decline in long-run savings.

The case of switching from proportional consumption to progressive consumption taxation is quite different. Since the elderly, according to the model's parameterization, consume more than the young, a change to progressive consumption taxation shifts more of the burden of paying, in present value, for the government's consumption onto the initial elderly; in Table 8.1 the marginal consumption tax rate is 25.9 percent at age 45 (real age 65), but only 21.6 percent at age 5 (real age 25). Hence, the increased savings arising from this intergenerational redistribution virtually completely offsets the reduced savings generated by the increased distortion of intertemporal consumption choices.

3. Progressivity and labor supply

An additional factor contributing to the stronger negative effect on savings under the progressive labor income tax is the change in the lifetime labor supply pattern. With higher marginal tax rates during the years of peak earnings, individuals are encouraged to engage in intertemporal labor substitution, working less in middle age and more when old. As a result, labor earnings, on the average, shift to later years, thereby lessening the need for life cycle savings. The changes in labor supply and consumption under the income tax are shown in Figure 8.2. Labor supply under the proportional labor income tax is 0.40 (40 hours a week) at age 25 (real age 45) and 0.14 (14 hours a week) at age 45 (real age 65). Under the progressive version of the tax, the corresponding numbers are 0.38 and 0.16, respectively. Even though labor supply declines substantially along with consumption in the aggregate, it actually increases among older individuals. The progressive consumption tax provides no such direct incentive for intertemporal labor substitution. The corresponding changes in labor supply at the same two ages under the consumption tax are from 0.41 to 0.40 and from 0.17 to 0.16.

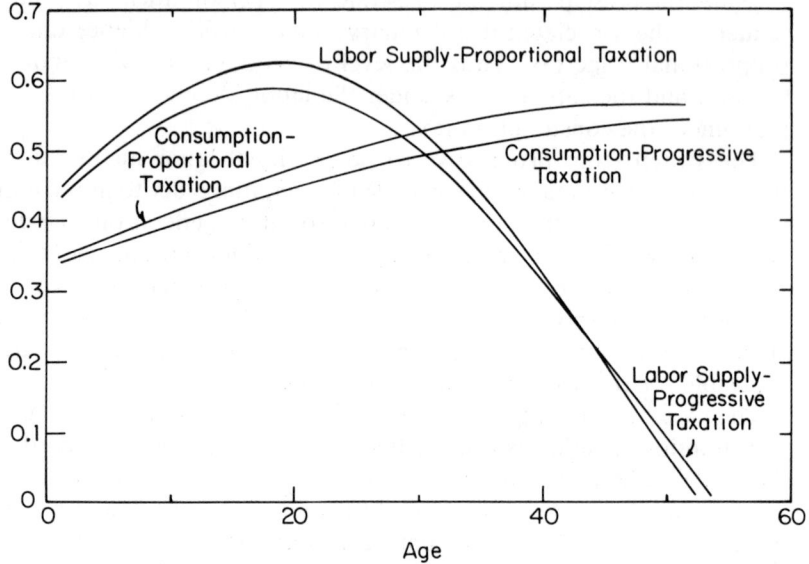

Figure 8.2. Comparison of labor supply and consumption profiles under proportional and progressive income taxation.

Intergenerational redistribution arising from making a tax base more progressive is less significant in the case of the income tax. In addition, the marginal tax rate under the progressive income tax peaks after labor earnings do (owing to the presence of the income from accumulated capital in the tax base); this offsets the tendency under the progressive labor income tax for labor supply to shift toward later years.

How robust to parameter changes are these qualitative results? The next section considers the effects of switching to a progressive tax base starting with a higher initial level of government consumption and revenue. It also examines the effects of variations in important preference parameters.

C. Sensitivity analysis

1. Scale of government consumption

Table 8.2 repeats the analysis of Table 8.1, but assumes a higher level of government consumption and revenue. Here, the government is assumed to require revenue resulting in a 25 percent tax rate under the propor-

8 Progressive taxation

Table 8.2. *Effects of progressive taxation – 25 percent proportional income tax revenue benchmark*

	Income tax		Consumption tax		Labor income tax	
	Proportional	Progressive	Proportional	Progressive	Proportional	Progressive
Average tax rate[a]	0.250	0.266	0.316	0.325	0.339	0.364
Marginal tax rate						
age 5	0.250	0.308	0.316	0.366	0.339	0.463
age 25	0.250	0.357	0.316	0.400	0.339	0.471
age 45	0.250	0.298	0.316	0.416	0.339	0.333
Capital stock	81.2	71.0	118.4	118.1	88.8	80.2
Labor supply	19.5	18.8	19.2	18.8	18.5	17.4
National income	24.9	23.4	27.1	26.5	24.4	22.8

[a] Aggregate average marginal tax rate.

tional income tax regime. The corresponding proportional rates of consumption and labor income taxation are 31.6 percent and 33.9 percent, respectively. Progressivity is introduced by keeping the tax base constant and setting ψ equal to 0.8 times the corresponding proportional tax rate. This adjustment was chosen so that the absolute change in ψ under the income tax (0.05) would be the same as in the previous experiment that assumed lower government consumption and tax revenue. The objective here is to compare the effects of introducing a given level of progressivity starting at different levels of required government revenue.

Assuming a higher level of government revenue strengthens the previous conclusions about switching from proportional to progressive tax systems. In comparison with the simulations of Table 8.1, the tax base and the capital stock each fall by a larger percentage, with the income tax still imposing the largest reductions in these variables and the consumption tax the smallest; in the case of income taxation, the shift to progressivity now reduces the long-run stock of capital by 12.6 percent; the reduction with the smaller revenue requirement is 8.5 percent. There is little impact on the lifetime pattern of marginal tax rates; maximum rates now reach nearly 50 percent under the labor income tax, more than 35 percent under the income tax, and more than 40 percent under the consumption tax. Although the effects on the timing of labor and consumption are similar to those observed in the low-revenue experiment, the changes are larger. For example, under the labor income tax, labor supply at age 25 (45) is now reduced from 0.40 to 0.36, whereas it increases at age 45 (65) from 0.11 to 0.15. These are roughly double the size of the labor supply changes of the corresponding smaller government consumption experiment, even though government revenue has increased by only 60 percent. This greater distortion occurs because increases in marginal tax rates of given amounts are more distortionary when the initial rates themselves are higher.

2. Parameterization

Table 8.3 presents additional sensitivity analysis for the income tax. The table presents the impact on both 15 percent and 25 percent proportional taxes of the move to progressive taxation for alternative assumptions about the intertemporal elasticity of substitution, γ; the intratemporal elasticity of substitution, ρ; the pure rate of time preference, δ; the leisure intensity parameter, α; and the technical elasticity of substitution in production, σ. Alternative parameter values are chosen to permit comparisons with the sensitivity analysis presented for the proportional income tax in Chapter 5. The first line in each of the two sets of simulations presented in Table 8.3 represents the baseline set of parameters, the results for which have already been discussed in this chapter.

From a comparison of the average tax rates under progressive taxation, it is clear that the percentage decline in the tax base decreases with decreases in ρ, α, δ, σ, and γ. The reasons for many of these relationships are clear. If the labor supply of individuals is less sensitive to the wage, either because of a lower taste for leisure (α) or a lower elasticity of substitution between goods and leisure (ρ), the higher marginal rate of tax on labor income associated with the progressive tax will have a smaller effect on labor supply. Likewise, as future consumption becomes more important (δ declines) or the ability to switch away from higher capital income taxes via consumption today becomes less desirable (γ declines), the tax on future consumption embodied in the higher tax on capital income will exert proportionately less force. The reason for the effect of the decline in σ is less obvious. A tax on either labor or capital income will lead to less substitution away from the taxed factor in this case. However, since each type of income is being taxed more heavily, it is not clear a priori what the effect on the overall tax base or its components (labor and capital income) should be.

Table 8.3. *Sensitivity analysis of effects of switching to progressive income taxation*

Parameterization						Proportional income tax				Progressive income tax			
γ	ρ	σ	δ	α		τ_y	Y	K	L	τ_y^a	Y	K	L
0.25	0.8	1.0	0.015	1.5		0.150	25.5	95.1	19.1	0.157	24.4	87.0	18.5
0.50	0.8	1.0	0.015	1.5		0.150	28.6	147.8	19.2	0.157	27.2	134.0	18.6
0.25	0.3	1.0	0.015	1.5		0.150	28.1	99.9	21.4	0.153	27.6	93.4	21.8
0.25	0.8	0.8	0.015	1.5		0.150	24.2	79.6	20.0	0.156	23.2	73.4	19.4
0.25	0.8	1.0	−0.030	1.5		0.150	31.0	201.7	19.4	0.155	29.9	190.4	18.8
0.25	0.8	1.0	0.015	0.5		0.150	37.9	113.6	30.6	0.155	36.7	106.0	30.0
0.25	0.8	1.0	0.015	1.5		0.250	24.9	81.2	19.5	0.266	23.4	71.0	18.8
0.50	0.8	1.0	0.015	1.5		0.250	27.9	126.5	19.6	0.267	26.1	109.0	18.9
0.25	0.3	1.0	0.015	1.5		0.250	28.7	86.9	23.0	0.256	28.0	80.0	23.0
0.25	0.8	0.8	0.015	1.5		0.250	23.8	69.7	20.3	0.264	23.8	62.0	19.5
0.25	0.8	1.0	−0.030	1.5		0.250	30.2	171.4	19.7	0.262	28.8	157.3	19.0
0.25	0.8	1.0	0.015	0.5		0.250	36.8	96.6	31.0	0.261	35.2	87.7	30.2

[a] Aggregate average marginal income tax rate.

122   Dynamic fiscal policy

Despite widely varying predictions about the levels of capital, labor, and output under the different parameter assumptions, there is relatively little variation in the size of the tax base reduction associated with the income tax under the move to progressivity. Under the 15 percent proportional tax, the reduction varies from 2 percent to 5 percent, while under the 25 percent proportional tax it ranges from 4 to 7 percent.

D.   Welfare and efficiency effects of progressivity

1.   *Base case results*

The discussion of the choice of tax base in Chapter 5 pointed out that most of the change in steady state individual welfare associated with a switch to either consumption or labor income taxation from proportional income taxation was due not to efficiency gains, but to the intergenerational redistribution associated with changes in the timing of tax collections. Since increasing the degree of progressivity also involves intergenerational redistribution, changes in long-run individual welfare associated with changes in tax progressivity cannot be attributed to efficiency differences alone. Under two of the three tax bases, a move from progressive to proportional taxation is associated with an increase in long-run individual welfare. When government revenue equals that raised under a 15 percent proportional income tax, a switch from the progressive income tax with $\psi = 0.1$ to a proportional income tax results in a wealth equivalent increase in steady state utility of 0.69 percent. In addition, nearly all generations alive at the initiation of this policy have greater utility.

Keeping constant the welfare of these initial generations (using the LSRA introduced in earlier chapters) makes it possible to provide each subsequent generation a sustainable increase in utility equivalent to a 1.24 percent increase in full-time resources in the initial progressive income tax steady state. The switch to proportional wage taxation from its progressive version makes long-run cohorts better off by 0.84 percent of lifetime full resources, but neutralizing, via the LSRA, the gains and losses (again, primarily the former) of initial generations allows a sustainable increase of 1.35 percent in the welfare of all subsequent generations.

As discussed above, the difference in the macro characteristics of the economy, such as the size of the tax base and the capital stock, is much smaller after a switch from proportional to progressive consumption taxation (or vice versa) than after such a switch in the case of income or labor income taxation. Again, this is because the initial elderly generations in particular suffer from the progressivity of the tax, which thereby lessens the burden on future generations and offsets the efficiency losses

8 Progressive taxation

from progressive taxation. In fact, long-run generations are worse off by 0.12 percent of lifetime resources under proportion consumption taxation than under progressive taxation. This loss turns to a gain of 0.50 percent when the gains and losses of preexisting generations are neutralized by the LSRA during the switch from progressive to proportional consumption taxation.

Thus, for all three tax bases, the LSRA could generate a large sustainable increase in the welfare of generations born after a switch to proportional taxation. However, without the LSRA in place, much of this potential gain is actually received by members of transitional generations. In the case of the consumption tax, enough is received by those alive initially that long-run cohorts are actually slightly worse off in the absence of the LSRA. Even with such transitional gains neutralized, the gains from reducing progressivity are smaller under a consumption tax than under the income tax. At the same time, progressivity of the wage tax seems particularly distortionary in comparison with its proportional counterpart. This can be explained by the fact that the burden of progressive consumption taxes falls even more heavily on the elderly, imposing a larger implicit lump sum tax on their assets, than the burden of the proportional consumption tax, whereas the burden of progressive wage tax falls even less heavily on this group than the proportional wage tax. Thus, the same factors that explained (in Chapter 5) why a switch to proportional consumption taxation produces a greater efficiency gain than one to proportional wage taxation explains the difference in gains from getting rid of progressive taxation under each of the two bases.

2. Sensitivity analysis

Once again, the effect of assuming a higher level of government revenue is to magnify these results. For example, under the income tax, the long-run gain of switching to a proportional 25 percent tax from a progressive tax is 1.62 percent, as compared with 0.69 percent for the 15 percent income tax; the corresponding "efficiency gain" (after using the LSRA to neutralize transitional gains and losses) is 3.72 percent, compared with 1.24 percent. Thus, the gain is two to three times larger even though the proportional tax rate is just 60 percent higher.

The reason why the efficiency gain is so much larger than the ordinary long-run gain in all of the foregoing examples is that virtually all generations gain from a switch to proportional taxation. This is especially true under the consumption tax, but even under the income tax transition just considered no generation loses more than 0.01 percent of lifetime wealth, and all generations under age 42 (62) enjoy a lifetime increase in welfare

Table 8.4. *Efficiency gains of a switch from income taxation (percentage of lifetime wealth)*

	Consumption taxation		Labor income taxation	
	Proportional	Progressive	Proportional	Progressive
Lower taxes	0.29	0.77	−0.25	−0.42
Higher taxes	1.04	2.42	−1.18	−2.91

Note: Lower taxes and higher taxes correspond, respectively, to the revenue in the base case steady state with 15 and 25 percent proportional income tax rates.

when the switch is made. The efficiency costs of progressivity are so large that even those retirees whose average tax rates increase in switching to proportional taxation lose very little. This result is important, for it suggests that a decision to increase or reduce the progressivity of the tax base does not hinge on issues of intergenerational redistribution to the same extent as the choice of the tax base.

E. The choice of tax base, once again

The simulation experiments of Chapter 5 suggest that a switch from a proportional income tax to a proportional consumption tax will increase steady state welfare in the hypothetical case in which transitional gains and losses are neutralized through LSRA intergenerational transfers. An LSRA switch to labor income taxation would, however, reduce long-run welfare.

The results of this chapter indicate that progressive taxation is most distortionary under the labor income tax, because of the very low burden placed on the elderly, even relative to the proportional wage tax. The consumption tax has the least overall distortion associated with progressivity. Thus, it should be expected that the difference between the welfare effects of switching to these two alternative tax bases from the income tax will be even larger when taxes are progressive than when taxes are proportional.

Table 8.4 presents statistics for the long-run welfare gains, in the presence of LSRA transfers, associated with a switch to consumption and labor income taxes from the income tax for two levels of government revenue and for proportional and progressive taxes. Both the efficiency gains from switching to proportional consumption taxation and efficiency losses from switching to labor income taxation are significantly greater in absolute value if one is switching from a progressive income tax to a progressive consumption or wage tax than if the initial income tax and subsequent taxes are proportional. These are sizable efficiency gains and losses. With the higher revenue requirement, the wealth equivalent gain to switching to progressive consumption taxation is 2.42 percent, while the loss from switching to progressive wage taxation is 2.91 percent.

F. Progressive taxes and intragenerational redistribution

The results presented thus far suggest that the gains obtained in switching from an income tax to a consumption tax and the losses from switching instead to a labor income tax are increased by the existence of tax progressivity. Yet these calculations introduced progressivity in a somewhat arbitrary fashion. Rather than introduce progressivity, as above, by setting ψ at two-thirds of the corresponding proportional tax rate, it would probably be more appropriate to consider the efficiency costs of a tax base switch for a given degree of inequality.

Although the simulation model used in this book has but a single individual per generation, an earlier version of the model, less satisfactory in several respects than the current version, had three representative members per cohort, differing in ability levels. In that model (see Auerbach and Kotlikoff, 1983a) the degree of progressivity of a consumption tax was chosen to deliver the same degree of lifetime wealth inequality as the progressive income tax.

This analysis resulted in little difference in the resulting rate structure progressivity across tax bases. For example, top lifetime marginal income tax rates were 0.24, 0.34, and 0.43 for the poor, median, and rich individuals, respectively, in the long run, while they were 0.34, 0.54, and 0.71 under the consumption tax. Given that consumption tax rates, unlike those of the income tax, are expressed on a "tax exclusive basis" (i.e., as a fraction of consumption, not gross expenditures on consumption), these rates are not directly comparable to those of the income tax unless they are adjusted. Expressing these three rates on a "tax inclusive basis" (i.e., as a fraction of consumption plus taxes) yields top rates of 0.25, 0.35, and 0.42, respectively, which are virtually identical to those of the income tax.

These findings suggest that equity considerations would not greatly affect the ranking of tax bases arrived at in this chapter, but for several reasons caution is still advisable. First, these results do come from an earlier model, one that had fixed labor supply and less realistic age-earnings and age-consumption profiles. Second, and perhaps more important, rich and poor individuals may differ systematically in dimensions beyond ability. Empirical evidence suggests, for example, that the rate of time preference may be substantially higher for low-income individuals (Hausman, 1979; Lawrence, 1986). Finally, and perhaps most important in this context, is the exclusion of bequests in these models.

Empirical evidence suggests both that bequests represent an important component of national wealth (see Kotlikoff and Summers, 1981) and that the wealth elasticity of bequests is substantially above one (Menchik and David, 1983). In a setting with significant intergenerational transfers, switching from income to wage or consumption taxation can have quite different effects on inequality than those considered here. Indeed, the implicit taxation of individuals with vast inherited wealth via the consumption tax was a goal of one strong proponent (Kaldor, 1957). As stressed in Chapter 2, the bequest mechanism is still poorly understood, and more research in this area is required before the welfare effects of progressive taxation can be analyzed satisfactorily.

CHAPTER 9

Investment incentives

Chapters 5 and 8 analyzed the effects of tax reform on economic behavior. The reforms studied included changes in the tax base and changes in the degree of progressivity of the rate structure for a given tax base. In comparison with such tax reforms, the introduction of investment incentives may appear to be a rather minor modification of an existing tax structure. Such is not the case. One of the central messages of this chapter is that changes in investment incentives can fundamentally change the nature of the tax base. For example, introducing 100 percent expensing of new investment in the presence of an income tax transforms the effective tax base from income to consumption.

That the government can effectively introduce a consumption tax by altering investment incentives is one of the lessons of this chapter. Another is that the government can redistribute resources across generations without any direct transfer by using investment incentives or the tax rate on business profits to induce stock market revaluations. A third feature of investment incentives is that they can be self-financing over the long run.

The distinction between savings and investment incentives provides a useful starting point for this discussion. Investment incentives treat newly produced capital more favorably than existing capital. A consequence of this discrimination against old capital is that it will fall in value relative to new capital. Thus, investment incentives directly alter stock market valuations, whereas savings incentives do not. Since revaluations in the asset (stock) market also arise because of adjustment costs, it seems natural also to include adjustment costs in the discussion of asset revaluations in several of this chapter's simulation exercises. In addition to simulations comparing savings and investment incentives with and without adjustment costs, the chapter presents simulations in which savings and investment incentives are deficit financed as well as simulations in which investment incentives are gradually phased in.

The principal findings of this chapter are

> Investment incentives represent a shift from income to consumption taxation, while savings incentives represent a shift from income to wage taxation.

Investment incentives can dramatically alter stock market values. Such revaluations are dampened somewhat by assuming significant adjustment costs.

Investment incentives, even those financed by short-run increases in the stock of debt, significantly increase capital formation in life cycle economies.

Deficit-financed investment incentives can be self-financing for particular, but not unreasonable, parameterizations of neoclassical life cycle growth models.

The underlying explanation of the relative efficacy of investment as opposed to savings incentives in stimulating capital formation in life cycle models is that investment incentives redistribute from the old to the young via asset (stock) market revaluation.

A. Distinguishing savings and investment incentives

In closed economies, saving and investment represent, respectively, the supply of and demand for new domestic capital. Saving incentives shift the supply curve for new domestic capital, while investment incentives shift the demand curve. The basic public finance equivalence theorem – that the real effects of a tax (subsidy) are independent of who nominally pays the tax (receives the subsidy) – applies equally well to the market for new capital. Hence in closed economies, saving and investment incentives do not represent conceptually distinct policies, and the real effects of taxes or subsidies are the same whether applied to saving or the demand for new capital, investment.

Although economically meaningful distinctions between saving and investment incentives do not arise, there are meaningful distinctions between policies that affect savings, the sum of past and current saving, and those that directly affect only current saving, or, in equilibrium, current investment. Policies that distinguish new capital from old are denoted investment policies, while those that do not are labeled savings policies. Although both types of policies alter marginal incentives to accumulate new capital, investment incentives can generate significant inframarginal redistribution from current holders of wealth to those with small or zero claims on the existing stock of capital. In the context of the simulation model, this redistribution runs from the elderly to younger and future generations. The direction of the intergenerational transfer generated by investment incentives is the same as that associated with switching from wage to consumption taxation. Indeed, an easy way to explicate invest-

9 Investment incentives

ment and savings incentives is to clarify their relationship to consumption and wage taxation.

We have already indicated in Chapter 5 how a consumption tax and a tax on labor income differ primarily because of their effects on the holders of existing wealth at the time of their introduction. Even though each has a nondistortionary impact on new saving and investment decisions, the labor income tax is typically less efficient than the income tax, in part, because it provides a windfall to the initial elderly by eliminating taxation of income on preexisting capital, that is, capital that was accumulated in the past. The consumption tax, in contrast, reverses this windfall by increasing the tax burden on old wealth. In this way, the tax incentive for capital formation under the consumption tax is "targeted" at new capital accumulation.

Although it may at first appear quite surprising, savings incentives as typically observed in the United States and other countries are structurally equivalent to shifts from income taxation to labor income taxation, while investment incentives are structurally equivalent to shifts to consumption taxation. For the same reason that consumption taxes are more efficient than labor income taxes, investment incentives are more efficient than savings incentives.

1. *Structural equivalences*

a. *Savings incentives:* Consider first a savings incentive policy. This is any type of policy aimed at encouraging an increased supply of funds for investment. The crucial feature of savings incentives is that they do not distinguish new from old capital. Most such policies involve either a reduction in the rate of tax on the income generated by savings, or a tax deduction for savings itself.

Examples of rate reductions in the United States are favorable capital gains tax rates, the tax exemptions granted holders of municipal bonds, and, for a brief period after the 1981 tax legislation was passed, bank savings accounts called "all savers' certificates." Examples of deductions for savings are Individual Retirement Accounts and Keogh plans. Clearly, the former involve a movement in the direction of labor income taxation, since the return to capital is being removed from the income tax base. The latter appear to resemble a consumption tax approach, since the saver receives a deduction from the income tax when establishing the account and pays a tax on the entire subsequent withdrawal when the funds are spent on consumption. Such is not the case, however, because the savings deduction is not limited to new saving, but is permitted for old savings as well, that is, for all preexisting assets.

This is easily illustrated using the simple two-period model introduced in Chapter 2. With a proportional income tax, the individual's first-period budget constraint is

$$C_{yt} + C_{0t+1}/[1 + r_{t+1}(1-\tau)] = W_t(1-\tau), \tag{9.1}$$

where C_{yt} is consumption when young, C_{0t+1} is consumption when old, W_t is wages, r_t is the interest rate, τ is the tax rate, and t indicates the year.

For individuals entering the second period of life in period t, the budget constraint is

$$C_{0t} = A_t[1 + r_t(1-\tau)], \tag{9.2}$$

where A_t is the net saving in the first period. Consider first the impact of a consumption tax enacted in period t on these two budget constraints. They become

$$C_{yt}(1+\tau_c) + C_{0t+1}(1+\tau_c)/(1+r_{t+1}) = W_t \tag{9.3}$$

$$C_{0t}(1+\tau_c) = A_t(1+r_t). \tag{9.4}$$

Note that (9.3) is the same budget constraint that would be associated with a labor income tax – at a rate of $\tau_c/(1+\tau_c)$ – but that (9.4) indicates a period t tax on the consumption of the initial elderly that would be absent under a labor income tax.

Next consider the impact of a savings incentive program that allows taxpayers to deduct from the income tax the accumulation of any assets, new or old, and taxes these assets plus accumulated interest when withdrawn. The amount available to the young individual for second-period consumption, C_{0t+1}, is the amount saved from the first period, plus interest, after taxation of the entire amount, or $A_{t+1}(1+r_{t+1})(1-\tau)$. A_{t+1} equals first-period after-tax labor income plus the tax break from the asset deduction, less first-period consumption; that is,

$$A_{t+1} = W_t(1-\tau) + \tau A_{t+1} - C_{yt}. \tag{9.5}$$

Since $C_{0t+1} = A_{t+1}(1+r_{t+1})(1-\tau)$, the budget constraint in C_{yt} and C_{0t+1} can be written, using (9.5), as

$$C_{yt} + C_{0t+1}/(1+r_{t+1}) = W_t(1-\tau). \tag{9.6}$$

Dividing both sides of (9.6) by $(1-\tau)$ yields (9.3), where τ equals the tax-inclusive consumption tax rate (as defined in Chapter 8), $\tau_c/(1+\tau_c)$.

Next consider the situation of the initial older individual who at the beginning of his old age has savings, A_t, from the first period of life. Putting

9 Investment incentives

this amount A_t into an account that qualifies for the savings tax deduction yields net assets in the amount of $A_t/(1-\tau)$; at the end of the period after interest has been received and after taxes on withdrawal of the assets have been paid, the consumption of the initial elderly individual is given by

$$C_{0t} = A_t(1+r_t). \tag{9.7}$$

Comparing (9.7) to (9.4), we see that the older individual is treated not as he would be under a consumption tax, but rather as he would be treated under a labor income tax. This same result would arise if the government simply eliminated the capital income component of the income tax, or, alternatively, subsidized the return to savings at the rate τ. In order to get consumption tax treatment it would be necessary to deny the deduction for the assets A_t to the older individual, but still require that the assets be treated as if they were included in the savings plan and fully tax interest and principal upon withdrawal for consumption.

In actual implementation of such savings incentives governments often limit the extent to which all existing assets can be deducted immediately from the tax base. Permitting very large deductions could make taxable income negative, and tax systems typically do not provide a full tax refund for losses. Nevertheless, the approach falls far short of consumption tax treatment of existing assets.

b. *Investment incentives:* An investment incentive, by its nature, is a tax plan associated with specific types of investment. Since it is very difficult to trace the components of income for a typical business back to the different assets used to produce the income, the only feasible way of achieving such an incentive is to provide favorable tax treatment associated with the new ownership or acquisition of the assets themselves.

Historically, we have observed a variety of such schemes, all typically applied to asset purchases rather than asset ownership. Examples from the United States are the investment tax credit, which refunds a certain fraction of the cost of an asset in the year purchased, and the acceleration of depreciation allowances, which defers tax liabilities on new investments into the future without assessing the taxpayer interest on this deferral. The key feature of these and other investment incentives that differentiates them from savings incentives is that they are effectively available only to new investment. Although it is possible for a firm to obtain such tax benefits for preexisting assets (old savings) by reselling them, there are additional (recapture) tax costs in doing so, not to mention potentially large transaction costs. As discussed in Auerbach and Kotlikoff (1983b), this considerably limits the extent to which old assets can qualify for desirable new tax incentives. For the purposes of this analysis, the assumption that investment incentives are available only to new capital is maintained.

The economic effects of investment incentives can be illustrated by a government policy that permits each investor to expense (deduct) a certain fraction of the cost of new investment. Except for the distinction between a deduction and a credit (which is trivial under a proportional income tax), this is precisely what investment tax credits do. Although accelerated depreciation is more complicated than expensing, both share the salient characteristic of reducing the present value of the investor's tax burden through increased deductions.

Consider the impact of a program of partial expensing of new investments on the budget constraints of old and young individuals in the two-period model. If z is the fraction of investment that can be expensed, the saving of the young individual can be written as

$$A_{t+1} = W_t(1-\tau) + \tau z A_{t+1} - C_{y,t}. \tag{9.8}$$

The accumulated value of this investment in the second period, which is used to finance second-period consumption, equals the return to capital, after capital income taxes, plus the value of the capital itself:

$$C_{0t+1} = qA_{t+1} + r_{t+1}A_{t+1}(1-\tau), \tag{9.9}$$

where q is the price at which old (previously expensed) capital goods can be resold. Heretofore, this term has not appeared in our analysis; we have implicitly assumed it to be 1. But once investment incentives are present, this is no longer an appropriate assumption, since old and new capital are no longer perfect substitutes because of their differential tax treatment.

New capital goods (new investment) have a pre-tax (before-expensing) cost of 1, but a net, after-tax (after-expensing) cost of $1 - \tau z$ per dollar of capital purchased. A simple arbitrage relationship dictates that the net of tax (stock) market value of comparable existing old (previously expensed) capital goods must be the same. A company that has one dollar of existing capital must be worth the same amount as one with $1 - \tau z$ dollars of cash, since that amount of cash is just sufficient to purchase a comparable piece of capital.[1] Stated differently, a young saver must be

---

[1] A similar tax capitalization effect is associated with the taxation of land (Feldstein, 1977; Calvo, Kotlikoff, and Rodriguez, 1979; and Chamley and Wright, 1986) and dividends (Bradford, 1981; King, 1977; and Auerbach, 1979a, b). The relationship between the capitalization of investment incentives and dividend taxes is discussed in Auerbach (1983b). Because we have only one level of taxation, not the "classical" system of two separate corporation and individual income taxes, dividend tax capitalization is absent. The economic effects, however, are similar.

9 Investment incentives

indifferent between (1) investing in a new unit of this economy's single commodity (where "new" means not yet expensed) and (2) investing in an old unit of the single commodity (where "old" means it can no longer be expensed). Indifference requires that the price of old capital equals $1 - \tau z$, the after-tax cost of investment in new capital. Hence, the market value of old capital, q, is τz less than the market value of new capital.

Substituting this value of q into (9.9) and combining (9.9) with (9.8) yields the two-period budget constraint of a young individual at time t:

$$C_{yt} + C_{0t+1}/[1 + r_{t+1}(1-\tau)/(1-\tau z)] = W_t(1-\tau), \quad (9.10)$$

which is equivalent to a reduction in the tax rate on capital income from τ to $\tau(1-z)/(1-\tau z)$. Alternatively, it has the same impact as the combination of a consumption tax at the tax-inclusive rate τz, combined with an income tax at rate $\tau(1-z)/(1-\tau z)$.[2] If z equals 1, 100 percent expensing, the tax structure is equivalent to a labor or consumption tax from the perspective of the young at time t. Note that although capital income taxes are still collected, the subsidy to the purchase of capital offsets, in present value, the capital income tax, leaving a zero effective tax on capital income.

For the older individual at time t, the budget constraint becomes

$$C_{0t} = qA_t + rA_t(1-\tau) = (1-\tau z)A_t[1 + r_t(1-\tau)/(1-\tau z)], \quad (9.11)$$

which is, again, equivalent to that imposed by a combination of an income tax at rate $\tau(1-z)/(1-\tau z)$ and a consumption tax at the tax-inclusive rate τz.

Thus, encouraging capital formation in this manner rather than through a reduction in the capital income tax rate imposes an additional tax on existing assets at rate τz, just as a consumption tax imposes a tax on existing assets relative to the labor income tax. One should think of a partial expensing scheme as a combination of a reduction in the income tax and the introduction of a consumption tax. Indeed, a system of full expensing, with $z = 1$, is in effect identical to a consumption tax.[3] This can be

---

[2] To see this, note that the price of consumption goods in terms of wages equals the product of $1 - \tau_c$ and $1 - \tau_w$, where τ_c is the tax rate on consumption (measured tax inclusively) and τ_w is the tax rate on labor income; and $(1-\tau z) \cdot [1 - \tau(1-z)/(1-\tau z)] = (1-\tau)$.

[3] This last equivalence does not depend on the assumption that capital does not depreciate. In a model with depreciable capital, the same result would be true if there were normal depreciation allowances for replacement investment plus immediate expensing of all new *net* investment. This general result was discussed by the Meade Committee (1978) in the United Kingdom and has been applied by Hall and Rabushka (1983) in their proposal for a flat rate consumption tax for the United States. They proposed to attain a consumption tax by combining a labor income tax and a tax on business income with immediate expensing of investment.

readily verified by comparing (9.10) and (9.11) with $z=1$ and $\tau = \tau_c/1+\tau_c$ with (9.3) and (9.4). The elderly at time t, in the case of a switch from $z=0$ to $z=1$, bear the burden of the effective consumption tax through a capital loss on the value of their assets rather than through a higher after-tax relative price of consumption, as would occur if consumption were taxed directly.

This distinction between the consumption tax and the income tax plus expensing with respect to the manner in which the tax is effectively collected applies equally well in the multiperiod life cycle model. Although the ultimate asset owners bear the tax on existing capital in both cases, in the latter case it is a tax paid by the business, and the burden of the tax is passed through to the owners of capital via the reduction in asset (share) prices, whereas in the former it is paid by the individual directly. This may be a reason why investment incentives with these characteristics have been politically acceptable whereas the consumption tax has not; the large implicit wealth tax has been disguised because of its indirect mechanism.

In any event, the differential between old and new capital assets due to capital recovery provisions (the investment tax credit and accelerated depreciation) has been increasing over the years in the United States. Auerbach (1983a) estimated that the "q" value of the existing corporate capital stock was close to 1 during the 1950s, dropping to below 0.9 in the 1960s and below 0.8 with the passage of the Economic Recovery Tax Act of 1981, which dramatically increased the acceleration of depreciation allowances.

Note that changes in capital income tax rates will have marked effects on saving incentives depending on the presence of investment incentives. Consider again the case of $z=1$. With this value for z, changes in τ will leave unaltered, at zero, the effective capital income tax rate. A lower capital income tax rate means capital income is taxed at a lower rate, but it also means a smaller initial subsidy to the purchase of capital.

B.   Adjustment costs, investment, and stock market values

The question of costly adjustment of investment to desired changes in long-run capital intensity is frequently treated in the literature on investment incentives. Hence, it is appropriate to consider adjustment costs here. However, given the preceding discussion showing the equivalence of a partial investment incentive to a reduction in the income tax coupled with an increase in the consumption tax, the topic could equally well have been raised in Chapter 5. Any results discussed here relating to investment incentives clearly apply to the equivalent income–consumption tax policy.

9 Investment incentives

As discussed in Chapter 3, the presence of convex adjustment costs to changing the capital stock leads firms to smooth their investment program, since large changes are disproportionately costly. These adjustment costs provide another reason for a difference in the pre-tax (pre-expensing deduction) value of new capital and the value of old capital. Ignoring issues of taxation, old capital in this context corresponds to capital that has already been installed in the firm. If the firm is attempting to expand its stock of capital, old (installed) capital sells at a premium relative to new (noninstalled) capital because of the adjustment costs required to install the new capital. If the firm is trying to reduce its stock of capital, it values a unit of noninstalled capital more highly than installed capital because of the installation costs it is paying to disinstall capital.

Thus, the impact of an investment incentive on the value of the firm is no longer clear. Although the reduction in the effective capital income tax rate and the wealth effects of the redistribution from old to young will encourage investment and drive up q because of adjustment costs, investment incentives will directly lower the value of existing assets through the term $\tau_t z$, which measures the tax disadvantage of old capital. Which effect dominates depends on the magnitude of adjustment costs. At one extreme is the case of zero adjustment cost already considered throughout the book. At the other is the case of prohibitive adjustment costs, where no change in investment is possible and the incentives simply increase the value of the firm by increasing its after-tax cash flow. In the simulations described below, however, the tax-induced changes in the relative price of new and old capital outweigh the offsetting capital revaluation due to adjustment costs.

The general formula for q_t, given in Chapter 3 as (3.17), is repeated here for convenience:

$$q_t = [(1 - \tau_t z) + (1 - \tau_t) b(I_t/K_t)], \tag{9.12}$$

where b is the marginal adjustment cost to adding a unit of capital (if we assume that total adjustment costs are quadratic), and $\tau_t z$ is the tax-induced differential in the value of new and existing capital goods arising from expensing at rate z. The adjustment cost is expressed net of tax because it is reasonable to assume that it is deductible as an expense by the firm.

As further discussed in Chapter 3, the relation between the interest rate and the marginal product of capital is less direct if $q \neq 1$. Arbitrage between real and financial assets requires that they have the same annual return, inclusive of capital gains, or, repeating (3.18):

$$r_t = (mpk_t + q_{t+1} - q_t)/q_t, \tag{9.13}$$

where mpk_t is the real marginal product of capital. Hence, a mechanism through which expectations affect investment is introduced. Suppose it is expected that the capital income tax will be eliminated one period hence. This will drive up q_{t+1}, as investment in period $t+1$ rises in response. But this, in turn, makes the current holding period yield on real capital too high. Equilibrium is reestablished by an increase in current investment, and a higher value of q_t. Without adjustment costs, much more of the increase in investment would occur in period $t+1$, since q would never change.

Note that things would turn out quite differently were an investment incentive in period $t+1$ to be announced in period t. Although this will increase period $t+1$ investment, it could easily reduce q_{t+1} substantially via the term $\tau_t z$, requiring a lower equilibrium value of q_t and thereby discouraging investment in period t. The effect of adjustment costs is to cushion the period t impact on investment. In the absence of adjustment costs there could be very substantial disinvestment in period t as investors respond to the anticipated capital loss (the anticipated fall in q_{t+1} due to the increase in $\tau_t z$).

C. Simulation results

1. The impact of tax incentives on investment

The following simulations serve to illustrate the various points made above. We consider combinations of two types of policies: reductions in the rate of capital income taxation and increases in the fraction of investment that may be deducted as an expense.

Four policy simulations are presented in Table 9.1, two with adjustment costs and two without. Columns 1 and 3 report, respectively, the results of removing the capital income tax component of the income tax and of providing full expensing. Both simulations assume no adjustment costs. The initial steady state is our base case economy with a 15 percent income tax and no expensing or government debt. In column 1, annual budget balance is maintained by changing the labor income tax rate, while budget balance in column 3 is maintained by adjusting the income tax rate. As should be clear from the discussion above, these are just the basic simulations presented in Table 5.2 for transitions to the labor income and consumption taxes, respectively. The market value of assets is different under expensing and the consumption tax only because of differences in the units of measurement, as already discussed.[4] Columns 2

---

[4] In addition, the measured rate of interest differs slightly. Since the consumption tax is "prepaid" at the firm level under an expensing regime, the rate of interest received by savers is measured in net of tax dollars. Under a consumption tax, the interest rate would be measured in pre-tax dollars. There is no difference in the two measures when

9 Investment incentives

Table 9.1. *The impact of adjustment costs: switch from 15 percent proportional income tax to specified tax regime*

Initial steady state	Elimination of capital income taxation		Full expensing	
	$b=0$	$b=10$	$b=0$	$b=10$
r	6.7	6.7	6.7	6.7
q	1.000	1.085	1.000	1.085
S/Y	3.7	3.5	3.7	3.5
Transition year 2				
r	6.6	6.4	6.9	6.1
q	1.000	1.114	0.840	0.990
S/Y	5.2	4.0	9.0	6.0
Year 5				
r	6.5	6.4	6.6	6.1
q	1.000	1.112	0.842	0.982
S/Y	5.0	4.0	8.2	5.8
Year 10				
r	6.4	6.4	6.3	6.0
q	1.000	1.110	0.844	0.974
S/Y	4.7	3.9	7.2	5.5
Year 150				
r	6.3	6.3	5.7	5.7
q	1.000	1.100	0.850	0.935
S/Y	4.0	3.6	4.4	4.0

and 4 report results for the corresponding transitions in the presence of adjustment costs, with the parameter b set equal to 10.[5] This value of b implies that 5 percent of steady state investment expenditures are allocated to adjustment costs. It is on the low end of the range of empirical

the tax rate is constant over time. Should it rise (fall), however, the interest rate under an expensing scheme will be lower (higher) than under the equivalent consumption tax; only the first measure will take account of the price-level effect caused by the change in tax rates.

It is readily shown that the two tax rates are related by the expression

$$(1+r_t^e) = (1+r_t^c)\left(\frac{1+\tau_{t-1}}{1+\tau_t}\right),$$

where τ is the tax-exclusive tax rate and r^e and r^c are the interest rates under expensing and the equal-revenue consumption tax.

[5] For the adjustment cost simulations, we assume that the policy change in year 1 occurs after purchases of old capital from the dying generation have taken place. Thus, the initial change in q occurs at the beginning of period 2.

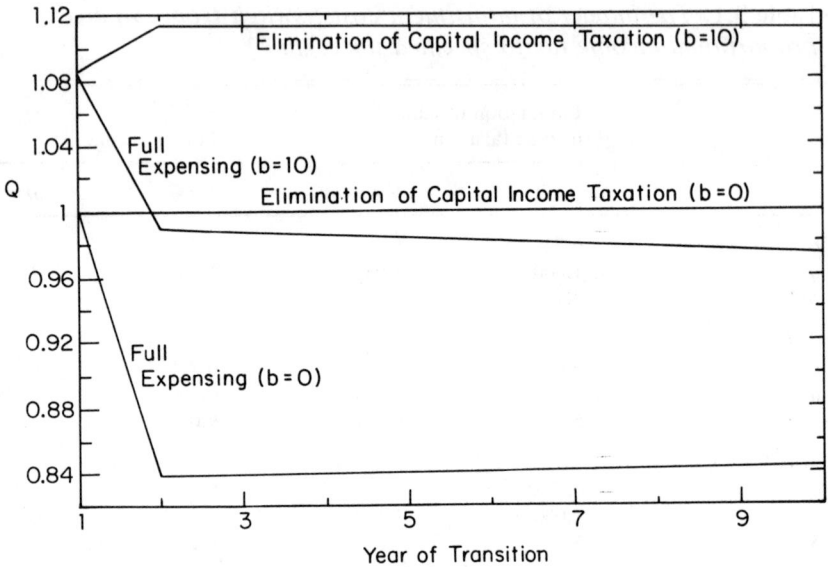

Figure 9.1. The impact on Q of savings and investment incentives with and without adjustment costs.

estimates, but there is reason to suspect that such estimates are biased upward.[6]

For selected years of each transition, Table 9.1 presents the interest rate, r; the ratio of market value to replacement cost of the capital stock, q; and the net national savings rate, S/Y, which equals the increase in the capital stock (at replacement cost) as a fraction of income.[7] Values for q and interest rates in the first 10 years under each transition are graphed in Figures 9.1 and 9.2, respectively.

Consider first the impact of adjustment costs on the steady states of each of the three tax systems considered here. Although steady state interest rates are not substantially affected by the presence of adjustment costs, this does not mean that steady state capital–output ratios are insensitive to adjustment costs. Since q is higher with adjustment costs, the implied marginal product of capital must be too (see equation 9.13); therefore, the capital–output ratio must be lower. This is confirmed by the lower savings rates in each case.

[6] See Auerbach and Hines (1986).
[7] During period 1 there are unanticipated capital gains, so that the ex-post interest rate and saving rate are not a reflection of perfect foresight behavior. To maintain comparability we therefore present results starting in year 2.

9 Investment incentives

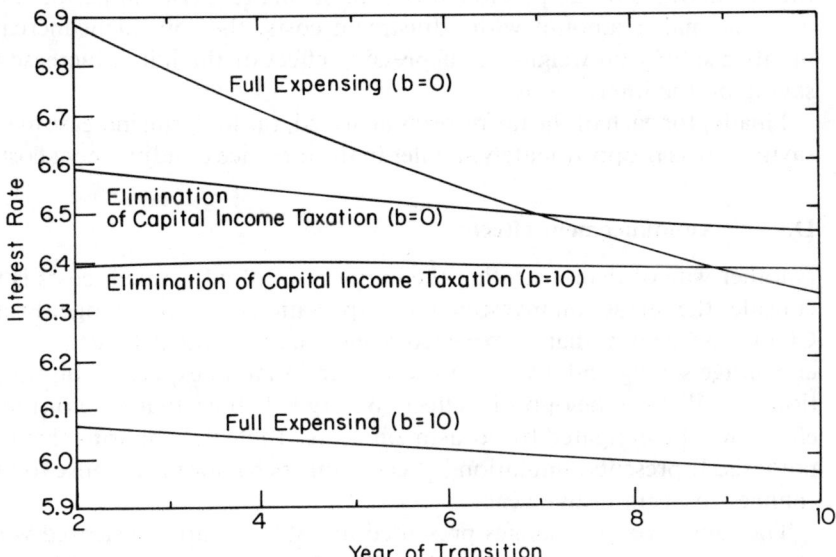

Figure 9.2. The impact on interest rates of savings and investment incentives.

In the transitions from the initial tax system to either of the two alternative tax regimes, there are additional differences arising from adjustment costs. Under the capital income tax cut, q rises initially by 2.7 percent as investment increases. This smoothes the increase in capital intensity relative to the case of no adjustment costs; the saving rate rises by much less in the first year and is below that in the no-adjustment cost case throughout the first 10 years of the transaction. At the same time, interest rates drop more quickly because the anticipated decline in q means capital losses must be subtracted from the marginal product of capital in determining the overall yield on assets. This reduced return to saving further contributes to the smoothing of the investment increase.

The switch to expensing has a more dramatic effect, with or without adjustment costs; we know this from the previous consideration of the consumption tax. The drop in q that occurs without adjustment costs because of the tax distinction between new and old capital is partly, but not completely, offset in the presence of adjustment costs by the increase in the before-tax cost of capital goods that comes from the rise in investment. Were adjustment costs zero, q would have fallen by 0.16 between the initial steady state and period 2. With adjustment costs the fall in q is 0.095. Hence, the presence of adjustment costs dampens by two-fifths the fall in q. As in the previous case, the saving rate rises in period 2 by a much smaller amount with adjustment costs, the coincident increase in labor supply outweighs the depressing effect of the initial increase in saving on the interest rate.[8]

Finally, for each of the tax reforms analyzed, the long-run increase in the saving rate is proportionately smaller in the presence of adjustment costs.

D. Announcement effects

Another way of demonstrating the importance of adjustment costs is to consider the impact on investment of expectations of a tax change. From Chapter 5 we know that an expected reduction in capital income taxes will encourage saving and investment today, and that an expected consumption tax will have the opposite effect. We argued above that each of these effects will be mitigated by adjustment costs. Table 9.2 confirms this hypothesis. It presents simulations of economic behavior in response to tax changes to begin in five years.

The same two tax changes presented in Table 9.1 are considered with and without adjustment costs. The only difference is that during the first five years of the transition the original tax regime remains in place. Remember, however, that q is measured at the beginning of the period, before any tax changes of that period occurs, while interest rates and saving are measured at the end. Thus, for example, the high level of saving in year six under the expensing regime directly affects the value of q in year 7, which is also the first year in which q includes the implicit tax on old assets.

The impact of the delayed implementation of a tax change depends on the change considered. For a removal of capital income taxes (switching to an effective wage tax base) saving increases immediately in anticipation of the higher after-tax returns that will soon be available. Absent adjustment costs, the saving rate rises from 3.7 percent to 6.8 percent in year 5; with adjustment costs, the increase is much smaller, from 3.5 percent to 5.1 percent. In each case, however, both the saving rate and q peak at the end of year 5, when adjustment costs may still be expensed and labor supply has yet to be discouraged by the switch to labor income taxation.

In contrast, delaying the switch to full expensing (switching to an effective consumption tax base) causes current saving and investment to fall. As predicted, the decline in saving is more severe without adjustment costs, as is the jump in saving occurring in year 7, once expensing is provided. In year 6, with and without adjustment costs, the interest rate actually becomes negative. This is due to the capital losses that will occur with the

---

[8] This temporary increase in labor supply comes about because leisure and consumption are complementary goods. As households save more to take advantage of high interest rates, they are also led to work more.

9 Investment incentives

Table 9.2. *Announcement effects: switch in year 6 from 15 percent proportional income tax to specified tax regime*

Initial steady state	No capital income tax		Full expensing	
	$b=0$	$b=10$	$b=0$	$b=10$
r	6.7	6.7	6.7	6.7
q	1.000	1.085	1.000	1.085
S/Y	3.7	3.5	3.7	3.5
Transition year 2				
r	6.8	7.0	6.6	6.6
q	1.000	1.110	1.000	1.079
S/Y	5.8	4.6	2.5	3.2
Year 5				
r	6.7	7.0	6.7	6.6
q	1.000	1.122	1.000	1.075
S/Y	6.8	5.1	1.8	3.0
Year 6				
r	6.4	5.1	−10.3	−2.0
q	1.000	1.126	1.000	1.074
S/Y	5.0	4.0	9.0	5.9
Year 7				
r	6.4	6.3	7.0	6.2
q	1.000	1.113	0.838	0.988
S/Y	4.9	4.0	8.8	5.9
Year 150				
r	6.3	6.3	5.7	5.7
q	1.000	1.100	0.850	0.935
S/Y	4.0	3.6	4.4	4.0

introduction of expensing at the period's end. The change in interest rates is much less severe with adjustment costs, since the contemporaneous rise in investment reduces the magnitude of these capital losses.

Figure 9.3 shows the paths for q in the presence of adjustment costs for each of the four tax experiments considered.

E. The impact of disguised wealth taxation

1. *Are wealth taxation and increased investment compatible?*

We conclude this chapter with two examples that illustrate how easy it is to be confused about the real effects of investment incentive policies,

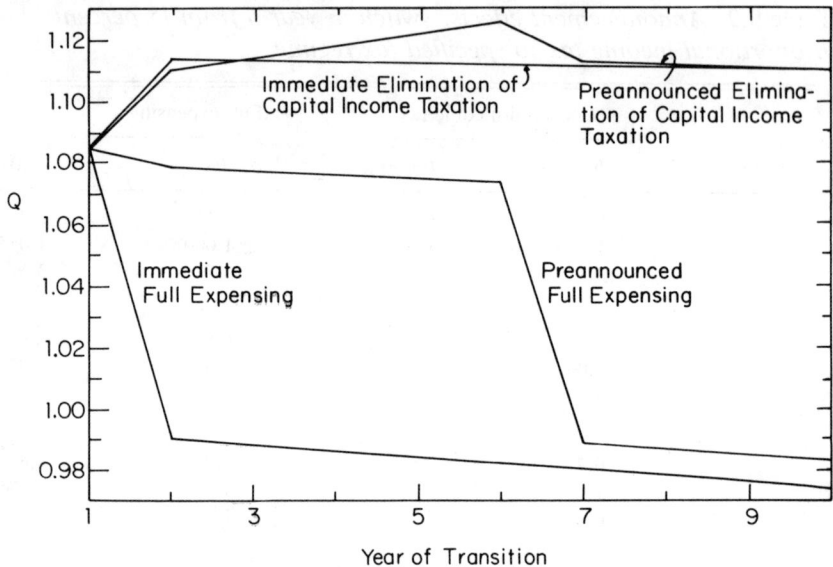

Figure 9.3. The impact on Q of immediate and 5-year preannounced savings and investment incentives with adjustment costs.

particularly the disguised wealth taxes they represent. Suppose the initial tax system had accelerated depreciation to the point where, as in the above simulations with full expensing, the effective tax rate on new investment was zero. Suppose, also, that the government, perhaps decrying the reduction in corporate tax collections, proposed to increase the rate of capital income taxation. What would the effects be? The intuition that asset owners would not like such a proposal is quite sound. But would it also hurt business investment and, more generally, economic efficiency?

On the contrary, such a policy is equivalent to a capital levy, a one-time tax on existing wealth, which allows a reduction in future distortionary taxes on labor income. In terms of the two-period model discussed above, the constraints facing young and old with full expensing ($z=1$) and with different statutory rates of tax on capital and labor income, τ_r and τ_w, respectively, are

$$C_{yt} + C_{0t+1}/(1+r_{t+1}) = W_t(1-\tau_w) \tag{9.14}$$

$$C_{0t} = qA_t + rA_t(1-\tau_r) = (1-\tau_r)A_t(1+r_t). \tag{9.15}$$

An increase in τ_r has no effect on the effective tax rate on capital income, which is still zero; it simply reduces q, and with q the value of existing

9 Investment incentives

assets. This reduction reflects the capitalization of an increase in the taxation of the quasi rents from existing capital that will be collected in the future. These tax revenues will enable the government to lower labor income taxes. The result will be a long-run increase in welfare for two reasons: the intergenerational transfer from old to young and the reduced distortion of future labor supply decisions.

For example, under a simulated increase (without adjustment costs) in the capital income tax from 15 percent to 50 percent in the presence of complete expensing, with the wage tax adjusted to keep revenues constant in each year, the wage tax will eventually drop from its initial value of 15 percent to below 4 percent, the wealth-equivalent measure of steady state utility will increase by 7.5 percent, and the long-run saving rate will increase from 4.4 percent to 5.9 percent. However, all those over adult age 15 (35) at the time of the capital levy are made worse off. Thus, a policy that may appear to be good for equity and bad for savings and efficiency is, actually, quite the opposite.

2. *Self-financing business tax cuts*

A popular notion of U.S. "supply siders" of the early 1980s was that tax cuts could be self-financing; everyone could be better off. It has been known by economists for well over a century that it is possible to raise tax rates so high that revenue decreases. At such high rates the marginal cost of a dollar of revenue from raising taxes is infinite, since such an increase in revenue is not possible. Conversely, lowering tax rates raises revenue. At the same time, taxpayers' real income increases, so everyone wins.

Although there is no serious evidence to suggest that such a situation prevails in the United States, given the current level of tax rates, it is not hard to find investment incentive policies that seem to generate the "supply side, free lunch" result. Consider, in our model without adjustment costs, an economy with an initial income tax rate of 30 percent and no expensing. Suppose the government introduced a policy of 50 percent expensing ($z = 0.5$) and for 20 years kept the tax rate at 30 percent and financed any shortage of revenue by issuing debt. If, at the end of the 20-year period, the government resolved thereafter to maintain constant the level of debt per capita by adjusting income tax rates, how much would these rates have to rise to allow a servicing of the debt? The answer is that they would not have to rise at all, and indeed they would have to fall to prevent the accumulation of a government surplus! The long-run, sustainable tax rate would be 29.3 percent, beginning in year 21, which is below the initial 30 percent income tax rate.

Lest it be thought that a free lunch has really been identified, one should remember than an investment incentive is equivalent in its effect to a cut in the income tax rate combined with a consumption tax increase that keeps the labor supply distortion unaffected. What we have found is that the consumption tax increase is slightly more than enough to finance the income tax decrease. This indicates that the distortion to saving can be reduced without increasing the distortion to labor, while at the same time running no long-run deficit. But there is a tax increase included in the package, on consumption. Initial elderly and late middle-aged shareholders will hardly find the tax policy beneficial or even innocuous since they will suffer a capital loss on their shares of stock. Once again, it is important to see the equivalences of different tax structures. The study of investment incentives obviously requires an understanding of simple principles of tax incidence.

CHAPTER 10

Social security

After defense, social security is the largest program in the U.S. federal budget. For more than half of U.S. working-age households, social security taxes exceed personal income taxes. Further, for most elderly U.S. households, the future payments they will receive from social security constitute their most valuable asset, with the possible exception of their house. Although this major U.S. fiscal institution has been highly successful in providing income security to the elderly, it has been criticized for reducing U.S. savings (Feldstein, 1974b), exacerbating the trend toward early retirement (Boskin and Hurd, 1978), and possibly distorting labor supply decisions (Auerbach and Kotlikoff, 1985b).

As is well known, the social security system is not funded; its financial assets at any point in time amount to only a trivial fraction of the future payment obligations of the system. The true source of funds to meet these future obligations is the social security tax contributions of future workers. The unfunded, "pay-as-you-go" method of financing social security is an implicit form of deficit finance that has transferred immense sums from current younger and future generations to current older generations as well as recently deceased generations. As described in Chapter 6, such intergenerational redistribution reduces savings in life cycle models because of generational differences in marginal consumption propensities.

The social security system's earnings test raises concerns about whether social security induces early retirement. Although social security participants are generally eligible to start receiving benefits at age 62, these benefits are "earnings tested" in the sense that benefits beyond a specified "exempt amount" are reduced 50 cents on the dollar for every dollar earned until benefits are totally exhausted.

The combined employer–employee payroll tax used to finance U.S. social security retirement and disability benefits is greater than 10 percent. Given the rather complex linkage between social security tax payments and eventual benefits, it may well be that most U.S. workers believe that marginal social security tax payments provide no marginal benefits; that is, paying additional social security taxes, like paying additional income taxes, provides no additional individual-specific benefit. In this case, the greater than 10 percent payroll tax may be greatly increasing the distortion of labor supply associated with the tax system since such distortions rise with the square of combined effective tax rates.

This chapter considers the impact of social security on savings and its potential distortionary impact on labor supply. The impact of social security on retirement is not considered here because of the difficulty of including nonlinear budget constraints in what is already a fairly complex simulation model.

The principal findings of this chapter are as follows:

> In its ability to crowd out savings, an unfunded social security system is equivalent to cutting taxes significantly for an extended period of time and, thereby, running substantial official budget deficits.
>
> An unfunded social security system with a 60 percent benefit to earnings replacement rate reduces the simulated long-run level of capital in the base case economy by 24 percent.
>
> For the base case economy, the welfare loss to generations living in the long-run steady state with a 60 percent social security replacement rate is 6.02 percent of full-time resources.
>
> The failure to link marginal social security taxes to marginal social security benefits significantly increases labor supply distortions.
>
> Greater than proportional linkage of marginal social security taxes to marginal benefits could substantially reduce labor supply distortions and generate quite large efficiency gains.

A.   Social security and savings

1.   *Conceptual issues*

The impact of introducing an unfunded social security system in a life cycle model can be easily understood by adding social security to the simple two-period model of Chapter 2. Let B_t stand for the social security benefit paid to a member of generation $t-1$ who is old at time t. At time t the budget constraint for each elderly individual is

$$C_{0,t} = A_t(1+r_t) + B_t, \qquad (10.1)$$

where A_t are private assets per old person at time t. For young individuals born at the beginning of period t, the lifetime budget constraint is

$$C_{y,t} + C_{0,t+1}/(1+r_{t+1}) = W_t(1-\Theta_t) + B_{t+1}/(1+r_{t+1}), \qquad (10.2)$$

10 Social security

where Θ_t is the social security tax rate at time t. Assuming a constant n percent population growth rate, the formula for the economy's capital stock per young worker is now

$$K_{t+1} = A_{t+1}/(1+n) = [W_t(1-\Theta_t) - C_{y,t}]/(1+n) \qquad (10.3)$$

Since the social security system is financed on a pay-as-you-go basis, social security tax revenues per young worker must equal benefit payments per young worker:

$$B_t = \Theta_t W_t (1+n). \qquad (10.4)$$

Combining equations (10.2) and (10.4) and considering steady state values (indicated by ˆ) gives

$$\hat{C}_y + \hat{C}_0/(1+\hat{r}) = \hat{W}[1-(\hat{r}-n)\hat{\Theta}/(1+\hat{r})]. \qquad (10.5)$$

From (10.5) and ignoring for the moment potential general equilibrium effects on the values of $\hat{W}$ and $\hat{r}$, one can see that introducing unfunded social security lowers the steady state level of lifetime resources if the interest rate exceeds the growth rate. This is intuitive; in the steady state each worker hands over $\hat{\Theta}\hat{W}$ to social security when young and receives back $\hat{\Theta}\hat{W}(1+n)$ when old. The benefit received when one is old exceeds the tax payment made when one is young by the growth rate because there are $1+n$ younger workers contributing at any point in time for every older beneficiary. However, if the interest rate exceeds the growth rate, the present value to a young worker of the old age benefit is less than the tax payment made when one is young.

When r exceeds n, as in our simulation model, initial young and future generations are worse off not only because the return they receive on their social security tax contributions is less than they could have received had they invested these funds in the private economy, but also because the policy of running unfunded social security crowds out capital formation, lowering through time the pre-tax wage. As in the case of tax cuts, the crowding out process under unfunded social security involves an initial increase in national consumption.

The consumption of the initial elderly generation increases because this generation receives benefits without having to pay taxes. Equation (10.1) makes this clear; if, starting at time t, B_t is raised from zero to a positive value $\bar{B}$, the consumption of the elderly at time t, $C_{0,t}$, rises by $\bar{B}$ since the marginal consumption propensity of the elderly is unity. If we ignore for the moment changes through time in benefit levels, tax rates, and factor rewards, the present value loss to the initial young from this policy is $\bar{B}(r-n)/(1+r)$. The young, whose marginal propensity to consume is less than unity, will reduce their consumption by a fraction of this present value loss. Hence, in the initial period in which social security is introduced each elderly individual increases his consumption, measured per young person, by $\bar{B}/(1+n)$, while each young person reduces his consumption by a fraction of $\bar{B}(r-n)/(1+r)$. Total private consumption in the initial period therefore increases, and saving is crowded out.

Although each future generation suffers a loss in present value of $\bar{B}(r-n)/(1+r)$, at any point in time there will always be future generations that have yet to arrive on the scene and experience this resource loss. Thus, at any point in time the initial period increase in private consumption will not yet have been fully offset by reduced consumption of future generations. This explains why the economy ends up in a new steady state with a permanently lower stock of savings.

Adding general equilibrium effects to this partial equilibrium story only reinforces the intergenerational transfer away from future generations. As the capital stock is crowded out, the wage falls and the interest rate rises. Those generations that are elderly when interest rates rise benefit from the greater return on their savings, while the corresponding young and future generations are worse off because the concomitant fall in their wages is more detrimental to their economic welfare than the reduced price of old age consumption reflected in the higher interest rate. In the case of a two-period model in which the social security tax rate is levied at time t at rate Θ and kept constant thereafter, the first generation of young workers benefits from the general equilibrium changes in factor returns; since the crowding out takes one period to get under way, the interest rate is high when they are old, but the wage this first set of young workers receive when young is unaffected by the introduction of social security. In contrast, generations born after the first generation, while benefiting from higher interest rates, receive lower wages during their initial working period.

The transitional and long-run crowding out of capital from running unfunded social security is determined by equation (10.3). If the economy is Cobb-Douglas as in the example of Chapter 2 with the share of C_y in the utility function equal to β and the share of capital in the production function equal to α, the formula for the long-run stock of capital per young worker, $\hat{K}$, under social security is implicitly defined by

$$\hat{K}^{(1-\alpha)} = (1-\alpha)\left\{1-\beta-\hat{\Theta}\left[1-\frac{\beta(\alpha\hat{K}^{\alpha-1}-n)}{1+\alpha\hat{K}^{\alpha-1}}\right]\right\}\bigg/(1+n). \quad (10.6)$$

It is easy to show that the larger is $\hat{\Theta}$ the smaller is the steady state capital stock.

10 Social security

The precise time path of crowding out as well as the precise course of intergenerational redistribution depends on the course of social security benefit levels, which determine, according to (10.4), the course of social security tax rates. If, for example, the government pursues a policy of gradually raising benefit levels over a period of time until they reach a level that is subsequently maintained, then social security may be beneficial to more than the initial generation of elderly. In the U.S. system, the level of real social security benefits grew at a faster rate than the economy over the period 1940–80, and, like the initial older generations, most of the generations that were middle-aged at the time social security was enacted also received more in present value in social security benefits than they paid in social security taxes.

In the United States the discussion concerning the proper level of social security benefits has focused on replacing, during retirement years, a specified level of earnings. In terms of this simple model, if the government specifies a benefit-to-earnings replacement rate of R, then the level of benefits at time t is given by

$$B_t = RW_{t-1}. \tag{10.7}$$

This rule for setting benefit levels through time also determines the time path of tax rates by equation (10.4).

2. *The relationship of unfunded social security to traditional deficit finance*

In the context of this simple model, unfunded social security could easily be run as an explicit government debt policy. Suppose that at the initiation of social security the government labels its initial benefit payments "transfer payments," but labels its initial and subsequent social security receipts from young workers "borrowing" rather than "taxes." In addition, the government labels benefit payments, with the exception of those made in the initial period, "principal plus interest payments" on the government's borrowing. Let the government also levy a special tax (possibly transfer) on each elderly generation to reflect the fact that social security benefits do not correspond precisely to tax payments when young plus interest.

With the new language, the same model, after the initial period, can be described in the following five equations:

$$C_{o,t} = A_t(1+r_t) - T_t \tag{10.1'}$$

$$C_{y,t} + C_{o,t+1}/(1+r_{t+1}) = W_t - T_{t+1}/(1+r_{t+1}) \tag{10.2'}$$

$$K_{t+1} = [(W_t - C_{y,t}) - D_{s,t}]/(1+n) \tag{10.3'}$$

150   Dynamic fiscal policy

$$T_{t+1} = \Theta_t W_t(1+r_{t+1}) - \Theta_{t+1} W_{t+1}(1+n) \tag{10.8}$$

$$D_{s,t} = \Theta_t W_t, \tag{10.9}$$

where T_t is the special old age tax, and $D_{s,t}$ is the stock of official government debt owed to the public by the social security system. A_t is still private assets, but A_t now equals $W_{t-1} - C_{y,t-1}$ rather than $W_{t-1}(1-\Theta_{t-1}) - C_{y,t-1}$. A comparison of the above five equations with equations (10.1)–(10.4) shows that the economy's real behavior is not altered by the relabeling. However, the relabeling makes explicit the debt policy associated with running unfunded social security; that is, it increases the level of officially reported debt in period t from zero to $D_{s,t}$.

For the United States, such a change in the labeling of social security taxes and benefits would have enormous implications for the level of government debt reported to the public. In this case, the amount of additional government debt that would show up on the U.S. books equals the sum over all cohorts of the accumulated (at historic interest rates) amount of social security taxes paid less benefits received. Formulas presented by Kotlikoff (1979) suggest that for 1986 this number could be as large as $8 trillion (30 × social security tax revenues), which is more than 4.5 times larger than the 1986 official stock of U.S. debt. Calculations of this kind should make one wary of relying on official government debt numbers as indicators of the government's true policy with respect to intergenerational redistribution.

B.   Including social security in the simulation model

In the simulation model, social security benefits are received starting at age 46 (age 66 in real time) and continue until death at age 55 (age 75 in real time). As in the U.S. system, benefits are related to an average of past earnings. The U.S. average is called the average index of monthly earnings. We use the symbol AIME to stand for the average of earnings over the first 45 years of the life span. Social security benefits are related to AIME by the replacement rate R. Denoting by AIME_t the level of AIME of the generation reaching age 46 in year t, the formula for AIME_t is

$$\text{AIME}_t = \sum_{j=1}^{45} W_{t-45+j,j}(1-l_{t-45+j,j})/45. \tag{10.10}$$

$W_{t,j}$ and $l_{t,j}$ stand for the wage and leisure, respectively, of an individual age j in year t. The benefit received each year until age 55 by the generation reaching age 46 in year t, B_t, is related to AIME_t by

10 Social security 151

$$B_t = R \text{ AIME}_t. \tag{10.11}$$

Since social security is self-financing, annual social security taxes must equal annual benefit payments:

$$\Theta_t \sum_{j=1}^{45} W_{t,j}(1-l_{t,j})/(1+n)^{j-1} = \sum_{j=1}^{9} B_{t-j}/(1+n)^{45+j}. \tag{10.12}$$

In the simulation model a value for R is specified, and the benefits of each generation above the social security retirement age (the age at which benefits are provided) are determined for each year according to equations (10.10) and (10.11). Equation (10.12) then determines the time path of social security tax rates. In each iteration of the convergence algorithm updated values of AIME_t, B_t, and Θ_t are calculated.

Workers are assumed to treat social security contributions as marginal taxes that provide no additional benefits in return for additional taxes paid. This assumption, which is explored in the next section, seems reasonable when the U.S. social security system is modeled; few U.S. workers appear to be aware of the complex relationship between taxes paid in and benefits ultimately received. Understanding this relationship requires knowledge of the determination of AIME, the nonlinear formula relating social security's primary insurance amount (PIA) to AIME, and the primary and various dependent benefits that one can receive on the basis of the determination of the PIA. In addition, for many U.S. spouses who are secondary earners, modeling social security OASI (Old AGE Survivor Insurance) taxes as marginal taxes yielding no marginal benefits is factually correct, since such secondary earners will collect retirement and possibly survivor benefits solely on the basis of their spouses' contributions to social security.

C. Simulating the transition to unfunded social security

1. *Impact on factor supplies and factor prices*

Table 10.1 presents simulations of three transitions to an unfunded social security system with a 60 percent benefit-to-earnings replacement rate.[1] The transitions differ with respect to which tax base is used to finance government consumption. In the three cases of income, wage, and consumption taxation the same level of government consumption is financed. In each of the three simulations, the capital stock falls by 23 units, which is

---

[1] The simulations reported in this section assume a slightly larger value for A in the production function given in (3.13). This has a negligible impact on the results.

Table 10.1. Simulating unfunded social security under different tax bases

Year of transition	Capital stock			Labor supply			Wage rate		
	Income	Wage	Consumption	Income	Wage	Consumption	Income	Wage	Consumption
Initial steady state	95	101	118	19.1	18.6	19.0	1.00	1.02	1.06
1	95	101	118	18.6	18.2	18.5	1.01	1.03	1.06
2	93	99	115	18.6	18.2	18.6	1.00	1.02	1.06
3	91	97	113	18.7	18.3	18.6	0.99	1.01	1.05
4	89	95	111	18.8	18.4	18.7	0.99	1.01	1.05
5	87	93	110	18.8	18.4	18.7	0.98	1.00	1.04
20	75	81	97	19.2	18.7	19.1	0.94	0.96	1.01
50	72	78	95	19.3	18.8	19.1	0.93	0.96	1.00
150	72	78	95	19.3	18.8	19.1	0.93	0.96	1.00

10 Social security

24 percent of the initial capital stock in the income tax steady state, 23 percent of the initial capital stock in the wage tax steady state, and 22 percent of the initial capital stock in the consumption tax steady state. This long-run crowding out of capital is substantial; in comparison, the crowding out arising from a five-year 30 percent income tax cut (see Chapter 6) is only 7.3 percent of the initial capital stock in the income tax steady state. Although the crowding out process is somewhat faster in this case, less than half of the ultimate reduction in the capital stock occurs within the first five years of introducing unfunded social security.

The aggregate supply of labor falls slightly in the first few years of each simulation. During this period the substitution effects of the additional work disincentive from the social security payroll tax explain this decline. In time, however, as capital is crowded out, income effects appear to outweigh substitution effects, and the supply of labor begins to increase. Ultimately aggregate labor supply in each simulation ends up somewhat larger than its initial value. Social security's crowding out leads to a 7 percent drop in the pre-tax wage in the income tax simulation, a 5.8 percent drop in the wage tax simulation, and a 5.6 percent drop in the consumption tax simulation. In all three simulations the social security tax rate initially equals 9.9 percent and gradually declines to 9.7 percent. Since each of the three tax bases is eroded by the crowding out of capital, non–social security tax rates must increase in each simulation. In the income tax transition, the income tax rate rises from 15 to 15.9 percent. The tax under the wage tax transition increases from 20 to 21.1 percent; under consumption taxation the rate increases from 18 to 18.9 percent.

2. *Impact of intergenerational redistribution on welfare*

The effects of welfare of introducing unfunded social security in each of the three initial economies are presented in Table 10.2. For each case the cohort age 20 at the enactment of the policy is the break-even generation that is neither harmed nor helped by the adoption of social security. All initial older generations are better off because of social security, whereas all initial generations younger than age 20 and all subsequent generations suffer welfare losses because of the program. Although the welfare gains to initial generations, measured as wealth equivalents, are small, the welfare losses to generations alive in the long run under social security are substantial. In the income tax, wage tax, and consumption tax economies, these long-run welfare losses are equivalent to reducing full-time resources in the initial steady state by 6.02 percent, 6.29 percent, and 4.78 percent, respectively. Measured as a fraction of initial steady state

Table 10.2. *Welfare effects of unfunded social security (wealth equivalents, in percent)*

Year of birth of generation[a]	Tax base		
	Income	Wage	Consumption
−54	0.05	0.04	0.05
−50	0.28	0.24	0.26
−45	0.68	0.58	0.63
−25	0.42	0.43	0.43
−10	−1.03	−1.90	−1.37
0	−4.89	−5.17	−3.70
20	−5.90	−6.18	−4.65
50	−6.01	−6.28	−4.76
150	−6.02	−6.29	−4.78

[a] Policy is introduced in year zero.

lifetime earnings (which equals the present value of lifetime consumption), these welfare losses are roughly twice as large.

The wealth equivalent measures of welfare changes may be somewhat misleading in regard to the welfare gains of initial generations. For example, for the initial oldest generation alive at the introduction of social security, social security finances almost a 60 percent increase in consumption. Whereas the welfare increase from this addition consumption is small relative to lifetime welfare, it is substantial relative to the rest-of-life welfare. Indeed, the wealth equivalent is almost 60 percent when welfare under social security is compared with rest-of-life utility rather than lifetime utility.

D. The efficiency gains from benefit-tax linkage

The previous simulations assume that workers perceive no linkage at the margin between social security benefits and taxes. There is, however, no reason that benefit payments cannot be linked in an understandable way to social security taxes. In a fully funded social security system in which individual "tax" contributions were registered in individual accounts and paid out with market interest in old age, the government would simply be providing forced savings accounts for individuals, and, if there are no liquidity constraints, a dollar contributed to social security would be viewed as a dollar of saving with no distortionary effect on labor supply.

The linkage, in present value, of marginal benefits in return for marginal contributions ("taxes") in this case is dollar for dollar.

Although the notion of individual accounts and the practice of tightly linking marginal benefits to marginal taxes have often been considered incompatible with an unfunded, pay-as-you-go social security system, such is not the case. Marginal linkage can be equal to, greater than, or less than dollar for dollar in either a funded or an unfunded system. Consider, for example, a fully funded system in which uniform benefits are paid independently of individual tax contributions. In this case the marginal linkage is zero; full funding requires only that each cohort's old age benefits equal the cohort's accumulated tax contributions. It does not require that individual cohort members view their own tax payments as being effectively identical to payments to a personal saving account.

In an unfunded system the government can establish marginal linkage simply by specifying a benefit formula, which, at the margin, provides X dollars in present value of additional benefits for each dollar of additional tax contribution, where X can exceed, equal, or be less than one. The fact that one's marginal benefits and, indeed, one's total benefits are financed by members of the next generation is of no concern in formulating individual optimal intertemporal consumption and labor supply decisions.

Despite the fact that the U.S. social security system is essentially completely unfunded, marginal benefit-tax linkage in the United States appears to be significantly greater than one for one for some groups (e.g., older married males whose lifetime earnings are low and whose wives never worked); for other groups (e.g., low-earning wives who will collect dependent and survivor benefits on their husbands' accounts), the marginal linkage is zero. The first systematic study of marginal benefit-tax linkage (Blinder, Gordon, and Wise, 1980) shows that at least prior to 1977 the benefit formula provided a significant return on marginal social security "tax" contributions to men in their early 60s.

These actuarial calculations require a clear understanding of social security's benefit formula, including its method of wage indexing, its early retirement actuarial reduction provisions, its dependent and survivor benefit provisions, and its rules concerning the number and choice of years of earnings entering the calculation of AIME. It appears extremely unlikely that typical American workers are aware of the marginal benefits they can expect under current law in exchange for their marginal taxes. Since the calculation of even a rough estimate of this linkage is difficult, since social security neither provides such information on a systematic basis nor will calculate such a number on request, and since social security legislation is subject to future changes, typical workers may simply, if incorrectly, assume that the marginal linkage is zero.

1. Modeling social security benefit-tax linkage

Recall that social security affects household behavior through its appearance in the lifetime budget constraint; with the addition of social security under income taxation, the budget constraint (3.4) becomes

$$\text{PVB} + \sum_{t=1}^{45} \left\{ \prod_{s=1}^{t} [1+r_s(1-\bar{\tau}_s)^{-1}] \right\} [w_t e_t (1-\bar{\tau}_t - \Theta_t)(1-l_t) - c_t] \geq 0, \tag{10.13}$$

where w_t is the wage per standard labor unit at time t, PVB equals the present value of lifetime social security benefits, the social security retirement age is taken to be 45, and Θ_t equals payroll taxes paid at age t. In an unfunded system, as in a funded system, the government is free to specify a formula that relates social security benefits to lifetime labor earnings. The fact that, as a long-run proposition, the return paid by social security on tax contributions equals the economy's growth rate places some restrictions on the generosity of the benefit formula, at least in the long run. It does not, however, restrict the design of the benefit formula at the margin. Consider, for example, the following simple linear formula relating the present value of benefits (PVB_i) received by generation i to the present value of its social security taxes (PVT_i).

$$\text{PVB}_i = \alpha_i + \lambda_i \text{PVT}_i, \tag{10.14}$$

where

$$\text{PVT}_i = \sum_{j=1}^{45} \left\{ \prod_{s=1}^{j} [1+r_s(1-\bar{\tau}_s)]^{-1} \right\} \Theta_j w_j e_j (1-l_j). \tag{10.15}$$

Consideration of (10.14) and (10.15) indicates that this benefit formula offsets, at the margin, the age j social security tax by the factor $\lambda_i \Theta_j$. Hence, the effective social security marginal tax on age j labor supply is reduced from Θ_j to $(1-\lambda_i)\Theta_j$, and the payroll tax offset factor at age j simply equals $\lambda_i \Theta_j$.

The benefit formula given in (10.14) is convenient for simulating the efficiency gains from benefit-tax linkage. With this formula the total effective marginal labor income tax rate on a worker age s in year t is $\tau_{s,t} + \Theta_t(1-\lambda_i)$, where $\tau_{s,t}$ is the age s, year t, marginal income tax rate, and Θ_t is the year t social security tax rate. Note that $\lambda_i = 0$ is the case of no linkage, and $\lambda_i = 1$ is the case in which the payroll tax offset exactly equals the payroll tax. We examine each of these cases below. Another case examined here is $\alpha_i = 0$ and $\lambda_i = \text{PVB}_i/\text{PVT}_i$. Note that in the steady state PVB < PVT; hence, α is negative if λ exceeds PVB/PVT, and it is positive if λ is less than PVB/PVT.

2. Incorporating benefit-tax linkage in the simulation model

In the simulations considered below, we examine (1) the case of setting $\alpha_i = 0$ for all i, and $\lambda_i = \text{PVB}_i/\text{PVT}_i$, and (2) the case of setting $\alpha_i = \text{PVB}_i - \lambda \text{PVT}_i$, where λ is set equal to 1 for all generations. When the baseline benefit linkage is announced, there are, of course, initial social security beneficiaries in the model. These initial steady state social security recipients, who exceed age 45 (65 in real time) at the time of the new policy, are grandfathered under the old social security program; that is, they are permitted to continue receiving the same benefits they were collecting prior to the change in the benefit formula.

For each worker the present value of his or her benefits is related to the present value of taxes by the formula:

$$\text{PVB}_t = B_{t+46} \sum_{j=46}^{55} \left\{ \frac{1}{\prod_{s=0}^{j}[1+r_{t+s}(1-\bar{\tau}_{t+s})]} \right\}$$

$$= \alpha_t + \lambda_t \sum_{j=1}^{45} \frac{\Theta_{t+j} w_{t+j} e_j (1-l_{t+j,j})}{\prod_{s=1}^{j-1}[1+r_{t+s}(1-\bar{\tau}_{t,s})]}, \quad (10.16)$$

where PVB_t, α_t, and λ_t are the present value of benefits, of α, and of λ, respectively, for the generation born in year t; $\bar{\tau}_{t,s}$ is the average tax rate paid by the generation age s in year t. Substituting for B_{t+46} from (10.16) into (10.12) gives a sequence of equations of the form:

$$\Theta_t \sum_{a=1}^{45} \frac{w_t e_a (1-l_{t,a})}{(1+n)^{a-1}}$$

$$= \sum_{a=46}^{55} \left(\frac{1}{1+n}\right)^a \left(\alpha_{t-a} + \lambda_{t-a} \sum_{j=1}^{45} \left\{ \frac{\Theta_{t-a+j} w_{t-a+j} e_j (1-l_{t-a+j,j})}{\prod_{s=1}^{j-1}[1+r_{t-a+s}(1-\bar{\tau}_{t-a+s,s})]} \right\} \right)$$

$$\cdot \left\{ \sum_{j=46}^{55} \frac{1}{\prod_{s=0}^{j}[1+r_{t-a+s}(1-\bar{\tau}_{t-a+s,s})]} \right\}^{-1}. \quad (10.17)$$

Suppose that the time path of the social security tax rates, the values of Θ_t, is given. Also assume that either the sequences of α_t or λ_t are set exogenously according to the policy experiments (1) and (2) described above. If the time paths of w_t, r_t, $\tau_{t,a}$, and $l_{t,a}$ (which depends on λ_{t-a}) are also given, the sequence of equations (10.17) for each t can be used to solve for the endogenous sequence of either α_t or λ_t. In the simulation model, this sequence of equations plus other equations determining w_t, r_t, $\bar{\tau}_{t,a}$, and $l_{t,a}$ are solved simultaneously. Actually, the values of the time path of the social security tax rates, the Θ_t, are also endogenously determined. The time path of tax rates is set equal to the time path that

Table 10.3. *Efficiency gains from linking social security benefits to payroll taxes (percent)*

Tax regime	$\lambda = PVB/PVT$	$\lambda = 1$
Proportional income tax	1.3	7.6
Progressive income tax	2.0	15.1

would be required to finance annual benefits for each successive generation equal to 60 percent of its AIME. This choice for setting the time path of social security tax rates ensures that the general scale of the system is not affected by the particular formula chosen that links individual benefits to individual taxes.

3. *Benefit-tax linkage – simulation results*[1]

Table 10.3 reports the efficiency gains from switching from an unlinked ($\lambda = 0$) social security benefit formula to two alternative benefit-tax linked formulae. The two formulas have alternative values of λ equal either to 1 or to the realized ratio of the present value of social security benefits to the present value of social security taxes. Two alternative methods of financing government consumption are considered. The first is a 30 percent proportional income tax; the second is a progressive income tax in which the marginal tax rate, τ_m, is a linear function of income:

$$\tau_m = 0.25 + 0.4Y. \tag{10.18}$$

Here the LSRA efficiency gain is measured with reference to the initial ($\lambda = 0$) steady state. In the case that $\lambda = PVB/PVT$ and government consumption is financed by a proportional income tax, the efficiency gain is 1.3 percent of full lifetime resources, or more than 2.4 percent of the present value of actual lifetime earnings (or lifetime consumption since the two are equal). Since a new generation is born each year, the efficiency gain is equivalent, in present value, to an annual stream of additional income to the economy equal to 1.3 percent of full lifetime earnings. When this annual stream is measured as a percentage of GNP, the efficiency gain is equivalent to permanently increasing GNP by 0.78 percent. To put the 1.3 percent figure in further perspective, one can compare it to the comparable efficiency gain associated with a switch from a proportional

---

[1] The simulations reported in this section assume a slightly larger value for A in the production function given in (3.13). This should have a negligible impact on the results.

10 Social security

income tax to a proportional consumption tax starting in the same initial 30 percent income tax and unlinked social security steady state. The gain from such a policy is 5.3 percent of full lifetime resources. Hence, the gain from a proportional benefit-tax linkage ($\lambda = \text{PVB}/\text{PVT}$) is about one-fourth of that available from switching to a consumption tax.

The final steady state value of λ in this simulation equals 0.13, and the final steady state payroll tax rate is 9.8 percent. Since the final steady state income tax rate is 0.29, proportional benefit-tax linkage lowers the effective tax rate from an initial steady state value of 39.8 percent to a final steady state value of 37.4 percent. Setting $\lambda = 1$ produces a much larger efficiency gain, 7.6 percent. The effective tax rate, in this case, is reduced from 39.8 percent to 26.9 percent.

As one would expect, the efficiency gains from benefit-tax linkage are larger still if a progressive rather than a proportional income tax is used to finance the same level of government consumption as it would under the proportional income tax. In the initial steady state the marginal tax rates associated with the equal revenue progressive tax rate schedule considered here are 40 percent at age 1 (age 21), 50 percent at age 25 (age 45), 31 percent at age 50 (age 70), and 25 percent at age 55 (age 75). The efficiency gains reported in Table 10.3 from benefit-tax linkage in the presence of this progressive income tax are 2 percent for $\lambda = \text{PVB}/\text{PVT}$ and 15.1 percent for $\lambda = 1$. Measured as a percentage of annual GNP, these figures are 1.2 percent and 9.1 percent.

Table 10.4 contains information about the stock of capital and the supply of labor for the four economies referred to in Table 10.3. Note that when $\lambda = 1$, benefit-tax linkage significantly increases the supply of labor, particularly at the early stages of the transitions. This linkage, coupled with the LSRA's tax-transfer policy, leads to substantial long-run increases in the capital stock. In viewing these numbers, one should recall that the parameterization of the model is fairly conservative with respect to the extent of substitution possibilities between consumption and leisure, both at any point in time and over time. The significant substitution effects underlying the results of Table 10.4 appear to reflect the substantial changes that occur in the relative price of leisure when λ is set equal to 1.

Table 10.5 shows how setting $\lambda = 1$ affects cohort welfare. Note that without the LSRA, as with the LSRA, the economy's transition path involves a Pareto improvement. The reduced long-run welfare gain with no LSRA relative to that with the LSRA (1.5 percent rather than 7.6 percent) reflects the improved welfare of those generations that are initially alive at the time the $\lambda = 1$ benefit-tax linkage policy is implemented. The capital stock is also larger with the LSRA since the LSRA must tax initial

Table 10.4. *LSRA steady state and transitional values of capital and labor*

	Proportional income tax		Progressive income tax	
Capital stock	$\lambda =$ PVB/PVT	$\lambda = 1$	$\lambda =$ PVB/PVT	$\lambda = 1$
Year				
0	56.2	56.2	39.4	39.4
5	56.7	58.7	39.7	42.5
10	57.2	61.7	40.1	46.5
50	58.9	75.0	41.7	67.2
150	58.7	74.4	42.5	66.9
Labor supply				
Year				
0	18.4	18.4	16.8	16.8
5	18.6	20.1	17.1	18.9
10	18.6	20.0	17.1	18.7
50	18.5	19.5	17.0	17.8
150	18.5	19.4	16.3	17.9

generations to lower their welfare to the value it would have attained in the absence of the new policy. These taxes lower the consumption of such early generations and thus account for the larger accumulated saving.

E. Conclusions

The simulations of this chapter suggest that introducing unfunded social security can substantially crowd out long-run capital formation. Although unfunded social security doesn't increase officially reported deficits, the crowding out can be greater than that arising from sizable long-term tax cuts that significantly increase the size of officially reported government liabilities.

The chapter also indicates that there may be significant efficiency gains in tightening the connection between marginal social security taxes paid and marginal social security benefits received. Indeed, the simulated efficiency gains are very large in comparison with those obtained from analyses of the gains from structural tax reform. Greatly restructuring social security to enhance marginal benefit-tax linkage may be infeasible, at least in the short run. However, the results suggest that under the current

Table 10.5. *Efficiency gains from social security benefit–payroll tax linkage, LSRA versus no LSRA (percent)*

Generation born in year	No LSRA	LSRA
	Welfare gain	
−55	0.0	0.0
−25	0.3	0.0
−10	0.9	0.0
0	1.4	0.0
1	1.5	7.6
10	1.7	7.6
25	1.7	7.6
50	1.6	7.6
100	1.5	7.6
150	1.5	7.6
	Capital stock	
Transition year		
0	56.2	56.2
10	58.6	61.7
50	60.7	75.0
100	60.5	74.5
150	60.4	74.4

Note: $\lambda = 1$.

U.S. social security system, simply providing annual reports that indicate how a worker's projected benefits are affected by his or her tax contributions could increase economic efficiency considerably – perhaps as much as 1 percent of GNP on an annual basis.

CHAPTER 11

Effect of a demographic transition and social security's policy response

The remarkable changes in U.S. fertility rates over the past four decades are having increasingly important effects on U.S. social institutions and economic performance. Recent elementary school closings, less rapid wage growth of the young relative to the old, and alarming projections of long-run social security deficits are examples of the far-ranging implications of the demographic transition.

Another major swing in U.S. fertility occurred earlier in this century. The interwar period witnessed a sizable change in childbearing behavior; but the difference between the postwar peak total fertility rate (the expected number of births over a woman's life span as she experiences current age-specific birth rates) of 3.7 in 1957 and the trough of 1.7 in 1976 is almost twice the interwar peak–trough differential.[1] More important, the previous birthrate changes were cyclical, and the cycles extended only two decades. In contrast, the current decline in birth rates appears to be a permanent phenomenon. Under intermediate assumptions of the Social Security Administration's activities, the U.S. fertility rate will remain below 2.2 through 2060.[2]

In the United States, a two-decade-long baby "boom" followed by a permanent baby "bust" has produced a bulge in the age structure of the population that will pass into older age groups over the next 50 years. The elderly (those older than 64) now represent about one-fifth of all adults; by 2040 they could represent as many as two-fifths of all U.S. adults.[3] Given social security's pay-as-you-go method of finance, the 60 to 125 percent projected increase by 2040 in the ratio of beneficiaries to contributors portends increases in social security tax rates to levels as high as 25 percent.[4] Such a rise might have important economic effects, but alternative policy choices should be made with a clear understanding of the full economic implications of the demographic transition.

For example, this potential increase in social security taxes need not

[1] Board of Trustees, Federal Old-Age and Survivors Insurance and Disability Insurance Trust Funds, *1982 Annual Report*, p. 77.
[2] Ibid., p. 35.
[3] Ibid., p. 79.
[4] Ibid., p. 66; see Alternatives II and III.

11 Demographic transition and social security

reduce living standards of future generations. Fewer children per family implies a reduction in the fraction of a family's lifetime resources required for child raising. Reduced expenditures on child rearing permits households both to consume and to save more in their working years. In addition, if an important part of the economy's capital stock is generated by the accumulation of assets for retirement, then the rise in the ratio of old to young that accompanies a decline in population growth will lead to an increase in the economy's capital–labor ratio and, hence, in the level of wages. Stated differently, the demographic change means there are fewer young workers with limited asset accumulation relative to elderly individuals with sizable retirement savings.

Despite social security's financial requirements, living standards in the next century could also rise because of possible reductions in non-social security government expenditures and taxes. As a fraction of total aggregate output, other government expenditures could decline if much of the expenditure is on programs for the young – for example, education. The importance of these factors can be evaluated only if one makes explicit assumptions about the response of both private and government behavior to changes in the economic and demographic environment.

This chapter examines the economic effects of a demographic transition, particularly the interaction of demographics and social security.[5] The unsettled nature of social security's long-term finances certainly provides ample rationale for this emphasis. Moreover, there is a need for more information about the general equilibrium effects of demographic change per se on numerous macroeconomic variables, including savings, interest rates, wage rates, and non-social security tax rates. Although the United States is engaged in a dramatic demographic swing, the potential impact of the baby boom's baby bust on general economic performance has received little attention. The dearth of research in this area is probably a reflection of the difficulty in deriving analytic expressions for the time paths of economies experiencing complex demographic change.

This chapter opens with a discussion of the 1983 amendments to the U.S. Social Security Act. The underlying concern here is the impact of impending U.S. demographic change and the course of U.S. social security policy. The next two sections describe the modeling of demographics. Section D looks at the impact of demographic change on savings and other economic variables in the absence of social security, and section E brings social security into the picture. A variety of social security policy responses to demographic change are considered in section F. These

---

[5] The simulations in this chapter, as in section D of Chapter 10, are based on a slightly different value of the coefficient A appearing in the production function (3.13).

include reductions in benefit replacement rates, advances in social security retirement age, taxation of social security benefits, and the accumulation of a significant social security trust fund.

The key findings of this chapter are as follows:

> Major swings in fertility rates such as those currently under way in the United States can have considerable effect on long-run factor returns and produce precipitous changes in short-term saving rates.
>
> Although social security policy has important effects on the simulated demographic transitions, these effects are of secondary importance to the long-run level of economic welfare.
>
> Even if payroll tax rates rise dramatically, long-run welfare is nonetheless substantially higher in the case of a sustained drop in the fertility rate; while a sustained decline in fertility eventually means a larger ratio of elderly per capita, the concomitant decline in children per capita means an eventual overall decline in the ratio of dependents to prime-age workers in the economy. Long-run welfare is also greater because of the capital deepening associated with lower population growth rates.
>
> Baby busts require large changes in social security finances. These must take the form of significant payroll tax increases, sizable benefit cuts, substantial advances in the social security retirement age, or the accumulation of a large social security trust fund.

A. The U.S. social security system's policy responses to the demographic transition

The 1983 amendments to the Social Security Act contain a number of significant changes in the system's current and projected fiscal operations. These include federal income taxation of half of social security benefits of high-income recipients starting in 1984, gradual increases in the normal retirement age from 65 to 67 starting in 2000, and the expansion of coverage to new government workers and to employees of nonprofit organizations. If fully implemented, these provisions are projected (under intermediate IIB assumptions) to close social security's OASDI (Old Age, Survivors' and Disability Insurance), 75-year, open-group deficit, with little or no need for additional payroll tax increases beyond those currently stipulated in law.

Although the new legislation has greatly alleviated if not eliminated OASDI's short-term cash flow problems, the longer-term financial picture remains in doubt. There are four important reasons for the continuing

11 Demographic transition and social security

emphasis on the system's long-term finances. First, even if all aspects of the new law are actually implemented, economic and demographic conditions close to the social security actuaries' pessimistic assumptions may prevail. In this case the OASDI deficit, expressed as a fraction of taxable payroll, equals 10.0 percent over the period 2034 to 2058.

Second, most of the long-run financial savings from the new legislation arise from measures that are scheduled to be implemented. These measures include increases in the retirement age and the gradual rise, through inflationary bracket creep, in the fraction of social security recipients whose benefits are taxed under the federal income tax. If future administrations and Congress periodically legislate away this bracket creep or if they delay or eliminate raising the retirement age, the nation will again face, under intermediate assumptions, significantly higher OASDI tax rates in the early part of the next century.

The third concern is closely tied to the second. During the period 2000 to 2015, the ratio of the cumulative projected surplus of the OASDI trust fund to annual benefit payments will rise from 2.3 to 5.4. To put this figure in perspective, the current ratio of gross U.S. debt to current social security benefits is roughly 4.5. Since the OASDI trust fund holds its reserves in the form of government securities, the 1983 amendments implicitly project social security's holding of a significant fraction, if not all, of official government liabilities.

Although such an OASDI investment policy raises questions of its own, there is the logically prior question of whether future politicians will have the will to preserve a trust fund for future generations that would represent more than 5.4 years of benefits by 2015 (7.0 years under the II-A assumptions). Such a surplus is unprecedented in the history of the program; the current OASDI reserve can cover less than 3 months of benefit payments. Rather than accumulate a large trust fund, future politicians may dissipate the projected social security surplus by legislating larger benefit payments, by indexing federal income taxation of social security benefits, or by reversing the scheduled retirement age increases. There is another, more subtle way in which this trust fund could be dissipated: The government could run larger official deficits over this period if it found the Social Security Trust Fund a ready purchaser of these securities. From the perspective of the government's overall deficit policy, such a program, in the extreme, simply transforms an implicit liability into an explicit liability and transfers concerns about major increases in payroll tax rates into concerns about major increases in income tax rates.

The fourth concern about social security's long-run finances has to do with the sizable long-term Medicare (HI) deficit projected by the Senate Finance Committee. Under current law and the actuaries' intermediate

II-B assumptions, the HI deficit will reach 7.9 percent of taxable payroll by 2030 and rise to 8.3 percent of taxable payroll by 2055.

B. Modeling demographics

We assume that each adult has N children at age 21 and seeks to maximize the utility of his (her) immediate family, which consists of his (her) own utility, given by equation (3.3), but with age now running from 21 to 75 rather than from 1 to 55, plus that of his (her) children until they reach adulthood (age 21). The adult's utility of children is

$$u_c = \left(\frac{1}{1-\gamma}\right) \sum_{a=21}^{40} f(a-20)(1+\delta)^{-(a-21)} \cdot (C_{a-20}^{1-\rho^{-1}} + \alpha l_{a-20}^{1-\rho})^{1-\gamma/1-\rho}, \quad (11.1)$$

where $f(a-20)$ is the utility weight given to children aged $a-20$ and C_{a-20} and l_{a-20} represent children's consumption of goods and leisure. The parameters δ, ρ, γ, and α correspond to those in equation (3.3) for any given simulation.

The lifetime constraint facing an adult with children at age 21 is

$$\sum_{a=21}^{75} \left\{ \prod_{s=22}^{a} [1+r_s(1-\tau_{ys})] \right\}^{-1} [(1-\tau_{ya})w_a e_a(1-l_a) - T_a]$$

$$+ \sum_{a=a_R}^{75} \left\{ \prod_{s=22}^{a} [1+r_s(1-\tau_{ys})] \right\}^{-1} B_a$$

$$+ \sum_{a=21}^{40} \left\{ \prod_{s=22}^{a} [1+r_s(1-\tau_{ys})] \right\}^{-1} [(1-\tau_{ya})w_a e_{a-20}(1-l_{a-20}) - T_{a-20}]$$

$$\geq \sum_{a=21}^{75} \left\{ \prod_{s=22}^{a} [1+r_s(1-\tau_{ys})] \right\}^{-1} c_a$$

$$+ \sum_{a=21}^{40} \left\{ \prod_{a=22}^{a} [1+r_s(1-\tau_{ys})] \right\}^{-1} C_{a-20}, \quad (11.2)$$

where r_s is the gross interest rate, w_a is the standard wage rate, e_a is the human capital profile, and τ_{ys} is the proportional income tax rate when the adult is age s. The terms T_a and B_a represent social security taxes paid and benefits received, respectively, by an individual age a. Benefits are received after age a_R. In the individual's maximization problem, B_a are treated as lump sum payments and receipts (see Chapter 10). The human capital profile e is normalized so that $e_{21} = 1$; e_a equals zero for $a \leq 12$, and rises linearly from 0.3 at age 13 to 1 at age 21. After age 21, e_a rises

11 Demographic transition and social security

and then falls off somewhat following the pattern estimated by Welch (1979) and discussed in Chapter 3.

Besides the overall budget constraint, we maintain the requirement that labor supply can not be negative, including the labor supply of children. That is, if the notional demand for leisure, l, exceeds one, the individual must "retire" for that period, supplying zero labor.

The life cycle nuclear family's first-order conditions with respect to consumption and leisure at each age are given in Chapter 3 for the choice of the adult's consumption and leisure.

The first-order conditions for children's consumption imply

$$C_{a-20} = \left\{ \left[\frac{1+r_a(1-\tau_{ya})}{1+\delta} \right] \left[\frac{f(a-20)}{f(a-21)} \right] \right\}^\gamma \left(\frac{v_{a-20}}{v_{a-21}} \right) C_{a-21}, \quad a > 21, \tag{11.3}$$

where v_j is defined in (3.11). The relationship between children's consumption and leisure at a specific age is given in (3.9). The first-order conditions, household budget constraints, and labor nonnegativity constraints of the extended life cycle family are solved using the techniques discussed in Chapter 4. These decisions are recalculated in each iteration of the simulation model until the perfect foresight equilibrium is obtained.

C. Specifying a time path of fertility change

Fertility change is introduced into the model in the following way. For a certain period after the beginning of the transition, we exogenously specify the number of births per adult. Thereafter, a procedure is needed to make the population's age structure converge to that of the new steady state. Constancy of the birth rate will not suffice, since the perfect regularity in the birth cycle would perpetuate cohort size differences through an infinite series of "echo effects." In the real world, this happens to a much smaller extent because births are distributed over parents of different ages, but such a solution would be infeasible for a simulation model. Instead, we assume that, after a specified period, typically 50 years, births equal the number born the previous year times the annual population growth rate of the final steady state. Thus, after 75 additional years at most, the age distribution of the population stabilizes. This procedure makes the fertility rates themselves endogenous for a period, and they may fluctuate somewhat unrealistically for a time. However, experiments varying the critical date at which fertility rates become endogenous suggest that, as long as the date is well after the posited demographic transition has occurred, it has little influence on the basic results.

168   Dynamic fiscal policy

D. Baseline simulations: the economic effects of a demographic transition

1. *Impact on macro variables*

This section contains simulation results for two types of demographic transitions: a sudden and permanent reduction in the birth rate (bust) and a cycle of decline and increase in the birth rate followed by a permanent drop ("bust-boom-bust"). In the simulations of the bust transition, the fertility rate drops so that population growth declines from an annual rate of 3 percent to a stationary level. In the second set of simulations, which contain the "bust-boom-bust" (BBB) fertility behavior, the birth rate drops to one child per parent over a 5-year period. For the next 10 years the rate stays constant, after which it gradually rises, reaching its original level 20 years into the transition. Between years 20 and 35 the birth rate remains at this high value. It then gradually falls again to the zero population growth fertility rate between years 35 and 45. The birth rate remains at this level until year 50, after which birth rates are endogenously determined according to the requirement that a flat zero population growth (ZPG) age structure achieved by year 125 and thereafter. The model is given an additional 125 years (a total of 250 years) to reach a new steady state.

In all of these simulations we have had to introduce the assumption of a positive government capital stock to generate plausible values for the economy's capital–output ratio. This was not necessary in the simulations of the previous chapter because of the absence of children. With the consumption needs of nonproductive children added to the population, life cycle behavior based on plausible preference parameters yields extremely small capital stocks. The inability of the life cycle model, by itself, to explain U.S. wealth has been pointed out by several authors (e.g., Kotlikoff and Summers, 1981). This demographics-augmented model provides further indication of the inadequacy of the pure life cycle model without bequests to explain observed rates of capital accumulation.

We begin the analysis by examining how the composition of the population changes over time for each of these transitions. Table 11.1 presents the fraction of the population at different ages during the demographic transition. The top panel presents data for the bust transition, and the bottom panel considers the BBB transition. In the bust transition the age structure flattens smoothly over time until, in year 50, it is essentially flat and equal to its long-run structure. The bust-boom-bust transition is a more complicated situation; it starts out like the straight bust, but maintains a fairly steep age structure through year 50 because of the rebound

11 Demographic transition and social security

Table 11.1. *Population age structure in transition*

Year	Bust transition (by cohort)				Bust-boom-bust transition (by cohort)			
	1–20	21–40	41–60	61–75	1–20	20–40	40–60	61–75
0	0.50	0.28	0.15	0.07	0.50	0.28	0.15	0.07
20	0.37	0.36	0.20	0.09	0.41	0.33	0.18	0.08
50	0.28	0.28	0.28	0.16	0.40	0.30	0.19	0.11
70	0.26	0.27	0.27	0.20	0.27	0.34	0.26	0.13
110	0.27	0.27	0.27	0.21	0.25	0.25	0.25	0.25
150	0.27	0.27	0.27	0.20	0.27	0.27	0.27	0.20

Table 11.2. *Characteristics of demographic transitions without social security*

	Bust transition				Bust-boom-bust transition			
Year	Saving rate	Wage rate	Interest rate	Marginal tax rate	Saving rate	Wage rate	Interest rate	Marginal tax rate
0	7.6	1.00	9.9	15.0	7.6	1.00	9.9	15.0
1	6.1	1.00	9.9	13.0	6.2	1.00	9.8	14.7
5	6.6	1.00	10.0	12.4	6.7	1.00	9.9	12.7
10	7.4	1.00	10.0	11.8	7.7	1.00	10.0	12.1
20	7.9	1.02	7.4	11.6	8.7	1.02	9.3	14.1
50	3.0	1.10	7.3	10.6	4.3	1.04	8.9	11.8
70	−0.01	1.11	7.1	10.3	6.2	1.06	8.3	9.9
110	−1.5	1.11	7.1	10.5	−5.0	1.13	6.9	10.9
130	0.0	1.11	7.1	10.6	0.0	1.11	7.1	10.7
150	0.0	1.11	7.1	10.6	0.0	1.11	7.1	10.6

in the birth rate. The boom cohort is clearly evident in year 70's bulge in the fraction of young adults between 20 and 40 and, again in year 110, in the fraction of the population age 61 to 75. The different time patterns in age structures in these two cases suggest that large changes in macroeconomic variables will take longer to show up in the BBB transition, but that the swings in these variables will be larger as the boom cohort moves through the population.

This intuition is supported by the results of the basic simulations of the economy without social security (see Table 11.2). In these simulations we normalize the initial wage rate to unity and set the government surplus (capital stock) so that the gross interest rate is approximately 10 percent. The stock of government capital per capita is held constant throughout each simulation.

In the bust simulation, wages rise and interest rates gradually fall throughout the transition in response to the increase in capital per worker as the fraction of young workers, who own relatively little wealth, decreases. The association of capital deepening with lower population growth rates dates at least from Solow's (1956) growth model, with its Keynesian saving behavior. Marginal income tax rates decline because government consumption per capita is held fixed, but the fraction of the population with no taxable income – in this case, children – falls through time. Once the transition has begun, saving rates immediately fall. They then rise through year 20 to a value above that in the initial steady state. There follows a decline in saving rates, which reach negative values in year 110. Between 110 and 150 the saving rate rises to its ultimate steady state value of zero.

The initial drop in the saving rate is unrelated to concurrent demographic changes, which in period one are still unimportant, but is related to *anticipated*, general equilibrium increases in future after-tax wages. The projected increases in budget opportunities produce higher current consumption and lower current saving. Between years 1 and 20 the drop in fertility reduces the number of children and the importance of their dissaving, that is, consumption; by year 20, the fraction of the population between 20 and 60 has increased from 45 to 56 percent, and this group is doing more saving because of the reduced number of mouths they must feed. By year 70, however, the decline in birth rates has affected the size of the young and middle-aged adult-saving population, so that the only boom group remaining are the aged dissavers. This leads, temporarily, to a slightly negative saving rate.

The BBB transition, as suggested, occurs more slowly and is then characterized by erratic swings in macroeconomic activity as the bulge cohort ages. The wage rate rises gradually to 1.06 by year 70, rather than the 1.11 of the bust transition. It then overshoots its long-run level as the boom cohort, with its large accumulated savings of capital, retires. Similarly, marginal tax rates take longer to fall and undershoot their long-run value. Saving rates remain positive and quite high through year 70; they then fall precipitously to −5.0 percent of income in year 110 before converging to zero.

2. *Welfare effects of demographic transitions*

The well-being of individuals alive during either of these transitions can be compared to that of cohorts who die before there is any change in fertility. The method used in previous chapters is to ask what additional

11 Demographic transition and social security

fraction of lifetime resources an individual in the initial steady state would have to receive to be as well off as a member of a particular transition cohort. This approach has some ambiguity in the current context because the parent's utility function depends on the consumption and number of children. Our model does not, however, provide reasons for specified changes in fertility. Hence, equating a decline in the number of children with a decline in parental welfare seems rather arbitrary. In a more elaborate model that fully described the fertility decision, a decline in the number of children could be associated with both negative and positive changes in parental welfare. For example, if children provide pleasure to their parents, but changes in social customs make childbearing more difficult, this would imply a loss in welfare not present if reduced fertility came about because of, say, an income effect associated with increased living standards.

This problem is side-stepped by focusing on the welfare adults receive directly from their own consumption and leisure. The welfare changes of transition adult cohorts are measured by the increase or decrease in resources (spent on own adult consumption and leisure) that adults in the initial steady state would need in order to be left with the level of utility from adult consumption and leisure enjoyed by particular transition cohorts during their adulthoods. This is essentially the equivalent variation measure of the change in economic circumstances faced by a transition cohort.

Table 11.3 expresses these welfare effects as a percentage of the lifetime resources of initial steady state cohorts. The cohort born in year -75 (75 years prior to the date the transition begins) is the last generation not affected by the transition. The first part of the table, labeled "bust," shows the welfare effects of the transition under various fiscal regimes. The first column corresponds to the basic transition without social security discussed above. The drop in birth rates causes a large long-run welfare gain of 12.57 percent, about three-fourths of which is realized by those born in year -10. The primary reason for this upward shift in welfare is the reduction in children per adult. As we are considering welfare measured in terms of adult expenditure on consumption and leisure, such a demographic shift permits a higher level of welfare since adults now shift a greater fraction of their resources toward their own consumption and leisure. The corresponding BBB transition, represented in the first column of the second part of Table 11.3, evidences the same jump in welfare as birth rate declines, but also displays a temporary welfare drop associated with the temporary rise in fertility.

E. Including social security in the demographic transition

Consider next the effect of including unfunded social security in each of these transitions. The baseline model of social security assumes that the

Table 11.3. *Welfare effects of demographic transitions: equivalent variations as percentage of resources spent on adult consumption and leisure*

Generation born in year	No social security	With social security	Immediate cut in benefits	Immediate increase in retirement age	Trust fund policy	Taxation of social security benefits
Bust						
−75	0.00	0.00	0.00	0.00	0.00	0.00
−65	0.02	0.01	−0.16	0.01	0.01	−0.05
−50	0.16	0.12	−0.02	−0.00	0.06	0.08
−25	0.95	0.99	1.50	1.26	0.53	1.18
−10	9.23	9.50	10.61	10.22	10.46	9.88
0	10.33	9.95	11.35	10.87	13.06	10.41
10	11.32	9.87	11.67	11.03	12.81	10.42
25	12.36	8.70	11.29	10.37	11.97	9.54
50	12.76	7.29	10.46	9.24	11.07	8.29
75	12.66	6.72	10.09	8.82	10.56	7.79
100	12.57	6.94	10.23	8.93	10.77	7.97
125	12.57	6.94	10.21	8.93	10.78	7.98
150	12.57	6.95	10.21	8.94	10.79	7.99
Bust-boom-bust						
−75	0.00	0.00	0.00	0.00	0.00	0.00
−65	0.01	0.01	−0.16	0.01	0.00	−0.05
−50	0.11	0.08	−0.06	−0.04	0.03	0.03
−25	0.63	0.66	1.17	0.92	0.14	0.87
−10	8.54	8.80	9.89	9.51	9.49	9.23
0	2.09	1.46	2.85	2.39	4.37	2.03
10	2.43	1.40	2.99	2.47	4.51	2.03
25	9.91	9.02	10.60	10.06	12.30	9.55
50	12.09	9.54	11.67	10.90	12.58	10.23
75	13.03	6.66	10.17	8.88	10.20	7.79
100	12.57	6.84	10.09	8.82	10.42	7.87
125	12.57	6.84	10.12	8.84	10.44	7.89
150	12.57	6.95	10.15	8.88	10.48	7.93

replacement rate is 60 percent and the initial age of benefit receipt is 46 (66). This replacement rate may seem odd given that actual U.S. replacement rates are currently about 40 percent. A 60 percent rate is used to cover several types of social security benefits not explicitly modeled in our analysis. These include dependent and survivor benefits, medical benefits. The simulated base case payroll tax associated with the 60 percent replacement rate assumption is 5.2 percent, which is still quite low relative

Table 11.4. *Characteristics of demographic transitions with social security*

Year	Saving rate	Wage rate	Interest rate	Marginal tax rate	Payroll tax rate
Bust transition					
0	6.8	1.00	11.1	15.0	5.2
1	5.5	1.00	11.1	12.9	5.2
5	5.9	1.00	11.2	12.3	5.3
10	6.7	1.00	11.2	11.7	5.4
20	7.0	1.02	10.6	11.6	5.6
50	1.7	1.09	8.5	10.8	10.1
70	−1.3	1.08	8.8	10.1	14.0
110	−1.5	1.07	9.1	10.1	15.0
130	0.0	1.07	9.0	10.3	13.9
150	0.0	1.07	9.0	10.3	13.9
Bust-boom-bust transition					
0	6.8	1.00	11.1	15.0	5.2
1	5.5	1.00	11.0	14.7	5.3
5	5.9	1.00	11.2	12.6	5.2
10	6.8	1.00	11.2	12.0	5.3
20	7.8	1.02	10.5	14.1	5.5
50	3.6	1.03	10.1	11.8	7.5
70	5.1	1.05	9.6	9.9	8.6
110	−5.6	1.08	8.7	10.5	18.7
130	0.0	1.07	9.1	10.3	13.8
150	0.0	1.07	9.0	10.3	13.9

to the current U.S. combined employer–employee OASDHI (OASDI plus Health Insurance) payroll tax. This tax rate is much smaller than that reported in Chapter 10 because the assumed initial steady state population growth rate is 3 percent rather than 1 percent. Hence, from the perspective of approximating a realistic payroll tax rate, the replacement rate assumption is too low. As already mentioned, however, the aim here is not to provide empirical estimates, but to provide a qualitative sense of the relative impact of various demographic swings and alternative social security policies. Such qualitative findings are similar whether one uses a 40, 60, or 80 percent replacement rate for a baseline value.

Summary statistics for the bust and the bust-boom-bust simulations in the presence of social security are given in Table 11.4. The production function parameter A is chosen here so that the initial standard wage is again normalized to unity. Aside from the payroll tax, the two simulations with social security behave generally like their counterparts without social security presented in Table 11.2. The presence of social security means that, as fertility declines, part of the adult welfare gain previously discussed will be offset by the increased payroll taxes associated with the higher ratio of beneficiaries to workers. This is evident if one compares the first two columns of the two parts of Table 11.3, which corresponds to the welfare effects under the two transitions in the presence of social security. Although the qualitative patterns of welfare change are the same, cohorts gain uniformly less. About 45 percent of the long-run gain is lost. The effect is smaller in the short run, since the earlier generations escape the burden of higher social security taxes.

Payroll tax rates are quite different in the bust and the bust-boom-bust transitions. In the first case, the number of retirees per worker increases fairly smoothly, and the rise in the payroll tax behaves similarly. In the second, the population bulge represented by the baby boomers holds down payroll tax increases while they are working, and causes them to jump sharply once this cohort retires. In year 110 the payroll tax rate is 18.7 percent, almost 3.5 times the initial steady state value.

F. Social security policy responses to the demographic transition

Table 11.5 shows saving, wage, interest, and tax rates arising under the two demographic transitions if social security's replacement rate is cut from 60 to 40 percent in year zero. These benefit cuts apply to all cohorts receiving benefits at the time they are implemented. Table 11.5 also presents comparable figures for a gradual reduction in the replacement rate to 40 percent starting in year zero and ending in year 20. Table 11.4 indicates the time paths of these variables when the replacement rate is held fixed. A quick comparison of Tables 11.4 and 11.5 indicates that the social security tax rate is sensitive to the benefit-cut policy, while the impact on other variables is relatively minor. Rather than rising to 13.9 percent, as in Table 11.4, the long-run social security tax rate in Table 11.5 increases from 5.2 percent to 9.2 percent. The social security tax rate is significantly lower throughout the transition under the policy of immediately cutting the replacement rate than in the transitions of Table 11.4.

The benefit cuts, by reducing the scale of unfunded social security, generates a pre-tax wage rate that is 3 percent higher than would otherwise occur. The additional capital deepening associated with this higher long-run wage rate explains the slightly larger saving rates in Table 11.5 compared with those of Table 11.4. If the replacement rate cut is phased in rather than implemented immediately, the economy is left with a roughly 20 percent higher payroll tax rate during the first 10 years of the transition. The welfare effects of these benefit cuts are predictable. For both

Table 11.5. *Effects of reducing social security's replacement rate*

	Baby bust					Bust-boom-bust				
Year	S/Y	w	r	τ_y	τSS	S/Y	w	r	τ_y	τSS
Immediate cut in replacement rate from 60% to 40%										
0	6.8	1.00	11.1	15.0	5.2	6.8	1.00	11.1	15.0	5.2
1	6.6	1.00	11.2	12.7	3.5	6.7	1.00	11.1	14.5	3.5
5	6.8	1.00	11.1	12.3	3.5	6.8	1.00	11.1	12.6	3.5
10	7.2	1.01	10.9	11.9	3.6	7.4	1.01	10.9	12.1	3.5
20	7.3	1.03	10.2	11.8	3.8	8.1	1.03	10.5	14.3	3.7
50	3.0	1.12	10.2	10.9	6.7	4.5	1.05	9.6	12.0	5.0
70	−1.1	1.11	8.0	10.4	9.4	5.4	1.06	9.2	10.1	5.8
100	−.3	1.11	8.2	10.9	9.4	−1.4	1.17	7.7	11.2	8.9
110	−1.5	1.10	8.2	10.5	10.0	−5.5	1.11	8.1	10.9	12.5
130	0.0	1.10	8.4	10.6	9.2	−0.1	1.10	8.4	10.7	9.2
150	0.0	1.10	8.4	10.6	9.2	−0.01	1.10	8.4	10.7	9.2
Gradual (20-year) cut in replacement rate from 60% to 40%										
0	6.8	1.00	11.1	15.0	5.2	6.8	1.00	11.1	15.0	5.2
1	6.2	1.00	11.2	12.8	4.7	6.3	1.00	11.1	14.5	4.7
5	6.6	1.00	11.2	12.3	4.4	6.6	1.00	11.2	12.6	4.3
10	7.2	1.03	11.0	11.8	4.0	7.4	1.00	11.0	12.1	3.9
20	7.4	1.11	10.2	11.8	3.8	8.2	1.03	10.2	14.3	3.7
50	2.7	1.11	8.0	10.9	6.8	4.3	1.05	9.7	12.0	5.0
70	−1.1	1.11	8.2	10.4	9.4	5.4	1.06	9.2	10.1	5.8
100	−.3	1.11	8.2	10.9	9.4	−1.4	1.13	7.7	11.2	8.9
110	−1.5	1.10	8.4	10.5	10.0	−0.1	1.11	8.1	10.9	12.5
130	0.0	1.10	8.4	10.6	9.2	−0.1	1.10	8.4	10.7	9.2
150	0.0	1.10	8.4	10.6	9.2	−0.01	1.10	8.4	10.6	9.2

demographic transitions, the immediate cut in benefits causes a welfare loss to older generations alive in year zero (Table 11.3), but a welfare improvement for younger cohorts, even for those who are 25, and hence already working, at the time of the change. In the long run, such a policy leads to substantially greater welfare than does a policy of simply passively adjusting social security tax rates to meet the benefits associated with a 60 percent replacement rate.

An alternative to the explicit reduction in benefit levels would be an increase in the retirement age. Table 11.6 presents the characteristics of the demographic transition for two such policies, an immediate increase in the retirement age from 65 to 67, and the same rise occurring in year 20, after being announced in year zero. The welfare effects of the first of these policies is shown in the fifth column of Table 11.3. Both in terms

Table 11.6. *Effects of increasing social security's retirement age*

	Baby bust					Bust-boom-bust				
Year	S/Y	w	r	τ_y	τSS	S/Y	w	r	τ_y	τSS
Immediate increase in retirement age from 65 to 67										
0	6.8	1.00	11.1	15.0	5.2	6.8	1.00	11.1	15.0	5.2
1	5.9	1.00	11.2	12.8	5.2	6.0	1.00	11.1	14.6	5.2
5	6.4	1.00	11.2	13.3	4.2	6.3	1.00	11.2	12.6	4.1
10	7.0	1.00	11.1	11.8	4.1	7.2	1.00	11.1	12.0	4.1
20	7.3	1.02	10.3	11.7	4.3	8.0	1.03	10.3	14.3	4.2
50	2.4	1.11	8.2	10.9	7.7	4.1	1.04	9.8	11.9	5.8
70	−1.2	1.10	8.4	10.3	11.6	5.3	1.06	9.4	10.0	7.2
100	−.4	1.10	8.4	10.8	10.9	−1.5	1.12	7.8	11.1	10.1
110	−1.5	1.08	8.7	10.3	12.3	−5.6	1.10	8.3	10.7	15.9
130	0.0	1.09	8.6	10.5	11.0	0.1	1.09	8.7	10.5	11.1
150	0.0	1.09	8.6	10.5	11.0	0.0	1.09	8.6	10.6	11.0
Gradual increase in retirement age from 65 to 67										
0	6.8	1.00	11.1	15.0	5.2	6.8	1.00	11.1	15.0	5.2
1	5.6	1.00	11.1	12.9	5.2	5.7	1.00	11.0	14.6	5.2
5	6.1	1.00	11.2	12.3	5.3	6.1	1.00	11.2	12.6	5.2
10	6.8	1.00	11.1	11.8	5.3	7.0	1.00	11.1	12.0	5.3
20	7.3	1.02	10.5	11.6	5.0	8.0	1.02	10.4	14.2	4.9
50	2.1	1.10	8.2	11.9	7.9	3.8	1.04	9.9	11.9	5.8
70	−0.2	1.10	8.4	10.3	11.6	5.3	1.06	9.4	10.0	7.2
100	−0.3	1.10	8.4	10.8	10.9	−1.5	1.12	7.8	11.1	10.1
110	−1.5	1.08	8.7	10.3	12.3	−5.6	1.10	8.3	10.8	15.9
130	0.0	1.09	8.6	10.5	11.0	1.2	1.09	8.7	10.5	11.0
150	0.0	1.09	8.6	10.5	11.0	0.0	1.09	8.6	10.6	11.0

of macroeconomic and welfare effects, an immediate increase in the retirement age by two years has a similar but smaller impact than the immediate 40 percent benefit cut. In the long run, the payroll tax rate rises to 11.0 percent, which is higher than the 9.2 percent in the former case. Likewise, the long-run welfare gain of 8.94 percent is smaller than the previous gain of 10.21 percent. If one extrapolates from our results, maintenance of the original payroll tax rate appears to require a benefit cut of close to 75 percent, or an increase in the retirement age by 6 years.

Another alternative that has been suggested to reduce the growth in payroll taxes is the taxation of social security benefits. Indeed, because of the Tax Equity and Fiscal Responsibility Act of 1982, higher-income families now face regular income taxation on half of their social security benefits. Table 11.7 and the last column of Table 11.8 show the effects of taxing all social security benefits beginning at the start of the demo-

Table 11.7. *Immediate taxation of social security benefits*

	Baby bust					Bust-boom-bust				
Year	S/Y	w	r	τ_y	τSS	S/Y	w	r	τ_y	τSS
0	6.8	1.00	11.1	15.0	6.0	6.8	1.00	11.1	15.0	6.0
1	5.8	1.00	11.1	12.8	4.5	6.0	1.00	11.1	14.6	4.5
5	6.2	1.00	11.2	12.3	4.6	6.2	1.00	11.2	12.6	4.6
10	6.8	1.00	11.1	11.8	4.7	7.0	1.00	11.1	12.1	4.7
20	7.1	1.02	10.4	11.7	5.0	7.9	1.02	10.4	14.2	4.7
50	2.2	1.10	8.3	10.9	9.0	3.9	1.04	9.9	11.9	6.6
70	−1.3	1.09	8.6	10.2	12.6	5.2	1.05	9.5	9.9	7.8
100	−0.4	1.09	8.6	10.7	12.6	−1.6	1.12	8.0	11.0	11.8
110	−1.5	1.08	8.9	10.2	13.5	−5.6	1.09	8.5	10.7	16.7
130	0.0	1.08	8.8	10.4	12.5	0.1	1.08	8.9	10.4	12.4
150	0.0	1.08	8.8	10.4	12.5	0.0	1.08	8.8	10.5	12.5

graphic transition and of keeping the receipts within the social security system to reduce payroll taxes. Such a policy leads initially to reductions in social security taxes, but in the long run has a smaller impact than any of the policies previously examined, because of the relatively low rate of income taxation. As this suggests, the long-run welfare impact of this policy is smaller than the others, but generations reaching adulthood early in the transition actually do almost as well as under the other policies.

Table 11.8 investigates a policy that some have advocated as a long-run solution to the long-run social security deficit: the accumulation of a trust fund. The simulated policy introduces a one-third surcharge on the payroll tax for the first 20 years of the transition, the proceeds of which are contributed to the trust fund. That is, in the initial 20-year period this policy raises revenues by one-third more than is necessary, in equilibrium, to pay for current benefits. After year 20, the accumulated trust fund is held constant per capita, and the income and principal beyond that needed to maintain a constant per capita trust fund is used to help pay for benefits. Under this policy, the social security tax rate drops to essentially zero in year 20 of both transitions so that as the retiree–worker ratio rises, the payroll tax is kept from rising. In each simulation, the long-run payroll tax (8.4 percent for the bust case, 8.8 percent for the BBB case) is the lowest of any of the simulations presented. As one would expect, the trust fund transitions produce the highest long-run welfare gains of any of the social security transitions considered (Table 11.3). At the same time, they are the only policy simulations, excluding simply passively adjusting payroll tax rates, under which each generation gains from the changes in fertility.

Table 11.8. *Accumulation of social security trust fund*

	Baby bust					Bust-boom-bust				
Year	S/Y	w	r	τ_y	τSS	S/Y	w	r	τ_y	τSS
0	6.8	1.00	11.1	15.0	6.0	6.8	1.00	11.1	15.0	6.0
1	5.9	1.00	11.2	12.8	7.0	6.0	1.00	11.1	14.6	7.0
5	6.4	1.00	11.2	12.4	7.0	6.4	1.00	11.2	12.7	7.0
10	7.2	1.00	11.1	12.0	7.1	7.5	1.00	11.1	12.3	7.1
20	7.5	1.03	10.2	12.5	−0.0	8.5	1.03	10.1	15.2	0.9
50	2.1	1.11	8.0	11.4	5.3	3.4	1.05	9.5	12.9	1.8
70	−1.4	1.11	8.1	10.9	8.3	5.3	1.07	9.0	10.7	3.6
100	−0.0	1.11	8.1	11.4	8.8	−1.6	1.13	7.6	11.7	8.7
110	−1.5	1.10	8.3	11.0	9.2	−5.6	1.11	8.1	11.4	13.2
130	0.0	1.10	8.3	11.2	8.4	0.2	1.10	8.4	11.2	8.6
150	0.0	1.10	8.3	11.2	8.4	0.1	1.10	8.3	11.2	8.8

G. Summary and conclusion

A central lesson of the simulations presented here is that demographic conditions are potentially significant determinants of economic performance and welfare. Indeed, the time path of demographic change dominates the outcomes of each of the five social security policy transitions, despite the fact that these five simulations involve significantly different and quite substantive social security policy responses. The simulated demographic transitions suggest that the swings in U.S. fertility currently under way can have major impacts on factor returns over the long run and can produce precipitous changes in saving rates in the short run. To place our findings on demographic change in perspective, it should be noted that the simulated long-run changes in factor returns and capital-labor ratios from major fertility declines are of the same order of magnitude as the simulated effect of entirely abolishing unfunded social security. Whereas considerable research has been conducted on the saving impact of this and other government fiscal policies, few studies have investigated the effect of demographic change on saving.

The presence of a social security system does have important effects on the economic transition associated with either baby busts or cycles of baby booms and busts; but the attendant financial squeeze placed on social security in these transitions is of secondary importance with respect to the long-run level of economic welfare. Although payroll tax rates may rise dramatically, long-run welfare is nonetheless substantially higher, as measured by equivalent increases in levels of adult consumption and leisure. This reflects, in part, the fact that each adult parent has "fewer

11 Demographic transition and social security

mouths to feed" and therefore can enjoy a higher individual standard of living. In addition, although the replacement fertility rate prevailing in the long run leaves more elderly per capita in society, the sharp drop in children per capita means an overall decline in the ratio of dependents to prime-age workers in the economy. For the government, these changes potentially imply smaller demands on its regular fiscal operations (e.g., educational expenditures), which we model here as involving a fixed level of government consumption expenditure per capita. In our model the marginal income tax rate used to finance this spending falls from 15 percent to roughly 10.5 percent in each of the simulations in response to the lower overall dependency ratio. Hence, although the typical worker must support more elderly through social security, he (she) supports fewer children, both directly as a parent and indirectly as an income tax payer. Under a passive policy of adjusting social security payroll taxes, combined income and payroll tax rates rise from an initial 20.2 percent to a long-run value of 24.2 percent (see Table 11.4). Had the income tax rate not dropped to 10.3 percent, the combined long-run tax rate would have equaled 28.9 percent.

Although the combined long-run tax rate is 4.2 percentage points higher in this simulation, the pre-tax wage rises by 7 percent, in response to the significant increase in capital intensity associated with the long-run decline in fertility rates. It is this general equilibrium impact on factor returns that is primarily responsible for the higher long-run level of welfare.

Although reasonable alterations in social security policy appear incapable of significantly altering the basic economic impact of substantial demographic swings, the particular choice of social security policy is nonetheless important. In comparison with simply allowing payroll taxes to adjust upward to meet required benefit payments, major reductions in replacement rates, major increases in the retirement age, or the accumulation of a significant trust fund can all raise the long-run level of welfare by an amount equivalent to almost 4 percent of lifetime expenditure on consumption and leisure. A 4 percent long-run increase in welfare is a large amount when compared with the simulated long-run welfare effects of a variety of major fiscal policy changes. The potential long-run welfare gain is not, however, freely obtained; rather, such long-run welfare gains come at the price of reductions in the welfare of transition cohorts, typically those alive at the time of the demographic change as well as those born within 25 years of the initial date of the change. Hence the choice of social security policy in the midst of the demographic transition is of considerable importance to the intergenerational distribution of welfare.

CHAPTER 12

Summary and conclusion

The purpose of this book has been to explain and illustrate the dynamic impact of alternative fiscal policies. The simulation results, although based on a highly simplified economic model, suggest that fiscal policies can have powerful effects on the economy. Prolonged and significant tax cuts, changes in the tax structure, increases in the degree of tax progressivity, increases in government consumption, enhancement of investment incentives, and the introduction of unfunded social security are each policies that can substantially alter the course of saving, investment, and factor rewards. Many of these policies are effective primarily because they transfer resources across generations. Others are effective, in large part, because they change economic incentives. Such changes in economic incentives can significantly alter the degree of economic efficiency, albeit in directions that may not necessarily correspond to the direction of change in long-run welfare.

The simulation methodology has proved useful not only for tracing the channels through which fiscal policy operates, but also for obtaining a quantitative sense of the relative impacts of alternative fiscal actions. Although absolute levels of capital stocks and other economic variables appear to be quite sensitive to the choice of parameter values, the relative efficacy and efficiency of alternative fiscal policies appear much less sensitive to the precise parameterization of the model.

Despite the apparent power of fiscal choices to alter the course of the economy, such effects may be hard to discern. Many fiscal policies operate slowly, and others act subtly through, for example, revaluations in asset markets. Another difficulty in assessing the reaction to fiscal policies is that short-run policy outcomes depend critically on expectations concerning the future course of policy, and such expectations are difficult to ascertain.

An implication of the slow nature of fiscal policies is that current economic performance may be largely the legacy of policies enacted decades ago, rather than the result of more recent policy modifications. This suggests that policies should be assessed largely in terms of their longer-range impact on the economy. Unfortunately, most participants in the political system have short time horizons, and may as a consequence become too quickly skeptical of policies that will ultimately prove highly beneficial.

12 Summary and conclusion

Alternatively, they may incorrectly equate short-run policy results with long-run policy outcomes. Consider, for example, the short-term tax cut simulations of Chapter 6; policymakers looking only at short-run results would draw the incorrect conclusion that deficit-financed tax cuts increase savings, although such policies do so only in the short run and, indeed, can greatly reduce savings in the long run.

Another concern about correctly assessing fiscal policy involves the issue of fiscal illusion. We are accustomed to distinguishing policies on the basis of their labels, but identical or essentially identical policies can be conducted under quite different names. Thus Chapter 9 points out that enhancing investment incentives is equivalent to introducing consumption taxation, and Chapter 5 indicates that consumption taxation is equivalent to wealth taxation in conjunction with wage taxation. Chapter 7 addresses fiscal illusion in the context of intergenerational transfer policies, pointing out that a variety of policies, not simply deficit-financed tax cuts, redistribute resources across generations. Structural tax changes and unfunded social security are two prime examples, but such policies can be conducted with no impact on officially reported levels of government debt. In addition, officially reported government debt can change enormously with no necessary change in the intergenerational distribution of resources. Despite this fact, in countless empirical analyses that are allegedly based on the life cycle model, ill-defined accounting constructs such as official government deficits are related to actual economic outcomes.

A failure to understand the structural similarities of policies can lead to the simultaneous enactment of largely offsetting policies. Thus, the Reagan administration's increase in investment incentives and longer-term cuts in social security benefits in the early 1980s constitute redistribution away from current old and young generations toward future generations that may more than offset the redistribution toward current generations from future generations associated with the Reagan tax cuts.

The stance of fiscal policy cannot be properly evaluated without an understanding of the structural similarities of policies, the length of time required for policies to be effective, the role of expectations, and the interactions of policies. Such an understanding is also important simply to describe fiscal policy properly; fiscal policies are sufficiently complex and have sufficiently diverse effects on the economy that they cannot be accurately or adequately described by simple terms such as "tight" or "loose." Nor can they be well understood by pointing to their effects on particular accounting entities, such as "deficits." The results in this book suggest that fiscal policies should be described in terms of their effects on the budget constraints of current and successive generations as well as in terms of the course of the government's consumption.

To describe fiscal choices in this manner one must specify the time path of policies and consider the feasibility of such policy paths. An important component of the price of many short-term decisions is that they render less feasible other policy choices in the future. Thus a decision not to accumulate a social security trust fund along the transition path of a baby bust limits the government's ability to sustain social security benefits in the future. Furthermore, in characterizing the budget constraints of successive generations, policymakers will be less likely to overlook longer-term losers and focus attention solely on short-term winners.

Whether such an approach to the description and analysis of fiscal policy will ultimately prevail is uncertain. What seems more likely, however, is that policy analysts will increasingly rely on more comprehensive general equilibrium dynamic models of the sort presented here. There is a danger, of course, that one may mistake models of this type for the real world and may end up providing policy prescriptions that are appropriate to a particular model, but not to the true underlying model of the economy. The present model differs from economic reality in a number of obvious ways. There is no unemployment, only a single asset, only a single homogeneous labor input, no international trade, no uncertainty, no differences across individuals in tastes or earnings potential, no market imperfections, no disequilibria, and no money. For these reasons and many others, this model cannot be used for economic predictions or for providing explicit policy recommendations. However, the model can greatly expand one's intuition about the ways in which fiscal policy may operate, and it is for this purpose that we have offered it to the reader.

References

Abel, Andrew B., *Investment and the Value of Capital,* New York: Garland Publishing, 1979.

Abel, Andrew B., and Olivier Blanchard, "The Present Value of Profits and Cyclical Movements in Investment," *Econometrica,* 1986.

Ando, Albert, and Franco Modigliani, "The 'Life Cycle' Hypothesis of Saving: Aggregate Implications and Tests," *American Economic Review,* vol. 53, 1963.

Atkinson, Anthony B., and Joseph E. Stiglitz, *Lectures on Public Economics,* New York: McGraw-Hill, 1980.

Auerbach, Alan J., "Share Valuation and Corporate Equity Policy," *Journal of Public Economics,* vol. 11, 1979a.

"Wealth Maximization and the Cost of Capital," *Quarterly Journal of Economics,* 1979b.

"Corporate Taxation in the United States," *Brookings Papers on Economic Activity,* 1983a.

"Taxation, Corporate Financial Policy, and the Cost of Capital," *Journal of Economic Literature,* September, vol. 21, no. 3, 1983b.

"Investment, Taxation, and Growth," in *Removing Obstacles to Economic Growth,* ed. M. Wachter and S. Wachter, Philadelphia: University of Pennsylvania Press, 1984.

"Saving in the U.S.: Some Conceptual Issues," in *The Level and Composition of Household Saving,* ed. P. Hendershott, Cambridge: Ballinger Press, 1985.

"The Dynamic Effects of Tax Law Asymmetries," *Review of Economic Studies,* April 1986.

Auerbach, Alan J., and James R. Hines, Jr., "Tax Reform, Investment, and the Value of the Firm," National Bureau of Economic Research Working Paper no. 1803, January 1986.

Auerbach, Alan J., and Dale Jorgenson, "Inflation-Proof Depreciation of Assets," *Harvard Business Review,* vol. 50, no. 5, Sept./Oct. 1980.

Auerbach, Alan J., and Laurence J. Kotlikoff, "National Savings, Economic Welfare, and the Structure of Taxation," in *Behavioral Simulation Methods in Tax Policy Analysis,* ed. Martin Feldstein, Chicago: University of Chicago Press, 1983a.

"Investment versus Savings Incentives: The Size of the Bang for the Buck and the Potential for Self-Financing Business Tax Cuts," in *The Economic Consequences of Government Deficits,* ed. L. H. Meyer, Boston: Kluwer-Nijhoff, 1983b.

References

"An Examination of Empirical Tests of Social Security and Savings," in *Social Policy Evaluation: An Economic Perspective,* ed. Elhanan Helpman et al., New York: Academic Press, 1983c.

"Social Security and the Economics of the Demographic Transition," in H. Aaron and G. Burtless, eds., *Retirement and Economic Behavior,* Washington, D.C.: Brookings Institution, 1984.

"Simulating Alternative Social Security Responses to the Demographic Transition," *National Tax Journal,* June 1985a.

"The Efficiency Gains from Social Security Benefit-Tax Linkage," National Bureau of Economic Research Working Paper no. 1645, June 1985b.

Auerbach, Alan J., Laurence J. Kotlikoff, and Jonathan Skinner, "The Efficiency Gains from Dynamic Tax Reform," *International Economic Review,* vol. 24, no. 2, February 1983.

Azariadis, C., and J. Stiglitz, "Implicit Contracts and Fixed-Price Equilibria," *Quarterly Journal of Economics,* vol. 98, no. 3, Supplement, 1983.

Ballard, Charles A., Don Fullerton, John B. Shoven, and John Whalley, *A General Equilibrium Model for Tax Policy Evaluation,* NBER Volume, University of Chicago Press, 1985.

Berndt, E. R., and L. J. Christensen, "The Translog Function and the Substitution of Equipment, Structures and Labor in U.S. Manufacturing, 1929–1968," *Journal of Econometrics,* March 1973.

Bernheim, B. Douglas, "A Note on Dynamic Tax Incidence," *Quarterly Journal of Economics,* November 1981, 705–23.

Blinder, A., and R. Solow, "Does Fiscal Policy Matter," *Journal of Public Economics,* vol. 2, November 1973.

Blinder, Alan S., Roger H. Gordon, and David E. Wise, "Reconsidering the Work Disincentive Effects of Social Security," *National Tax Journal,* vol. 33, no. 4, December 1980.

Boskin, Michael J., "Federal Government Deficits: Some Myths and Realities," *American Economic Review,* vol. 72, no. 2, May 1982.

Boskin, M., and M. Hurd, "The Effect of Social Security on Early Retirement," *Journal of Public Economics,* vol. 10, no. 3, December 1978.

Boskin, M., and L. Kotlikoff, "Public Debt and United States Saving: A New Test of the Neutrality Hypothesis," *Carnegie Rochester Conference Series on Public Policy,* 1985.

Bradford, David F., "The Incidence and Allocation Effects of a Tax on Corporate Distributions," *Journal of Public Economics,* February 1981.

Untangling the Income Tax, Cambridge, Mass.: Harvard University Press, 1986.

Bradford, David, and U.S. Treasury Department Tax Policy Staff, *Blueprints for Basic Tax Reform,* 2d ed. rev., Arlington, Va.: Tax Analysts, 1984.

Buiter, Willem H., "Measurement of the Public Sector Deficit and Its Implications for Policy Evaluation and Design," Staff Papers, Washington, D.C.: International Monetary Fund, 1983.

Calvo, Guillermo A., "On the Indeterminacy of Interest Rates and Wages with Perfect Foresight," *Journal of Economic Theory,* December 1978a.

References

"On the Time Consistency of Optimal Policy in a Monetary Economy," *Econometrica,* vol. 46, 1978b.

Calvo, Guillermo A., Laurence J. Kotlikoff, and Carlos A. Rodriguez, "The Incidence of a Tax on Pure Rent: A New (?) Reason for an Old Answer," *Journal of Political Economy,* vol. 87, no. 4, August 1979.

Chamley, Christophe, "The Welfare Costs of Capital Income Taxation in a Growing Economy, *Journal of Political Economy,* vol. 89, no. 3, June 1981.

Chamley, Christophe, and Brian Wright, "Fiscal Incidence in Overlapping Generation Models with a Fixed Asset," mimeo, 1986.

Costrell, Robert, "Stability of Zero Production under Life Cycle Savings," *Review of Economic Studies,* vol. 48, October 1981.

Darby, Michael R., *Effects of Social Security on Income and the Capital Stock,* Washington, D.C.: American Enterprise Institute, 1979.

Economic Report of the President, 1982, 1985, 1986, Washington, D.C.: U.S. Government Printing Office.

Eisner, Robert, and Paul J. Pieper, "A New View of the Federal Debt and Budget Deficits," mimeo, January 1983.

"How to Make Sense of the Deficit," *Public Interest,* no. 78, Winter 1985.

Eisner, Robert, and Robert Strotz, "Determinants of Business Investment" (with bibliography by G. R. Post), in *Commission on Money and Credit, Impacts of Monetary Policy,* Englewood Cliffs, N.J.: Prentice-Hall, 1963.

Feldstein, Martin, "Social Security, Induced Retirement and Aggregate Capital Accumulation," *Journal of Political Economy,* vol. 82, 1974.

"The Surprising Incidence of a Tax on Pure Rent: A New Answer to an Old Question," *Journal of Political Economy,* vol. 85, no. 2, April 1977.

Fisher, Irving, "The Double Taxation of Savings," *American Economic Review,* 1939.

Flavin, Marjorie A., "The Adjustment of Consumption to Changing Expectations About Future Income," *Journal of Political Economy,* vol. 89, no. 5, October 1981.

Fullerton, D., "On the Possibility of an Inverse Relationship between Tax Rates and Government Revenues," *Journal of Public Economics,* vol. 19, no. 1, October 1982.

Fullerton, Donald, John B. Shoven, and John Whalley, "Replacing the U.S. Income Tax with a Progressive Consumption Tax," *Journal of Public Economics,* vol. 20, 1983.

Gahvari, Firouz, "Taxation of Housing, Capital Accumulation, and Welfare: A Study in Dynamic Tax Reform," *Public Finance Quarterly,* vol. 13, no. 2, 1985.

Ghez, G., and Gary S. Becker, *The Allocation of Time and Goods Over the Life Cycle,* New York: Columbia University Press, 1975.

Grossman, Stanford, and Robert J. Shiller, "The Determinants of the Variability of Stock Market Prices," *American Economic Review,* vol. 71, no. 2, May 1981.

Grossman, Sanford, and Laurence Weiss, "A Transactions-Based Model of the Monetary Transmission Mechanism," *American Economic Review,* vol. 73, no. 5, December 1983.

References

Grunfeld, Yehuda, "The Determinants of Corporate Investment," in *The Demand for Durable Goods,* ed. A.C. Harberger, Chicago: University of Chicago Press, 1960.

Hall, Robert E., "Intertemporal Substitution in Consumption," NBER Working Paper No. 720, July 1980.

Hall, Robert E., and Frederic Mishkin, "The Sensitivity of Consumption to Transitory Income: Estimates from Panel Data on Households." *Econometrica,* vol. 50, no. 2, March 1982.

Hall, Robert E., and Alvin Rabushka, *Flat Tax, Simple Tax,* McGraw-Hill, 1983.

Hansen, Lars P., and Kenneth J. Singleton, "Stochastic Consumption, Risk Aversion, and the Temporal Behavior of Asset Returns," *Journal of Political Economy,* vol. 91, no. 2, April 1983.

Hausman, Jerry, "Individual Discount Rates and Utilization of Energy Using Durables," *Bell Journal,* Spring 1979.

"Labor Supply," in *How Taxes Affect Economic Behavior,* ed. H. Aaron and J. Pechman, Washington, D.C.: Brookings Institution, 1981.

Hayashi, Fumio, "Tobin's Marginal and Average q: A Neoclassical Interpretation," *Econometrica,* vol. 50, January 1982.

Heckman, James, "Shadow Prices, Market Wages and Labor Supply," *Econometrica,* July 1974.

Hobbes, Thomas, *Leviathan,* Baltimore, Md.: Penguin Classics, 1651.

Jorgenson, Dale W., "Capital Theory and Investment Behavior," *American Economic Review,* vol. 53, 1963.

Kaldor, Nicholas, *An Expenditure Tax,* London: Allen and Unwin, 1957.

Kehoe, Timothy J., and David Levine, "Comparative Statics and Perfect Foresight in Infinite Horizon Economies," *Econometrica,* vol. 53, no. 2, March 1985, pp. 433-53.

Keynes, John Maynard, *The General Theory of Employment, Interest and Money,* New York: Harcourt, Brace, Jovanovich, 1964 (originally published in 1936).

King, Mervyn A., *Public Policy and the Corporation,* London: Chapman and Hall, 1977.

King, Mervyn, and L. Dicks-Mireaux, "Asset Holdings and the Life Cycle," *Economic Journal,* vol. 92, no. 2, 1982.

Kotlikoff, Laurence J., "Social Security and Equilibrium Capital Intensity," *Quarterly Journal of Economics,* May 1979.

Kotlikoff, Laurence J., John B. Shoven, and Avia Spivak, "The Effect of Annuity Insurance in Savings and Inequality," *Journal of Labor Economics,* vol. 4, July 1986.

Kotlikoff, Laurence J., and Lawrence H. Summers, "The Role of Intergenerational Transfers in Capital Accumulation," *Journal of Political Economy,* vol. 89, no. 4, 1981.

"The Contribution of Intergenerational Transfers to Total Wealth: A Reply," forthcoming in *Modelling the Accumulation and Distribution of Wealth,* ed. Dennis Kessler and Andre Masson, Oxford University Press, 1987.

Kydland, Finn E., and Edward C. Prescott, "Rules Rather than Discretion: The Inconsistency of Optimal Plans," *Journal of Political Economy,* vol. 85, 1977.

References

Laitner, John, "Transition Time Paths for Overlapping-Generations Models," *Journal of Economic Dynamics and Control,* 1984.

Lawrance, Emily, *The Savings Behavior of Rich and Poor: A Study of Time Preference and Liquidity Constraints,* Ph.D. dissertation, Yale University, 1986.

Lucas, Robert E., Jr., and Edward Prescott, "Investment under Uncertainty," *Econometrica,* vol. 39, 1971.

MaCurdy, Thomas E., "An Empirical Model of Labor Supply in a Life Cycle Setting," *Journal of Political Economy,* vol. 89, no. 6, December 1981.

"A Simple Scheme for Estimating an Intertemporal Model of Labor Supply and Consumption in the Presence of Taxes and Uncertainty," *International Economic Review,* vol. 24, no. 2, June 1983.

Mankiw, N. Gregory, "The Permanent Income Hypothesis and the Real Interest Rate," *Economic Letters,* vol. 7, 1981.

"Consumer Durables and the Real Interest Rate," *Review of Economics and Statistics,* August 1985.

Mankiw, N. Gregory, Julio J. Rotemberg, and Lawrence H. Summers, "Intertemporal Substitution in Macroeconomics," *Quarterly Journal of Economics,* February 1985.

Mariger, Randall, *Consumption Behavior and the Effects of Government Fiscal Policies,* Cambridge, Mass.: Harvard University Press, 1986.

Meade Committee, *The Structure and Reform of Direct Taxation,* Institute for Fiscal Studies, London: Allen & Unwin, 1978.

Menchik, Paul, and Martin David, "Income Distribution, Lifetime Savings and Bequests," *American Economic Review,* vol. 73, no. 4, September 1983.

Miller, Merton, and Charles Upton, *Macroeconomics: A Neoclassical Introduction,* Homewood, Ill.: R. D. Irwin, 1974.

Mirer, Thad W., "The Wealth-Age Relation Among the Aged," *American Economic Review,* vol. 69, June 1979.

Modigliani, Franco, "The Life Cycle Hypothesis and National Wealth – A Rehabilitation," Massachusetts Institute of Technology Discussion Paper, January 1983.

"The Contribution of Intergenerational Transfer to Total Wealth," paper presented to the Paris Conference on Modeling the Accumulation and Distribution of Wealth, September 1984.

Modigliani, Franco, and Richard Brumberg, "Utility Analysis and the Consumption Function: An Interpretation of Cross-Section Data," in *Post-Keynesian Economics,* ed. Kenneth K. Kurihara, New Brunswick, N.J.: Rutgers University Press, 1954.

Nerlove, Marc, "Recent Studies of the CES and Related Production Functions," in *The Theory and Empirical Analysis of Production,* ed. M. Brown, New York: NBER, 1967.

Pechman, Joseph A., ed., *What Should Be Taxed: Income or Expenditure?,* Washington, D.C.: Brookings Institution, 1980.

The Promise of Tax Reform, The American Assembly, Columbia University, Englewood Cliffs, N.J.: Prentice-Hall, 1985.

References

Phelps, E. S., and John G. Riley, "Rawlsian Growth: Dynamic Programming of Capital and Wealth for Intergenerational 'Maximin' Justice," *Review of Studies,* February 1978.

Poterba, James M., "Tax Subsidies to Owner Occupied Housing: An Asset Market Approach," *Quarterly Journal of Economics,* vol. 99, no. 4, November 1984.

Poterba, James M., and L. Summers, "Dividend Taxes, Corporate Investment and Q," *Journal of Public Economics,* vol. 22, no. 2, November 1983.

Rosen, Harvey, "Taxes in a Labor Supply Model with Joint Wage-Hours Determination," *Econometrica,* vol. 44, May 1976.

Sandmo, Agnar, "Progressive Taxation, Redistribution, Labor Supply," *Scandinavian Journal of Economics,* vol. 85, 1983.

Sargent, Thomas, and N. Wallace, "Some Unpleasant Monetarist Arithmetic," *Federal Reserve Bank of Minneapolis Quarterly Review,* vol. 5, 1981.

Scarf, Herbert E., "The Approximation of Fixed Points of a Continuous Mapping," *SIAM Journal of Applied Mathematics,* 1967.

The Computation of Economic Equilibria, New Haven, Conn.: Yale University Press, 1973.

Seidman, Laurence S., "Taxes in a Life Cycle Model with Bequests and Inheritances," *American Economic Review,* vol. 73, no. 3, June 1983.

Sheshinski, Eytan, "A Model of Social Security and Retirement Decisions," *Journal of Public Economics,* vol. 10, no. 3, December 1978.

Shoven, John B., "The Incidence and Efficiency Effects of Taxes on Income from Capital," *Journal of Political Economy,* vol. 84, 1976.

Shoven, John B., and J. Whalley, "A General Equilibrium Calculation of the Effects of Differential Taxation of Income from Capital in the U.S.," *Journal of Public Economics,* vol. 1, 1972.

Solow, Robert, "A Contribution to the Theory of Economic Growth," *Quarterly Journal of Economics,* February 1956.

Summers, Lawrence H., "Capital Taxation and Accumulation in a Life Cycle Model," mimeo, 1980.

"Capital Taxation and Accumulation in a Life Cycle Growth Model," *American Economic Review,* vol. 71, no. 4, September 1981a.

"Taxation and Corporate Investment: A q Theory Approach," *Brookings Papers on Economic Activity,* Washington, D.C., Spring 1981b.

"Taxation and the Size and Composition of the Capital Stock: An Asset Price Approach," mimeo, 1981c.

"Inflation, the Stock Market, and Owner-occupied Housing," *International Economic Review,* May 1981d.

"Tax Policy, the Rate of Return, and Savings," NBER Working Paper No. 995, September 1982.

Surrey, Stanley S., *Pathways to Tax Reform,* Cambridge, Mass.: Harvard University Press, 1973.

Tobin, James, "Life Cycle Saving and Balanced Growth," in *Ten Economic Studies in the Tradition of Irving Fisher,* ed. William Fellner et al., New York: Wiley, 1967.

References

"A General Equilibrium Approach to Monetary Theory," *Journal of Money, Credit and Banking,* vol. 1, February 1969.

Tobin, James, and Walter C. Dolde, "Wealth, Liquidity and Consumption," in *Consumer Spending and Monetary Policy: The Linkages,* Proceedings of a Monetary Conference, Nantucket Island, Massachusetts, June 1971, Conference Series No. 5, Boston: Federal Reserve Bank of Boston, June 1971.

"Monetary and Fiscal Effects on Consumption," in *Consumer Spending and Monetary Policy: The Linkages,* Federal Reserve Bank of Boston Monetary Conference, 1981.

Weber, Warren E., "The Effect of Interest Rates on Aggregate Consumption," *American Economic Review,* vol. 60, no. 4, September 1970.

"Interest Rates, Inflation and Consumer Expenditures," *American Economic Review,* vol. 65, no. 5, December 1975.

Welch, Finis, "Effects of Cohort Size on Earnings: The Baby Boom Babies' Financial Bust," *Journal of Political Economy,* vol. 87, October 1979.

White, Betsy Buttrill, "Empirical Tests of the Life-Cycle Hypothesis," *American Economic Review,* vol. 68, September 1978.

Index

Abel, Andrew B., 11, 36
adjustment costs: firm behavior and, 36–7; income tax cuts in absence of, 91–5; investment incentives and, 134–5, 138, 139, 140, 143; life cycle model and, 89; production parameters and marginal, 53; short-term tax cut in presence of, 90–1; tax cuts in presence of, 95–7
AIME (symbol standing for average index of monthly earnings), social security analysis and, 150, 151, 155, 157
Ando, Albert, 8, 10
announcement effects: capital income tax and, 83, 84; consumption tax and, 83, 86; efficiency and, 86–7; income tax and, 83, 86; investment incentives and, 140–1; savings and, 82–5; tax base choice and, 56–7, 82–7; wage tax and, 84
Arrow, Kenneth, 27
asset accumulation, 163
Auerbach, Alan J., 51, 77, 80, 131, 134

Becker, Gary S., 51
bequests, 16, 126
birth rate, 162, 167, 168–71, 177, 178
bonds, 16
Brumberg, Richard, 8, 10
budget constraints: fiscal policy and, 181, 182; government behavior and, 39–40; household behavior and, 28–30, 103
budget deficits; *see* deficits
business tax cuts (self-financing), 143–4
business tax incentives, 3
"bust-boom-bust" (BBB) fertility behavior, 168–70, 171, 173–4, 177

capital: investment incentives and, 135, 143; tax-cut example and, 94–5; two-period life cycle model and, 16
capital accumulation: Cobb–Douglas example of two-period life cycle model and, 17–18, 18–19; government policy and, 5; tax progressivity and, 5
capital decumulation, 19
capital formation: deficits and income tax cuts and, 4; government consumption and "crowding in" of, 74; social security and crowding out of long-run, 147, 148, 153, 161
capital gains tax, 129
capital goods installation costs, 36–7
capital goods investment, 139
capital income tax, 120, 135; announcement effects and, 83, 84; household behavior and, 33; investment incentives and, 133; tax base choice analysis and, 60, 62, 67, 72, 73, 76, 80, 81
capital intensity, 52
children, 26
children's dependency, 64
Cobb–Douglas example of two-period life cycle model, 17–22
computers, 25, 54
Congressional Budget Act of 1974, 107
consumption: balanced budget increases in government, 97–101; deficit-financed increases in government, 101; demographics and, 167, 179; demographic shifts and government, 170; progressive taxation and sensitivity analysis and, 119, 120; social security and, 147–8, 161; tax reform analysis and government, 73, 74
consumption choices, 61; budget constraints and, 29, 30; household behavior and, 30–1
consumption measurement (household behavior), 27–8
consumption tax, 5, 89; announcement effects and, 83, 86; balanced budget increases in government consumption and, 98, 101; defining deficits and, 109; household behavior and, 34; inherited wealth and, 126; investment incentives and, 127, 129, 131, 133, 136, 137; progressive taxation analysis and, 115, 117, 119, 122, 123, 126; savings stimulation and, 4; social security and, 152–3; tax base analysis and, 55, 57, 58, 59, 62, 67, 72, 73–6, 78, 79, 80, 81, 82; welfare effects and, 85
crowding in: deficits and savings and investment, 4; government consumption

191

crowding in *(cont.)*
  and capital formation, 74; short-term tax cuts and, 93, 95
crowding out: balanced budget increases in government consumption and, 98–101; deficit-financed increases in government consumption and, 101; from deficit financing, 89; deficits and domestic savings and, 88; short-term tax cuts and, 93, 94, 95; social security and savings, 146; two-period life cycle model example of tax cut and, 23, 24; unfunded social security and capital formation and, 147, 148, 153, 161

deficits: balanced budget increases in government consumption and, 97–101; definitions (economic versus accounting) of, 103–9; domestic savings and, 88; increases in government consumption and, 101; as measure of intergenerational transfer, 90; short-term tax cut policies and, 90–7; social security and, 149–50; temporary tax cut example of two-period life cycle model and, 22–4
demographic shifts: economic effects of, 168–71; fertility rates and, 162, 167, 168–71, 173–4, 177, 178; general equilibrium model and, 26; modeling of, 166–7; nature of, 162–4; significance of (social security policy), 178–9; social security and, 5, 6, 163, 164–6, 171–7; welfare effects of, 164, 170–1, 175, 176, 177, 179
dependency of children, 64
depreciation allowance acceleration, 37, 142
Dolde, Walter C., 8, 11
dynamic general equilibrium models: early, 7–8; government fiscal policy and, 1–2; Harberger and, 6–7; myopic, 9; parameters of, 7; sensitivity analysis and, 7; steady state characteristics and, 8–9; *see also* general equilibrium economic model (55-period life cycle)
dynamics: life cycle model and government policies and, 12; two-period life cycle model and, 18–19

earnings test (social security), 145
efficiency: alternative tax structures and, 77–82; announcement effects and, 86–7; defining economic, 1; distinguishing from redistribution, 62–4; investment incentives and, 128–9; progressive taxation and, 122–4; tax base choice and welfare changes and, 56
efficiency gains, 81–2, 112, 122, 125; social security analysis and, 154–61

elasticity of substitution: household preferences and intertemporal and intratemporal, 50–1; production parameters and, 52
equilibrium: demographic shifts and, 163, 179; fiscal policy choices and, 1–2; social security and, 148; under perfect foresight, 41; *see also* general equilibrium economic model (55-period life cycle)
exchange rates, 13
exports, 13

fertility rates, 162, 167, 168–71, 173–4, 177, 178
fifty-five period life cycle model; *see* general equilibrium economic model (55-period life cycle)
firms: adjustment costs and "q theory of investment" and, 36–7; investment decisions and, 36; investment incentive and market value and, 135; labor demand and, 35–6; life cycle model and, 11; the production function for, 35; real and financial variables and, 38; taxation and market value and, 37–8
fiscal policy: areas active in, 5–6; budget constraints and, 181, 182; defined, 1; dynamic effects of, 1–2; effects on economy of, 180; government behavior and, 40–1; time horizons for political system and, 180–1; time path of, 182
Fisher, Irving, 6
foreign investment, 13

general equilibrium economic model (55-period life cycle): benefit–tax linkages (social security) and, 154–61; computer technology and, 54; demographic shifts and, 166–7, 168–71; equilibrium under perfect foresight and, 41; firms and adjustment costs and "q theory of investment" and, 36–7; firms and investment decisions and, 36; firms and labor demand and, 35–6; firms and real and financial variables and, 38; firms and taxation and market value and, 37–8; fiscal policy and, 182; government budget constraints and, 39–40; government fiscal policy and, 40–1, 53; government and social security and, 41, 54; government structure in model and, 38–9; household budget constraints and, 28–30; household composition and, 26–7; household leisure and consumption choices and, 30–1; household preferences (leisure and consumption measurement) and, 27–8, 50–2; parameterization of, 50–3; production function for firms and,

Index

35; progressive taxes and, 112–13; sensitivity analysis and, 54; solution method and, 47–50; taxation and household behavior and, 32–5, 42–5; *see also* simulation methodology
Ghez, G., 51
government behavior in model: budget constraints and, 39–40; fiscal policy and, 40–1, 53; social security and, 41, 54; structure of government in model and, 38–9
government consumption: balanced budget increases in, 97–101; deficit-financed increases in, 101; demographic shifts and, 170; progressive taxation and sensitivity analysis and, 119; tax reform analysis and, 73, 74
government expenditure: 55-period life cycle model and, 38, 39–40; social security and decrease in, 163
government fiscal policy; *see* fiscal policy
Grossman, Stanford, 50
growth, fiscal policy and, 5

Hall, Robert E., 50
Hansen, Lars P., 50
Hayashi, Fumio, 11
head tax, 105
Hobbes, Thomas, 6
households: budget constraints and, 28–30; deficits and budgets for, 105; household composition and, 26–7; leisure and consumption choices and, 30–1; life cycle model and, 10–11; preferences (leisure and consumption measurement) and, 27–8, 50–2; taxation and, 32–5, 42–5
human capital profile, 29, 52

imports, 13
incentives; *see* business tax incentives; investment incentives
income effects from switching tax bases, 58–60
income tax, 5, 129; absence of adjustment costs and tax cuts and, 91–5; announcement effects and, 83, 86; balanced budget increases in government consumption and, 98, 101; deficit-financed increases in government consumption and, 101; deficits and cuts in, 4; household behavior and, 32–3; investment incentives and, 129, 133; long-term increases in, 90; negative, 112; "permanent," 39–40; presence of adjustment costs and tax cuts and, 95–7; progressive taxation analysis and, 111, 113, 115, 119, 120, 123; savings and, 4;

social security and, 151–3; tax base choice analysis and, 57, 58, 61, 62, 65, 67, 72, 73–6, 78, 79, 80, 81, 82; temporary tax cut example and, 22–4
individual accounts (social security concept), 154–5
Individual Retirement Accounts, 129
inflation (life cycle model), 12
inflation tax, 40
inherited wealth, 16, 126
installation costs for capital goods, 36–7
interest rate, 88; adjustment costs and, 89; government budget constraints and, 39; household budget constraints and, 29; investment decisions and, 36; investment incentives and, 139, 140; social security and, 147; tax-cut example and, 24, 91
intergenerational transfers: consumption tax and, 89; deficits as measure of, 90; progressive taxation and economic decisions and, 116–18, 119, 122, 125–6; savings and, 89–90; social security and, 148; social security and welfare, 153–4; social security and welfare increases and, 143; welfare gains and consumption taxation and, 4
investment: deficits and, 4; firm behavior and, 36; foreign (not included in life cycle model), 13; *see also* q theory of investment
investment incentives, 181; adjustment costs and, 134–5, 138, 139, 140; announcement effects and, 140–1; disguised wealth taxation impact and, 141–4; economic deficits and, 109; effects on investment and, 136–40; efficiency of, 128–9; firm behavior and, 36–7; firm's market value and, 135; savings incentives compared with, 127–8; savings incentives distinguished from, 128–34; self-financing, 4; self-financing tax cuts and, 143–4; simulation results and, 136–40; structural equivalences (savings and investment incentives), 129–34
investment tax credits, 132

Kaldor, Nicholas, 6
Keogh plans, 129
Keynes, J. M., 13
Kotlikoff, Laurence J., 8, 51, 77, 80, 131, 150

labor demand, firm behavior and, 35–6
labor income tax, 33, 61; investment incentives and, 129, 131, 133, 136, 137, 143; progressive taxation and, 112, 114, 116, 117, 118, 119, 120, 122, 124, 125
labor market equilibria or disequilibria, 13

Index

labor supply: firms and, 11; fiscal policy and, 5; household budget constraints and, 29–30; households and, 10; progressive taxation and, 118–19; tax-cut example and, 95; two-period life cycle model and, 16

leisure choices, 61; budget constraints and, 29, 30; household behavior and, 30–1; simulation methodology and, 52

leisure measurement: demographics and, 167, 179; household behavior and, 27–8

life cycle model: economic behavior not included in, 12–13; firm (production sector) and, 11; government (fiscal authority and social security) and, 11–12; households and, 10–11; perfect foresight concept and, 10; *see also* two-period life cycle model

living standard, 179; of future generations, 163

Lump Sum Redistribution Authority (LSRA) (model government institution), 56, 77–8, 81, 87, 122, 123, 124, 160

lump sum tax, 62, 63, 80, 81, 82, 123

MaCurdy, Thomas E., 51
Mankiw, N. Gregory, 50
market value, firm behavior and, 37–8
Medicare, 165–6
Miller, Merton, 9
models; *see* dynamic general equilibrium models; general equilibrium economic model (55-period life cycle); life cycle model; two-period life cycle model
Modigliani, Franco, 8, 10
money (not included in life cycle model), 12, 13

Old Age, Survivors' and Disability Insurance (OASDI), 164–5, 173

Parameters: general equilibrium model and, 50–3; progressive taxation and sensitivity analysis and, 120–2; solution for equilibrium and, 7

payroll taxes, 41, 145; social security and, 164, 165, 172–4, 176, 178, 179

perfect foresight: equilibrium under, 41; for government policy, 20; usefulness of concept of, 10

Phelps, E. S., 63
Poterba, James M., 11
prices: tax-cut example and factor, 24; tax reform analysis and factor, 70, 72; unfunded social security and factor, 151–3

production function: example of two-period life cycle model and, 17; firm behavior, 35; simulation methodology and production parameters and, 52–3

production sector, 11

progressive taxation: characteristics of, 111; economic decisions and, 114–19; modeling of, 112–13; sensitivity analysis and, 119–22, 123–4; switching from (to proportional taxation), 89; tax base choice and, 111–12, 124–5; welfare and efficiency effects of, 122–4

proportional income tax, 58, 89, 112, 117, 124, 125; *see also* income tax

q theory of investment, 11; firm behavior and, 36–7; *see also* investment

Reagan administration, 181
Riley, John G., 63
Rotemberg, Julio J., 50

savings: announcement effects and, 82–5; consumption taxation and stimulation of, 4; deficits and, 4; demographic shifts analysis and, 170, 174, 178; fiscal policy and, 5; households and, 10–11; intergenerational redistribution and, 89–90; investment incentives and incentives for, 127–34; low rate of, 88; progressive taxation and, 5, 115–16, 118; retirement and, 163; social security and, 145, 146–50; social security and crowding out of, 146; social security as forced, 154; tax base choice analysis and, 57, 60, 61, 64, 65; tax cuts and rate of, 91; two-period life cycle model and, 16, 17–18

Scarf, Herbert E., 7
Seidman, Laurence S., 9
sensitivity analysis: progressive taxation and, 119–22, 123–4; simulation methodology and, 54; simulation models for alternative policies and, 7; tax base choice and, 56, 67–74, 81–2

Sheshinski, Eytan, 8
Shiller, Robert J., 50
Shoven, John B., 7

simulation methodology: computer technology and, 54; demographics and, 166–71; equilibrium transition path and, 49–50; government behavior and, 53–4; initial and final steady state and, 47–9; investment incentives and, 136–40; parameterization and household preferences and production and, 50–3; progressive taxation and, 112–16; sensitivity analysis and, 54; short-term tax-cut policies and, 90–7; social security and, 151–4, 158; solution method and, 47–50; tax base choice and, 64–74

Index

Singleton, Kenneth J., 50
Skinner, Jonathan, 51, 80
social security, 64; amendments to, 163, 164–6; "bust-boom-bust" fertility behavior and, 168–70, 171, 173–4, 177; benefit formula and, 155–6; benefit-tax linkages and, 154–61; crowding out of long-run capital formation and unfunded, 147, 148, 153, 161; "deficits" reported in, 104; demographic modeling and, 166–7; demographic transition and, 5, 6, 163, 164–6, 171–7, 178–9; demographic transition and economic effects and, 168–71; demographic welfare effects and, 164, 170–1, 175, 176, 177, 179; factor supplies and prices and, 151–3; government behavior and, 41; household behavior and, 34–5; impact of introducing unfunded, 146–7; individual accounts concept and, 154–5; life cycle model and, 11; long-run cuts in, 181; "pay-as-you-go" financing and, 104; savings and, 145, 146–50, 154; simulation model and, 150–1, 156–8; transition to unfunded system (simulation) and, 151–4; welfare and, 143, 153–4, 160
Solow, Robert, 170
solution method (simulation methodology), 47–50
standard of living, 179; of future generations, 163
static models, 1, 9, 41
steady state characteristics: balanced budget increases in government consumption and initial, 98, 101; fiscal policy transition (temporary tax cut) in two-period life cycle model and, 22–4; limitations of using, 8–9; simulation methodology and, 47–9
stocks, 16
substitution effects from switching tax bases, 60–1
Summers, Lawrence H., 8, 9, 11, 50, 60
Surey, Stanley S., 107

taxation: deficits and, 88; defining deficits and, 103, 106, 107, 108; firm behavior and, 37–8; government behavior and, 38, 39–40; household behavior and, 32–5, 42–5; investment incentives and disguised wealth, 141–4; self-financing business tax cuts and, 143; single rate system of, 113; social security and benefit-tax linkages and efficiency gains and, 154–61; wealth, 62, 141–4, 181; *see also names of specific taxes, i.e.* consumption tax; income tax, *etc.*

tax base choice: announcement effects and, 56–7, 82–7; capital income tax and, 60, 62, 67, 72, 73, 76, 80, 81, 83, 84; comparing tax structures and, 61–2; consumption tax and, 55, 57, 58, 59, 62, 67, 72, 73–6, 78, 79, 80, 81, 82; efficiency and, 56, 62–4, 77–82, 86–7; fiscal policy and, 5–6; income and substitution effects and, 57–61; income tax and, 57, 58, 61, 62, 65, 67, 73–6, 78, 79, 80, 81, 82; lump sum tax and, 62, 63, 80, 81, 82; nominal versus effective tax bases and, 55–6; progressive taxation and, 111–12, 124–5; savings and, 5, 57, 60, 61, 64, 65; sensitivity analysis and, 56, 67–74, 81–2; simulation results and, 64–74; steady state values and, 64–5, 78; structural tax change and, 65–7; wage tax and, 57, 59, 62, 67, 72, 73, 76, 79, 80, 81, 82; welfare changes versus efficiency and, 56; welfare effects and, 74–7, 78
tax credits for investments, 37
tax cuts: dynamic fiscal policy transition and temporary, 22–4; self-financing business, 143–4; simulation findings of short-term policies and, 90–7
Tax Equity and Fiscal Responsibility Act of 1982, 176
tax reform, study and, 2–3; *see also* tax base choice; tax cuts
time preference (parameterization of model), 51
Tobin, James, 8, 11, 36
transfer payments, 107
transition path, 95; simulation methodology and, 49–50
two-period life cycle model: Cobb–Douglas example, 17–22; deficiencies of, 24–5; dynamics in, 18–19; early and late periods of life and, 16–17, 24–5; government fiscal policy in, 19–22; savings and, 17–18; tax cut as fiscal policy transition and, 22–4; *see also* life cycle model

unemployment, not included in life cycle model, 13
Upton, Charles, 9
utility, example of two-period life cycle model and, 17
utility function, household preferences and, 27–8

wage rates: budget constraints of households and, 29; demographic shifts analysis and, 170, 173, 174; investment decisions and, 36; tax-cut example and, 24

wage tax, 181; announcement effects and, 54; balanced budget increases in government consumption and, 98, 101; defining deficits and, 109; household behavior and, 33; investment incentives and, 129; progressive and proportional, 123; savings and, 4; social security and, 151-3; tax base choice analysis and, 57, 59, 62, 67, 72, 73, 76, 79, 80, 81, 82; welfare effects and, 86

wealth elasticity, 126

wealth taxation, 62, 141-4, 181

Weber, Warren E., 50

Welch, Finis, 52, 167

welfare: announcement effects and, 85-6; consumption taxation and, 4, 85; demographic shifts and, 5, 164, 170-1, 175, 176, 177, 179; progressive taxation and, 122-4; short-term tax cuts and, 93, 94; social security and intergenerational transfers and, 143, 153-4, 160; tax base choice and efficiency and, 56; tax reform analysis and, 74-7, 78; wage tax and, 86

Whalley, J., 7